AF607877

"OUR RELATIONS... THE MIXED BLOODS"

SUNY series, Tribal Worlds:
Critical Studies in American Indian Nation Building

Brian Hosmer and Larry Nesper, editors

"OUR RELATIONS... THE MIXED BLOODS"

INDIGENOUS TRANSFORMATION AND DISPOSSESSION IN THE WESTERN GREAT LAKES

LARRY NESPER

With research assistance from Amorin Mello

FOREWORD BY MIKE WIGGINS JR.

Chair of the Bad River Band of Lake Superior Chippewa Indians

Cover photo: Portrait of French Indians and Vincent Roy. Courtesy of the Wisconsin Historical Society.

Published by State University of New York Press, Albany

Printed in the United States of America

For information, contact State University of New York Press, Albany, NY
www.sunypress.edu

Library of Congress Cataloging-in-Publication Data

Names: Nesper, Larry, author. | Wiggins, Mike Jr., foreword.
Title: "Our relations . . . the mixed bloods" : indigenous transformation and dispossession in the western great lakes / Larry Nesper, foreword by Mike Wiggins, Jr., with research assistance from Amorin Mello.
Description: Albany : State University of New York Press, [2021] | Series: SUNY series, Tribal Worlds: Critical Studies in American Indian Nation Building | Includes bibliographical references and index.
Identifiers: ISBN 9781438482859 (hardcover : alk. paper) | ISBN 9781438482873 (ebook)
Further information is available at the Library of Congress.

10 9 8 7 6 5 4 3 2 1

For brother and sister, daughters,
their spouses, nephews, and grandchildren

Contents

Illustrations

Figures

Photographs

Maps

Acknowledgments

This book was inspired by the archival, cartographic, and investigative journalistic work of Amorin Mello, who collaborated with Bret Deutscher and Leo Filipczak as independent researchers and residents of the Lake Superior Basin in exploring the nineteenth-century history of the Chequamegon Bay area. Amorin published a paper entitled "Wisconsin's Government Presumes Adverse Impacts Necessary for Mining Jobs" on the *Woods Person* blog in May of 2012.[1] This paper was particularly important in my decision to explore this story in greater depth, and I have drawn upon his seminal work and the sources that he identified throughout the process of researching and writing. Amorin established the connection between the mixed-blood provision of the Treaty of 1854 and eighty-acre allotments in the Penokees. He then pointed the way to the questionable practices that were at the heart of the land transfer from mixed-blood tribal members to private interests. I was in regular contact with Amorin through the research phase of this project, and I am deeply grateful to him, especially for his cartographic and archival work identifying many primary documents that were critical for telling this story. It is in this sense that this work is written with his research assistance, though I am the sole author of the prose and fully responsible for it.

I also wish to acknowledge the following individuals for the different forms of assistance they provided in bringing this work to fruition. The leaders of Chippewa Federal in Wisconsin welcomed my exploration of this topic from the start, especially Chris McGeshick and Tom Maulson. Early on, Susan E.

Amorin Mello, 2013. "Wisconsin's Government Presumes Adverse Impacts Necessary for Mining, Jobs." *Woods Person: Thoughts and reports on what is happening in Wisconsin's North Woods*. http: //woodsperson.blogspot.com/2013/05/wisconsins-government-presumes-adverse.html. Visited July 1, 2018.

Gray shared a very capacious bibliography with me. Steve Kantrowitz, in the History Department, and Anatoly Khazanov, in the Anthropology Department, both at UW-Madison, encouraged me to pursue this topic, and I am grateful for their on-going support and interest. Jameson Sweet shared valuable historical documents on Dakota mixed bloods, and James McLurken offered excellent advice on archival records. John Broihahn, state archaeologist, made valuable suggestions about land use in the region. Grant Arndt created a venue for me to tell an early version of this story at Iowa State as did the Indigenous Law Students Association at the University of Wisconsin-Madison. Several accomplished scholars working on Ojibwe and related peoples have been supportive throughout the research and writing process. Here I am thinking of Theresa Schenck, Rebecca Kugel, Jacqueline Peterson, Susan Sleeper-Smith, Jennifer Brown, Lucy Murphy, Cary Miller, Bruce White, Rand Valentine.

Other fellow academics, legal and tribal government professionals, and activists took an interest and had valuable advice. They are William Leslie Balan-Gaubert, Mindie Lazarus-Black, James Botsford, John Coleman, William Cronon, Kennan Ferguson, Ray Fogelson, Al Gedicks, Sandy Gokee, Greggory Jennings, Robert J. Miller, Richard Monette, Matthew Newell, Eric Olmanson, Sheree Petersen, Brian Pierson, Kathy Reilly, Jason Sanders, Morgan Smallwood, Kekek Jason Stark, Paul Stenzl, Terry Straus, and John Suval.

Mike Wiggins, Edith Leoso, Tony Corbine, and Patrick Mayotte of the Bad River Band of Lake Superior Chippewa Indians were generous with their time and their archival sources. Kim Bouchard and Marian Duffy at the Great Lakes Bureau of Indian Affairs office in Ashland were most helpful in procuring archival sources only available there. Lisa Marine at the Wisconsin Historical Society helped with the illustrations. The University of Wisconsin-Madison granted me a semester sabbatical, and the Institute for Research in the Humanities offered me the opportunity to research and write for a semester. I am grateful to Brian Hosmer, who read a rough version of the manuscript and suggested that we consider it for the Tribal Worlds series. Two anonymous reviewers endorsed this judgment, and I hope I have adequately responded to their generous and thoughtful critiques. And finally, my dear and indefatigable partner, the recently retired Professor Shiela Reaves of UW-Madison's Life Sciences Communication Department, not only encouraged me all along but very generously read the entire manuscript aloud, line editing for clarity. I am forever grateful.

Foreword

This book illuminates a time and a series of events that represent the very worst of government abdication of this nation's federal-Indian trust responsibility. Telling this story will undo the darkness of amnesia that has shadowed Penokee mineral rights and, in turn, heighten Wisconsin tribes' connectivity to our watershed home. It centerpunches, the need for trust responsibility and the Bad River tribal people's inherent right to live on our land without poisons unleashed into our waters for corporate profit. This book's historical account, like Benjamin Armstrong's 1892 memoirs, will cement the story of the cataclysmic changes wrought upon our ancestors. This story of the Bad River tribe's journey represents a key piece of evidence and truth that will help unlock the possibilities of water protection and life well into the future. In effect, this book helps us look backward to remember and to know. While moving forward, it also sends a call to action along the arc of truth and justice.

Larry Nesper is a trusted friend, mentor, and educator in my world. His book *The Walleye War* on Ojibwe Indian spearfishing and treaty rights and related academic papers focus on issues that Anishinaabe/Chippewa have fought in our efforts to recognize ourselves again. There are three things that accompany Larry's interactions with our Bad River tribe: goodwill in his heart, goodwill in his mind, and his superb academic abilities. From helping piece together traditional cultural property designations, to ethno-historical research and work with our people, Larry Nesper is trusted and appreciated.

As this book details the malicious theft and ill intent regarding our watershed home and its metallic mineral body, one thing becomes clear. Our ancestors, all peoples and all living things in the Bad River Watershed deserve certainty—a certainty rooted in the future that will not see the manifestation of greed and destruction of the upper watershed and toxicity plumes, a certainty that the fish, macroinvertebrates, wild rice, migratory birds, and drinking water of this place stay intact and delivered to continue the Creator's intent of having this be a place for love, life, and growing.

To work against the natural laws and systems of the Bad River Watershed/ Lake Superior nexus is going against the entire spirit of the place. It's time for those with the power to change things to act decisively. It is time for the mineral-rights holders to deliver certainty of life for all inhabitants of this watershed home, including humans and rocks. The ability to convey certainty by letting go of the mineral rights is an opportunity of a lifetime that will propel a legacy rooted in memories of preservation and protection rather than calamity and destruction.

Our drumbeats represent the heartbeat of Mother Earth. When our drumbeats are sounded, they journey to the Center of the Earth and then bounce up and out to Ishpemiing, that highest place near the Creator. The Center of the Earth does important spiritual work for Anishinaabe/Chippewa receiving and conveying our drumbeats, songs, and prayers onward and upward.

The Center of the Earth is molten magma/lava with iron, nickel, gold, silver, copper, and an array of minerals churning and powering this planet. Almost four thousand miles below our feet, the Center balances the poles of the Earth and sends an electromagnetic force out that protects our fragile planetary home from interstellar forces that could end life. The Center is a place of very powerful fire. It is a place that the Creator uses to create love, life, and growth on this planet. It is a place that protects us.

Anishinaabe/Chippewa understand that the rocks and stones are our oldest relatives. They are the knowledge keepers and hold the most ancient wisdom and story from the beginning of Earth. All rocks, including the metal trapped in the Earth near our home, have a spirit. They were put here by the Creator for life. There are spirits and beliefs that accompany the rocks that are only mentioned in hushed, respectful tones—if they are mentioned at all. We are discouraged from talking about it. Prayers and acknowledgments to these special helpers of the Creator are usually quiet, sacred, and rooted in ancient protocol.

Anishinaabe/Chippewa people also understand that the rocks and the metallic minerals take care of our water—and that water is life. The metallic mineral body that lies in the Penokees, above the homeland we call Mashkiziibii in the Bad River Watershed, is a tangible manifestation of remnant fire from the Center of the Earth, delivered in that time when volcanic lava found its way to the surface of our home, 4.2 billion years ago. Cooled quickly by other orders of creation—air, land, water—the fire that used to burn here turned to metallic minerals near the surface of the Earth while the lava flows retreated deeper down. This place was birthing and becoming conducive for all life, including human life.

The volcanic fault lines that came from the fire at the Center of the Earth are still here. They are directly connected to the metallic mineral bodies cooled and trapped near the surface. From deep within the Earth in our Bad River Watershed/Penokee Mountain home, water has replaced lava. Pushed onward and upward by pressure, water also takes the path of least resistance. Ancient volcanic pathways are also the paths of least resistance. Invariably, the groundwater enters and percolates through the remnant fire and metallic mineral bodies. These aquifer pumps are strong enough to power the hydrological recharge of our watershed home into perpetuity. The connectivity to the Center of the Earth and volcanic memory herein are why the Penokee Mountains and Bad River Reservation are unbelievably water-rich areas, powered by groundwater from deep in the Earth and surface water from thunderstorm-rich microclimates.

There will never be a mine or mountaintop removal in the Penokee Mountains. The Creator took the mineral body, tilted it, and drove it deep down into the Earth at a sharp angle. Unlike other mineral bodies that lived on a horizontal plane slightly underneath the Earth's surface such as those obliterated in Minnesota, the Penokee mineral body dives deep. The amount of Earth that would have to be removed just to uncover it would mean the end to the hydrological processes that power the upper waterfall region, the red-clay river systems, the world-class wetland delta, and the Apostle Island Lake Superior area. Accompanying the destruction of the groundwater conductivity would be toxic plumes of asbestiform minerals, sulfuric acid, and heavy metals into the air and water.

Our reservation home and its people are downwind and downstream. We have been witnesses to all that has changed in our lands—and waters since the treaty era—and enough is enough. The fur trappers, shaft miners, brownstone miners, lumber barons, and others all had their day. The resource extraction in the form of mining stolen tribal lands and mineral areas in the upper watershed represents extremism and death to our home. Enough is enough.

Instead, the Bad River Watershed and Chequamegon Bay area make up a sustainable model of resource extraction. What makes the Bad River Watershed unique is that—despite all the past exploitation—it's still an intact living organism complete with world-class hydrology and pristine wilderness features. The metallic mineral body itself, ionized and connected to the electromagnetic power of the Earth, will spin a compass needle and call storms into the watershed nest to insure continued hydrological wealth, healing, and strength for all life.

In the face of climate change and extreme weather onset, the natural systems of our tribal home represent a foundation to ride into the future. The cold, clean groundwater infusion from the metallic mineral area that never stops flowing pours into the Big Lake and keeps the Apostle Island waters cool and healthy. Regardless of what climate changes bring, we are insulated and poised to be in a good place to go through cataclysmic changes because of the strength of our water and ecosystems. We pray that those with the power do the right thing for the right reasons.

Miigwech (Thank you).
Mike Wiggins, Jr.
Tribal Chairman
Bad River Band of Lake Superior Chippewa

Introduction

"Our relations . . . the mixed bloods": Indigenous Transformation and Dispossession in the Western Great Lakes is about racial ideology, settler colonialism, and the transformation of an indigenous polity and a sociocultural landscape as the outcomes of the treaty process and subsequent federal policy. It details the ways in which the terms "half-breeds" and "mixed bloods" emerged in the context of the fur trade and the treaty economies in the Great Lakes region over the course of the nineteenth century, then effervesced as social distinctions with the establishment and allotment of Indian reservations in the late nineteenth and early twentieth centuries, and then finally receded in the twentieth century. The emergence of these social distinctions was the outcome of competing conceptions of belonging and difference that interacted in the fur trade and treaty economy periods and transformed the indigenous polity as a result. I attempt to capture those conceptions in the title *"Our relations . . . mixed bloods"* as "our relations" is the term repeatedly used by Native people to refer to "the mixed bloods belonging to the Chippewa of Lake Superior," a phrase from the 1854 Treaty of LaPointe.

These distinctions made the transformation of the landscape of the Western Great Lakes region possible because the so-called mixed bloods were distinguished as a class and then recruited to influence the internal tribal politics and facilitate the treaty process. What had been a commons organized by kinship and customary law was appropriated and enclosed by settlers for purposes of settlement and resource extraction. Tactical use of the social distinction between Indians and mixed bloods played a critical role in the very material process of dispossession specifically enabling the capitalization of first mining companies in northern Wisconsin and then lumber companies in Minnesota, thus initiating a complete reimagining and subsequent transformation of the landscape and the peoples who lived upon it. This case study aspires to link ethnic formation and transformation to the forces of settler colonialism and the subsequent changes of the Western Great Lakes landscape. It also aspires to reveal a hitherto largely unrecognized capacity and agency on the part of indigenous polities to assimilate sources of power in the form of persons and things and, in doing so, simultaneously reproduce and transform themselves. This study is motived in relatively current historical events that threatened another major environmental if not indigenous transformation.

Shortly after Scott Walker was elected governor in November of 2010, with the campaign slogan Wisconsin: Open for Business, Gogebic Taconite announced that it intended to begin the process of seeking the permits to mine low-grade iron ore in the Penokee Hills, just south of the Bad River Chippewa Reservation and within the lands ceded by the Lake Superior Ojibwe in the Treaty of 1842 where the Chippewa bands had treaty-established rights to hunt, fish, and gather recently litigated in federal court. The proposed mine site lay in the headwaters of the Bad River, which flows north to Lake Superior where it enters "the 16,000-acre Kakagon-Bad River Sloughs, the largest undeveloped wetland complex in the upper Great Lakes."[1] In 2012, the sloughs were designated as an environmentally significant Ramsar site, recognizing their importance at the international level.[2] The sloughs are also the Bad River Band's breadbasket because they are the source of wild rice, "the food that grows on the water," and a condition of the possibility of the community's culturally distinct existence.[3] Wild rice is very sensitive to the acid drainage that a mining project would inevitably introduce into the watershed. Stopping the mine from being developed became the highest priority for the Bad River Band.

In February 2013, the Wisconsin legislature passed Wisconsin Act 1, an industry-friendly mining bill exempting ferrous mining from many of the state's environmental protection regulations and making the expansion of iron-mining state policy, despite the fact that the overwhelming majority of public testimony opposed the bill.[4] In the spring of that year, several members of the nearby Lac Courte Oreilles Band of Lake Superior Ojibwe Indians, who share treaty usufructuary rights in the ceded territories with the other Ojibwe bands, established the Education and Harvest Camp on county land in the Penokees. The symbolic action foregrounded the treaty rights that had been reserved on the lands ceded by the Chippewa to the federal government in the nineteenth century as participants actively harvesting fish, animals, and plants. Their goal was to educate the public about the meaning and value of the land, inviting them to imagine a more democratically organized landscape abundant in renewable resources. In doing so, Indian people would contest the state of Wisconsin and Gogebic Taconite's effort to define and designate the land for mineral resource extraction.

It had been only ten years since the Sokaogon community, another band of Lake Superior Chippewas, 150 miles to southwest of Bad River, had finally defeated the efforts of a series of mining companies that sought to extract metallic sulfide ore from lands immediately adjacent to their small reservation. The proposed mine in the Sokaogon community also threatened the community's wild rice.[5]

The May 2013 issue of the nationwide, independent, Hayward, Wisconsin-based *News from Indian Country* ran a short three-paragraph article entitled "Chippewa and Santee allotments discovered in Penokee Range." The article opened with the line, "The meaning of almost two hundred 80 and 160 acre allotments issued to Ojibwe and Santee Sioux Indians in the late 1854 [treaty] through 1880s on top of the Penokee Range ore deposit is still unknown." The article went on to assure readers that "members of several tribes are currently researching the history and the chain of title to clarify [under] what authority the allotments were made and under what conditions, legal or otherwise they were surrendered." Finally, the article promised a list of names of those allottees, noting that the allotment upon which the Harvest and Education Camp was sited belonged to Elizabeth Trudell, implying that she was an ancestor of the well-known indigenous activist/poet/musician John Trudell.

A map, reproduced below, originally showing the Ojibwe allotments in blue and the Sioux allotments in maroon, created by Amorin Mello, accompanied the article.

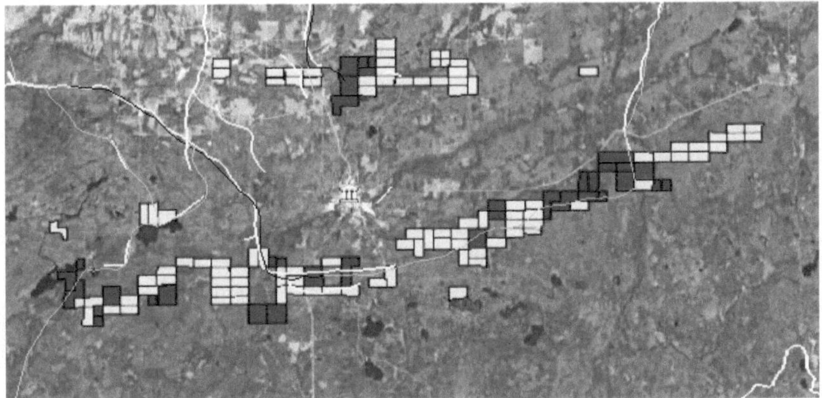

Map I.1. The mixed-blood allotments in the Penokee Range of Northern Wisconsin ca. 1858. Light rectangles represent Chippewa allotments and dark rectangles represent Dakota allotments. The array traces the iron formation in the Penokees. Map by Amorin Mello. Photo by the author.

Blog postings on *Save the Water's Edge* from May and June made reference to other allotments in the area and expressed the desire to learn why they are no longer in the possession of Indian people. Posting on May 23, Lac Courte Oreilles tribal member and publisher of *News From Indian Country* Paul DeMain listed the names of people who once held allotments in the area: J. B. Corbin, Robert Morrin, John Baptist Crane, John Baptist Denomie, John Hoskin, Michael Lambert, and Joseph Roy.[6] Some Ojibwe readers of the newspaper in the region still carried these surnames, and several of those names are common in the Ojibwe communities to this day. These readers would be the descendants of those "Ojibwe and Santee Sioux Indians" who had been allotted, though they apparently there was little current collective memory of that moment that took place about seven generations ago.

With the passage of Wisconsin Act 1, in the spring of 2013, the Bad River Band made the decision to hire a team of researchers to do a study of its traditional cultural resources and their relationship to environmental integrity. The goal was to produce a document to assist the band in reviewing its water quality standards since the band had been granted Treatment-as-State Status under the Clean Water Act.[7] The report would also be submitted to federal officials with the authority to grant permits to mining applicants reminding those officials of their trust responsibilities to the people of Bad River by calling attention to Section 106 of the National Historic Preservation Act. Section 106 requires government permitting agencies to "take into account" the historical significance of cultural properties at risk of being compromised by development.[8]

While doing the ethnographic component of that study, I visited the Harvest Camp in the Penokees and was given a copy of the above-mentioned map by Paul DeMain, co-founder and publisher of *News from Indian Country*. Paul had made multiple copies of the map and was distributing them to interested visitors. I would learn from Amorin Mello, who made the map using data from the Bureau of Land Management's online archive of land patents, that the allotments in the Penokees were authorized by the seventh article of the Treaty of 1854 that granted eighty-acre parcels to "mixed bloods, belonging to the Lake Superior Chippewa."

Amorin Mello has had an avocational interest in the history of the region for a number of years and is the co-author with Leo Filipczak of a blog on the history of the Chequamegon region since 2015.[9] What had been referred to as "Ojibwe and Santee Sioux Indians" in the newspaper article were, at the time the treaty was signed, mixed bloods, a marked class of indigenous political subjects. At the time, I noted the current indifference to distinguishing between mixed bloods and Indians and reflected upon the fact that this was a significant difference at the time of the treaties. The questions began to multiply.

How was it that lands had been allotted and lost south of the border of the Bad River Reservation on lands that had been ceded in a previous treaty? Did grantees ever live there? If so, would there still be evidence of their presence? How were the allotments in the Penokees alienated, that is, lost to their original owners? What role did the federal government play in the implementation of the treaty provision? What happened to those people who held title to those lands, and why was there apparently little or no collective memory of their tenure and dispossession?

Two relatively obscure published scholarly accounts, both longer than Edmund Danziger's[10] single-paragraph summary, address the implementation and effects of this provision of 1854 treaty. In 1906, Gustav O. Brohough wrote a master's thesis at the University of Wisconsin-Madison titled "Sioux and Chippewa Half-Breed Scrip and Its Application to the Minnesota Pine Lands." In this work, Brohough narrated the history of the creation and fraught establishment of the Sioux half-breed tract on Lake Pepin in Minnesota and then went on in twenty pages to describe the ways in which the provision in the 1854 treaty with the Chippewa led to the creation of half-breed scrip that was fraudulently used by lumber interests to secure access to the pine lands of Minnesota. Brohough pointed out a critical legal step that made this dispossession possible insofar as the scrip was written in a way that made it illegal to transfer: "To evade this provision, made to protect the half-breed from the acts of those who should attempt to take advantage of his ignorance and his necessities, two powers of attorney were attached to each certificate, one authorizing entries to be made of the lands, by an attorney on behalf of the half-breed, and the other authorizing conveyance to be made of these lands after patents should be procured."[11]

Apparently, something very similar must have taken place in Wisconsin very shortly after the treaty was signed for purposes of capitalizing mining companies and before lumbering interests entered the picture.

Brohough did impressive work for the time. However, he left unaddressed the manner in which this provision was administered, leaving unreconciled the great concern on the federal government's part that the scrip only be redeemed by eligible "half-breeds" for land and the outcome of the land being appropriated by corporate interests. And though Brohough questioned the legality of mixed bloods signing away power of attorney, he left the issue unexplored. Furthermore, the term "half-breeds" is left entirely unexamined as well. Thus, he unreflectively reproduced and transmitted a racial and social category whose existence was necessary to facilitate an indigenous transformation and dispossession.

William Watts Folwell gave an account of the "Chippewa Halfbreed Scrip" in appendix 9 to his 1956 *History of Minnesota* that offers some information about the administration of this policy. Folwell pointed out that the half-breeds were considered in the treaty in order to assure their assistance in "gaining the consent of the Indians to the treaty." He noted the General Land Office's desire that the 312 certificates enabling mixed-blood land claims not be transferable to anyone. Folwell then went on to discuss the effects of the 1864 ruling of the new secretary of the interior liberalizing qualifications for inclusion as eligible mixed bloods, which included the quadrupling of the number of certificates issued. Folwell repeated Brohaugh's recognition of the use of powers of attorney, adding that the legal validity of blank powers of attorney was not questioned at the time, an issue that I will explore in detail in chapter 5. The balance of Folwell's account describes the fraudulent scrip certificate production and governmental response to it in the late 1860s and early 1870s especially in regard to acquiring timber lands in Minnesota. He finally concluded that it is "no pleasure to tell this story."[12] Both of these essays were written long before the emergence of a critical ethnohistorical scholarship that would interrogate the history and organization of the indigenous polities that signed treaties with the federal government. These accounts were also written before efforts to critically examine the impact of racial ideologies on both the constitution of indigenous polities and the implementation of treaty provisions.

Richard White's *The Middle Ground: Indians, Empires, and Republics in the Great Lakes Region, 1650–1815* published in 1991 initiated a period of critical Great Lakes historical scholarship wherein he profoundly and permanently revised the declensionist, imperial narrative with the idea that relations between indigenous peoples in the region and Europeans were far more bilateral than had been represented in the past. He shows that Europeans were incapable of imposing their political will by force upon indigenous peoples, and the result was the creation of a middle ground, "a process of mutual invention," wherein there was "a willingness of those who created it to justify their own actions in terms of what they perceived to be their partner's cultural premises."[13] As this reflexivity inevitably led to misinterpretations and distortions, it resulted in improvised cultural, political, social, and economic forms both in the diplomatic register and in the ordinary lives of the French and Indian people interacting with each other.

Recently, Michael Witgen has critiqued and developed White's thesis of the middle ground to show that this region White referred to in French as the *pays d'en haut* is better thought of Anishinaabewaki, a complex, dynamic, decentralized sociopolitical formation organized by kinship giving even more agency to indigenous people than did Richard White. The peoples of Anishinaabewaki engaged with Europeans over the course of several centuries and created an indigenous New World, according to Witgen. In the very long run, the European-descended people would come to control the landscape, and indigenous societies would be diminished, marginalized, and largely segregated from the dominant society. But in that period of time that lasted for as long as two centuries in the Great Lakes region and characterized by the fur trade, the forces of assimilation emanated from both settler and indigenous societies. I am particularly interested in showing how the dynamism of this indigenous New World includes structural transformation, entailing the so-called mixed bloods.

The idea of Anishinaabewaki has also been taken up by Michael McDonnell in his effort to re-establish the centrality of Odawa Anishinaabeg people in the Great Lakes region in the history of America itself.[14] Both Witgen and McDonnell argue that until the mid-nineteenth century, native forces shaped European intentions more than the reverse. Furthermore, those intentions were oriented by fundamentally different conceptions of belonging and difference. This has important implications for how we understand the very idea of mixed bloods.[15]

Insofar as the problem this study addresses is the status of "mixed bloods, belonging to the Lake Superior Chippewa," as the treaty of 1854 describes them, the interaction between indigenous women and nonindigenous men is of particular interest. This subject has been thoughtfully explored by scholars such as Sylvia Van Kirk, Jennifer Brown, Jacqueline Peterson, Susan-Sleeper Smith, Susan Gray, Lucy Murphy, Carolyn Podruchny, and Rebecca Kugel to name only the most prominent, and I will draw upon their insightful works throughout. Becoming the husbands and partners of indigenous women—and therefore, brothers-in-law and sons-in-law of indigenous men—working class Frenchmen largely acculturated to an indigenous order of value and practice, albeit one that was changing by virtue of this engagement and related social, economic, and political processes. The exclusionary quality of the ascendant European conception of race prevented Indian people from traversing a symmetrical cultural trajectory within settler society. Instead, Indians appropriated elements of European culture and remained Indian.

The children born of this engagement were imagined and regarded very differently by indigenous people and colonizers. Indigenous people referred to them as "our relations," that is, they were incorporated into indigenous society in the comprehensive idiom of kinship. Here I will draw upon and extend Michael Witgen's analysis of Anishinaabeg ethnosociology and explore the full implications of the distinction between *inawemaagen* (relatives) and *meuyaagizid* (strangers or foreigners) in the political register.[16] By contrast, nonindigenous people called the category of people with ethnically heterogeneous parentage "mixed bloods" or "half-breeds" when speaking English or "chicot" when speaking French. Very late in the period, the term "Métis" would circulate after the emergence of a distinct ethnic group in the Red River Valley.

The point here is that mixed bloods' distinguishability from the indigenous population was contested as revealed in the difference in the terms used by indigenous people and Europeans. Over time, most mixed bloods were assimilated to indigenous society, and their genealogical pedigree was a distinction that made little difference to indigenous people, while the increasingly hegemonic conception of race excluded mixed bloods from full participation in non-Indian society. Mixed bloods were *inawemaagen*, relatives.

French men had to be assimilated to indigenous societies as kind of relative in order to exchange goods and extract furs. Anglo-American society increasingly understood similarity and difference in ranked racial terms. Indigenous society did not, for the most part, and as a result, the progeny were assimilated to indigenous society. And though these children of French men and Indian women were different from their indigenous kin in terms of their capacity for brokerage, they were not so different as to be considered anything but "our relations," thus enmeshed in the networks of obligation and exchange that make up indigenous society. The skills they acquired from their European fathers were often deployed by indigenous political leaders. At the same time, the dominant's society's view of their difference made them candidates for special consideration in the land cessions treaties, a strategic move with the goal of making the indigenous communities more manageable and transformable along lines envisioned by settlers.

"Mixed-blood" and "half-breed" are hegemonic racial terms: they come and go without much comment or justification on the parts of the people who used them at the time and, to some extent, by some scholars who write about them, as we shall see. The terms were naturalized in the process. Asking in what sense mixed bloods or half-breeds "belonged to the Lake Superior Chippewa" is to beg the question, for example. It is to smuggle in and tacitly assert the existence of a shared conception that one is seemingly questioning. From an indigenous perspective, the category of person that whites called "mixed bloods" belonged to the Lake Superior Chippewa in quite the same way the people that whites designated as "Indians" themselves belonged to the Lake Superior Chippewa. Both belonged. The Lake Superior Chippewa was circumscribed by kinship, other distinctions such as heterogeneous parentage without much significant standing, or at least not the significance that the settler population increasingly thinking in terms of race would give it.

The very question presumes the ascendancy of race as a means of figuring belonging and difference in the upper Great Lakes region and, of course, the idea of race has a history in any setting where it circulates. It is an ideology that serves the interests of some at the expense of others. It was both imposed upon and assimilated by indigenous people to different degrees.

Over the course of the first half of the nineteenth century, as non-Indian traders, missionaries and government officials came amongst indigenous peoples with their various interests, and in their various capacities, they came to imagine aboriginal society as constituted of groups of people, distinguishable by parentage, or "blood," hence "mixed bloods" and "full bloods." This imaginative model was a project, a discursive undertaking, a hegemonic practice, albeit a consequential one, and one that was variously engaged in by whites, the so-called mixed bloods themselves, and "Indians" or, later, "full bloods," at different times and for different reasons.

The presumptive distinguishability of mixed bloods was accomplished over time in ordinary acts of what Pierre Bourdieu describes as symbolic violence, wherein the subjects of an imposed distinction acquiesce in that distinction. Reproduced by missionaries, governmental officials, school personnel, members of the fur-trade business sector, and other non-Indigenous people, an emergent and minor internal indigenous social distinction became the basis for a dichotomous division of that indigenous world. When the distinction is inscribed in treaties, it takes on a far greater solidity. Pierre Bourdieu writes: "Law consecrates the established order by consecrating the vison of that order which is held by the State . . . Law is the quintessential form of the symbolic power of naming that creates the things named, and creates social groups in particular. It confers upon the reality which arises from its classificatory operations the maximum permanence that any social entity has the power to confer upon another, the permanence which we attribute to objects."[17]

Very consequentially, inscribed in treaties for a number of decades in the nineteenth century, the designation "mixed-blood" was imagined and then asserted to be a very clear distinction. And the term was deployed in the late nineteenth and early twentieth centuries as the Ojibwe reservations were allotted as it came to denote a progressive political orientation critical of the traditional leadership.

The term "mixed blood" was no longer significant by the middle and certainly the late twentieth century, though the term's disappearance was a fraught political process as we shall see in the last two chapters. So now, in the twenty-first century, the names of tribal members from the Ojibwe communities of Minnesota, Wisconsin, and Michigan include many French or French-originated patronyms—the legacy of these mixed bloods—and those patronyms are as Indian from the community's perspective as names such as Stone, Bearheart, Martin, and Moose, or Gashkibos.

This study is centered on the ways in which a single sentence in a land cession treaty signed between the Lake Superior bands of Ojibwe and the federal government in 1854 was interpreted and implemented and the consequences this process had for the larger landscape and the people who lived upon it. The provision appeared in Article II of the treaty, the section that created reservations, both the collectively and individually held parcels that were reserved for the benefit of native people. The Article "set[s] apart and withhold[s] from sale . . . the following-described tracts of land." After identifying what will become collectively-held tribal estates, the seventh paragraph reads: "Each head of a family, or single person over twenty-one years of age at the present time of the mixed bloods, belonging to the Chippewas of Lake Superior, shall be entitled to eighty acres of land, to be selected by them under the direction of the President, and which shall be secured to them by patent in the usual form."[18]

Most mixed bloods never received nor lived on those eighty-acre parcels because the right to those parcels was appropriated by would-be mining and lumbering interests almost immediately. In Wisconsin, parcels were consolidated by a small group of non-Indians who incorporated themselves as the state's first iron-mining companies. This was not the first time that the apparent intent of a land provision in an Indian treaty proved to be illusory.

Paul Wallace Gates identified what he called the "nonstatutory method of land disposal"[19] in his analysis of treaties signed with Miami and Potawatomi several decades earlier. Here a provision of the treaty authorized patenting of land to certain individuals or to a certain class of individuals within tribal society. The beneficiaries of the provision then conveyed their patents to the traders. Federal agents in collusion with the traders would then certify the transfer to gain the required presidential approval to alleviate any congressional concerns. Dispossession accomplished.

Was the mixed-blood provision of the Treaty of 1854, in fact, one of the last acts in this farce? The outcome would certainly support this contention. Yet, though it was local traders who would secure power of attorney from mixed-blood beneficiaries and so gain access to the patents to the lands, federal officials appear to have made a considerable effort to prevent this dispossession. They also repeatedly indicated their intention that the mixed bloods be secure in their possession of relatively small tracts of land then perceived to be viable for agricultural purposes both to pacify them and to make them models for their full-blooded kin nearby. This aspiration failed.

The trouble caused by the implementation of this treaty provision was the subject of a congressional investigation less than two decades after the treaty was ratified by the Senate and made law. *The Report of the Special Commission in the Matter of Chippewa Scrip, 1871*[20] included in the Report to the Secretary of the Interior detailed the ways in which the provision of the treaty was abused by speculators to the detriment of the intended beneficiaries. The report focused on the period *after 1863* when the commissioner of Indian affairs made a decision that had the effect of inviting widespread abuse with hundreds of individuals making claims.

As it would turn out, in the 1860s, entrepreneurial non-Indians began to counterfeit government-issued scrip and then gather up mixed-blood signatures in order to empower themselves to locate timber lands in Minnesota, capitalizing a lumber industry that would change the landscape and political economy of that state as well. The present study, however, draws attention to the first few years of the implementation of this treaty provision when the interest in the Lake Superior region was not yet in trees but in minerals. It may be thought of as a kind of rehearsal for what would turn out to be a more substantial dispossession process in Minnesota. Recognition of the failure to realize the stated goals of the policy may also have played a role in crafting the provisions and the implementation process of the Allotment Act of 1887 several decades later.

The dispossession of the Lake Superior mixed bloods had important consequences for the landscape of northern Wisconsin. Somewhat similar to what Kathleen Conzen revealed took place with the nearby Winnebago, called Ho-Chunk today. In that case, "the federal funds that the Winnebago represented" were converted into town sites and city lots.[21] In the present case, the mixed-blood right to land capitalized the earliest efforts at mining in the western part of the Gogebic Range called the Penokees.

The failure of the policy and the loss of that land simplified the ethnic landscape. Before the dispossession, there was Anishinaabewaki, a complex, evolving, and culturally heterogeneous, hybrid, indigenous sociopolitical formation largely organized by kinship and an increasing settler population of Euro-Americans variously articulated with Anishinaabewaki. After the dispossession, there would be a largely white civilization with social relations organized by contract and citizenship and Indian reservations, a truncated form of Anishinaabewaki situated on an extractive landscape in the hinterland of growing Midwestern urban centers.

This moment provides a window into society, culture, and change in the region south of Lake Superior at time when race, a new paradigm of belonging and difference, was on the ascent and culture and kinship as means of organizing groups were threatened. I am interested in the emergence in the eighteenth century, the subsequent effervescence, and the late nineteenth- and early twentieth-century reassimilation of the mixed-blood members of indigenous society that give context to this dispossession. This was accomplished by a network of actors with different intentions and powers to affect their interests both within the mixed-blood sector of Anishinaabe-waki as well as without.

This book will first sketch an overview of the Ojibwe or Chippewa of Lake Superior, the largest group of indigenous people of the region that articulated with the Europeans interested in extracting furs. It then goes on to a description of the fur trade in the Western Great Lakes and the consequent emergence of the so-called mixed bloods, first a social category of indigenous person, then, west of the Great Lakes region, a separate ethnicity in the form of the Métis of Canada. As the power of the United States increased in the early nineteenth century in the Great Lakes region, its policy initiatives shaped indigenous society, culture, and polities. It is here that the ascendant ideology of race played an important role in reshaping internal indigenous social categories. I then explore how so-called mixed-blood people were distinguished and reified in treaties over the course of the first half of the nineteenth century to show how the Treaty of 1854 represented both continuity and a rupture in federal Indian policy. Here sketching the contours of how the idea of race shaped the imagined horizons for Indian people, "full" and "mixed" bloods alike.

At the center of this book is an examination of the implementation of the 1854 treaty provision for the mixed bloods who belonged to the Lake Superior Chippewa and its consequences for both the Indian community and for the larger landscape. It will entail a detailed examination of archival sources revealing an administrative process characterized by the production of ambiguity and plausible deniability of failing to live up to the federal government's emerging trust responsibility. Finally, the last two chapters reveal how the mixed bloods "belonging to the Lake Superior Chippewa" were mostly assimilated through kinship to the reservation communities and the implications this demographic shift had for the Ojibwe polities in the upper Midwest.

The study is an effort to show how a changing economy, competing conceptions of belonging and difference, colonization, and law interact in the evolution of an indigenous polity. Focusing on the implementation a single provision of a single treaty and the subsequent consequences provides a window into the efforts of an indigenous polity to retain control of the means of its own social and cultural reproduction, even as that polity transformed.

1

Ojibwe Ethnogenesis and the Fur Trade

> When about to depart to return home, presents of a steel axe, knife, beads, and a small strip of scarlet cloth were given him, which carefully depositing in his medicine bag, as sacred articles, he brought safely home to his people at La Pointe.[1]

Lake Superior is the world's largest freshwater lake, and it is the defining natural feature for the indigenous groups in the region. The Wisconsin Ojibwe people live throughout the Lake Superior lowland and Northern Highland provinces adjacent to and south of the Highland. Though once mountainous, the Northern Highland province is now a peneplain of upland plains and ridges. One type of ridge is the monadnocks that crest above the level of the peneplain. The most prominent monadnock in the state is Rib Mountain[2] rising 640 feet above the level of most of the land in the region. The Penokee Range is also a monadnock. It is eighty miles long and about half a mile to a mile wide, located ten to fifteen miles from the southern shore of Lake Superior. "Old Baldy," also known as "St. Peters Dome," is on the eastern end of the Penokees. It is a red granite formation that rises to an elevation of 1565 feet and is a long-standing prayer site used by Bad River Ojibwe people and others over the centuries.[3]

The Northern Highland abounds in lakes and swamps, and few areas of the world have more lakes to the square mile. Numerous rivers flow north into Lake Superior and just as many form the headwaters of the St. Croix, Chippewa, Upper Wisconsin, and Menominee Rivers, which flow into the Mississippi.[4] Climate is seasonal, and the precipitation is moderate. This northern landscape shaped by the glaciers that left a "highly diverse set of landforms of moraines, outwash plains, drumlins, eskers, and glacial lake basins" is defined by the abundance of water manifested as rivers, streams, bogs, and lakes.[5] See the map on the next page.

The Northern Highland, with its generally infertile thin and acidic soils, is a mixed forest of fifty to sixty tree species including deciduous trees such as maple, hemlock, beech, yellow birch, and evergreens such as pines, spruce, and fir.[6] It is also abundant in blueberries, lingonberries, raspberries, juneberries, wild plums, cranberries, and wild strawberries.[7] According to Nicholas Perrot, trader, interpreter, and government agent, beaver were very plentiful in northern Wisconsin in the mid-seventeenth century. In the late seventeenth century, according to British traders, “the Chippewa country south of Lake Superior was scarcely to be surpassed or equaled for its fine furs.”[8] Indeed, John Pastor, author of *What Should a Clever Moose Eat? Natural History, Ecology and the North Woods*, asserted that the population density and quality of beaver fur was highest from the Great Lakes northward, and no other species in the region has played a larger role in shaping the land and waterscape.[9]

Map 1.1. Detail of “Landforms of the United States” show the region. Erwin Raisz, Fifth edition, 1957. Courtesy of Raisz Landform Maps.

And it was a watery world. A number of navigable streams flow into Lake Superior draining the Northern Highland, which, in turn is honeycombed with navigable streams ultimately connected to the larger rivers and finally the Mississippi. Douglas Birk described the "surface water system" of the Ojibwe in this region as "labyrinthine" thereby "living in scattered enclaves."[10] Though there were nearly always a number of portages, people tended to think in terms of time spent in birchbark canoes when they thought about distance. The names of the communities also reflected this orientation, with most of the Ojibwe groups in the region calling themselves and being called after bodies of water: Lac du Flambeau, Lac Courte Oreilles, Bad River, Fond du Lac, Mole Lake, St. Croix, Leech Lake, Red Lake, Sandy Lake.

Anishinaabewaki, or Great Lakes Indian Country

In commenting on her magisterial *Atlas of Great Lakes Indian History*, Helen Tanner once confided that though Indian settlements carried identifying tribal names, there are no single-ethnicity villages in the region. All villages designated by a tribal name had members of other communities within them, usually affines but also war captives. These ethnonyms that we use so casually and confidently—Ojibwe, Menominee, Sauk, Fox—are generalizations, arguments, representations, claims about social boundedness and homogeneity made by interested parties both within and without in the guise of authoritative and definitive descriptions. The same point was made in the linguistic register in 1847 by Reverend Frederick Baraga, who worked among Ojibwe people. Responding to the commissioner of Indian affairs' "Inquiries respecting the History, present Condition and future Prospects of the Indian Tribes of the United States" and asked about their dialects and languages, Baraga wrote in response: "This tribe speaks only Chippewa language, which is almost the same as the Ottawa, the algonquin, the potawatomi and the menomini languages. All these languages are only different dialects of the same language."[11]

Members of all of these groups could respond to a question about their identity with the autonym "Anishinaabe," that is, "people," or "real human being," connoting "us" to their interlocutor and distinguishing themselves from people who spoke incomprehensibly. In *Islands of History*, Marshall Sahlins wrote that "there is no such thing as an immaculate perception,"[12] a clever riff on the oft-made point about the social and cultural constitution of reality organized by unreflected-upon categories. I would add the corollary that there is no such thing as an uninterested representation, especially when constituting "us" and "them." Identity is always situational and relational, even when—or *especially* when—the person asserting or representing an identity is claiming that it is not contextual.

In the spirit of this cautionary remark, "Chippewa" and "Ojibwe" are versions of each other and are both used by Anishinaabeg people when speaking English. "Ojibwe" has become more commonly used over the last several decades, so I default to that much of the time but also use "Anishinaabe" for the people and "Anishinaabeg" as adjective. In that "Chippewa" is often the legal designation of bands in Wisconsin, I will use that especially when the term has been used in a document under discussion.

I will default to "mixed blood" as shorthand for people with both indigenous and settler parentage rather than "Métis," which I regard as anachronistic in this context. "Mixed-blood" is also used in the treaty provision that we are most interested in exploring. I recognize that the term smuggles in a racial ideology but not as crudely as "half-breeds," though this is a term used by some mid-nineteenth-century indigenous people of mixed parentage as well. I will use it, marked in quotes, when discussing people who use this term for themselves in the immediate context of discussing a document in which the term occurs.

In the hierarchy of registers of discerning similarity and difference, inclusion and exclusion, the manner in which a person spoke was at the top of the list, as it still is today. Putative linguistic homogeneity is relative and obscures diversity. With variation at the level of the village, even the Algonquian, let alone the "Sauk," or "Ottawa" or "Potawatomie" or "Ojibwe" were only relatively homogenous linguistic communities. Even today, in the first decades of the twenty-first century, after nearly a century of these languages being used chiefly for ceremonies in most these communities, speakers will say that the dialect of their community differs from that of the next community several score miles away. People related to each other in different ways navigated a rich soundscape that mapped onto a land and waterscape.

Then, of course, there is and was kinship as the hegemonic and very capacious mode of claiming and constituting similarity and difference. There were several categories of kin relations that all had similar physical substance. There were also other categories of relations that were different enough to marry. How one sounded on the topic of whom one and one's interlocutor were related, that is, kinship, established the basis of the relationship they would have with each other. Michael Witgen makes much of this point in using the metaphor of shape-shifters in describing indigenous polities to capture their inherent "mobility and social flexibility,"[13] the result of being organized by kinship. The result is "a dizzying number of amorphous and mobile social bodies."[14] There will be more to say about the exact nature of that kinship system in the next chapter, especially in regard to the shape of the kin group into which outsiders could be integrated.

Charles Callendar characterizes the Ottawa and Chippewa sociopolitical organization as small concentrations of several families at fishing sites and trading sites in the summer who then dispersed. He added that although patrilineal clans were present, their "corporate functions and features were at best very weak. Political organization was generally of the band type, with sporadic tendencies toward wider integration."[15] Theresa Schenck amends Callendar's characterization of the centrality of clans and bands in her etymology of the now famous analytical term "totem," reminding us that the term originates with the Algonquian word "oten," meaning village. "[N]ind oten or nind odem . . . was soon heard as totem or dodem" and referred to "a group of people tied together by bonds of kinship, and who moved together seasonally."[16] And I would note here that kinship is bigger than patriliny, descent figured through men, or the strength of this ideology and practice among the Ojibwe in the earliest contact period being a matter of debate.

Heidi Bohaker characterizes Algonquian society generally and Ojibwe society in particular as essentially organized by *nindoodemag*, the first-person form of the name for a patrilineally inherited kinship network that originate with an "other-than-human progenitor being."[17] The anthropological concept of totem derives from this ethnosociological term and is often used as a synonym for clan. The social, but even more, the *political* landscape was understandable, manageable, and manipulable to its inhabitants in terms of these *nindoodemag*. Yet this mode of figuring inclusion and exclusion, rights and responsibilities, was also flexible enough to accommodate the appearance of new people perhaps, in part, because Ojibwe social organization was changing from unilineal to bilateral descent as the single-clan villages were becoming multiclan settlements over the course of the seventeenth and eighteenth centuries, catalyzed by the fur trade.[18]

In the region south and west of Lake Superior, the combination of kinship norms and techno-ecological practices resulted in people being members of families, and families articulated with each other forming named bands that controlled territories. Bands were mobile, moving between seasonally resource-dense locations where they fished both in open water and through the ice, hunted terrestrial mammals, and gathered plant foods, especially wild rice, but also maple sap to make sugar, the last at least in the protohistorical and historical periods.[19] There was also relative ease of movement between bands, often named after charismatic individuals, in that the kinship ideology that organizes social relations provides individuals with a resource that facilitates changing their allegiance and residence.

People who came to see themselves as a single culturally similar group over the course of the eighteenth century, and calling themselves "Anishinaabe" but also "Ojibwe," extended from Ontario to North Dakota. They would become one of the largest indigenous ethnicities in North America and have been well studied by scholars from both within and without those societies for many years. Scholars manage the extent and sociopolitical diversity of this ethnic group by dividing them into the northern, southeastern, and southwestern Ojibwe, this last being the division of interest here.

Robert Ritzenthaler characterizes Ojibwe historic settlement pattern as "that of numerous, widely scattered, small, autonomous bands. Thus the term 'tribe' is applicable to the Chippewa-Ojibwas [these terms being versions of each other] in terms of a common language and culture, but it does not apply in the political sense that an overall authority was present."[20] Subsequently, indigenous ethnohistorian Theresa Schenck argued for the origin of the term and identity "Ojibwa" in "Ajijack," the name for the Crane Clan, which would spread east and west from the fishing grounds at Sault Ste. Marie for its prestige value in the context of the fur trade.[21]

The ethnonymic diffusion was catalyzed by the adoption of the Feast of the Dead and later the Midewiwin, or Medicine Lodge. Both of these ceremonial complexes effervesced with the fur trade. They actively reconstituted and reproduced boundaries and conceptions of communities, contra the materialist Harold Hickerson's[22] contention that these ceremonies are best understood as mainly expressive or reflective of sociopolitical change. This consolidation of an ethnic identity was also accelerated by the Iroquois destruction of Huronia in the 1640s creating a "shatter zone"[23] throughout the Great Lakes region that caused Algonquian speaking peoples—several groups that would coalesce as the Ojibwe among them—to migrate west along both the northern and southern shore of Lake Superior,[24] thus displacing resident Dakotas and Fox in the area that would become Wisconsin. Huronia's collapse and the diaspora of their trade allies were an important event and process as North America was brought into the international fur trade.

Fur Trade

The story of the very origin if not also the dispossession of the Lake Superior mixed bloods and their assimilation to neotribal polities over the course of the second half of the nineteenth century has to begin with that intercultural exchange network we call the fur trade in North America, although it might be just as well be called "the cloth trade,"[25] according to historian Susan Sleeper-Smith, since three-quarters of what was traded was cloth. There is a very large, daunting, and inviting North American fur-trade literature.[26] For the purposes at hand, the literature is especially interesting and relevant in regard to the extent to which economic practices were subsumed under political complexities and cultural orientations for both indigenous people and the Europeans. The issue calls our attention to the particular contexts within which exchange takes place between members of different societies. For the purposes of this study, however, only certain basics about the fur trade are necessary to consider.

The trade began in the northeastern region of the continent in the sixteenth century with European fishermen incidentally engaging in exchange of metal goods with indigenous people. With European interest in furs growing over the course of the sixteenth and early seventeenth centuries, more direct interest in trade developed with Indian groups proximate to French settlement in the St. Lawrence River Valley, who acquired furs from groups further inland. Similarly, the English established the trade from Hudson Bay and Albany, New York.

The Iroquois shatter zone created in the mid-seventeenth century was the result of the Iroquois effort to monopolize the trade throughout the entire Northeast and west to the Mississippi River motivated by the ordinary desire to replenish their own depleted population with captives and adoptees as well as ethnonationalistic grandiosity so common worldwide when a population taps into a new source of power. In the 1660s, the multiethnic refugee village of Chequamegon on Lake Superior was "the trade center for the entire upper Mississippi valley and western Great Lakes region."[27]

The northern tribes whose primarily subsistence came from hunting and gathering experienced a period that Marshall Sahlins refers to as "developman," a pigeonization of "development" representing an unprecedented period of material affluence that had the effect of social and cultural effervescence.[28] The immediate material benefits of new technology increased already abundant leisure time, the bands and clans were less isolated from each other, and there was more intertribal contact and intermarriage due to the capacity of gift exchange to establish and consolidate social relationships. "Religious and ceremonial life flowered, and tribal ties grew stronger. For them, the early fur-trade period was a golden age," according to Great Lakes fur-trade scholar Rhonda Gilman.[29] It was a time when Indians made great demands upon both the French and the English in the quality of the goods they were willing to exchange for their beaver pelts, indexing the relative equality of relations between Europeans and indigenous people.[30]

It was at this time that some *coureurs de bois* began to take up residence with Ojibwe in the region and culturally assimilate to indigenous society as they hunted more, used native technology, ate native foods, married, and had children with native women. From an indigenous point of view, and in the context of developman, in somewhat the same way that Ojibwe's relationship with their *manitu* had attracted animals to their traps, then material goods to their lodges, so, too, did they attract human beings to their families, clans, and villages, accessing new resources in the process. In his effort to foreground indigenous agency, scholar of the Ottawa Michael McDonnell points out that it was the Anishinaabe who invited the French to come live amongst them, rather to the dismay of colonial leaders who were attempting to consolidate settlements in the east.[31] The early extractive industry was bilateral, and both created relationships between societies and transformed those societies by virtue of exchanges that were the substance of those relationships. This is to say that there were important social implications to the exchange and use of guns, iron pots, cloth, furs, wild rice, alcohol, and venison, even as these objects were assimilated to both indigenous[32] and European orders of value.

Frederick Jackson Turner's dissertation "The Character and the Influence of the Indian Trade in Wisconsin" is the first and now widely criticized scholarly treatment of the fur trade in the Great Lakes region. For Turner, the trade "exploited the natives" and made an already socially inferior people dependent upon a superior people. To his credit, he also recognizes pre-Columbian intertribal trade, the importance of the social relationships entailed in such trade, and that indigenous exchange was the foundation of subsequent commerce.

Turner begins his discussion of the fur trade in Wisconsin by centering it as the link between the Great Lakes and the Mississippi and whose "river valleys teemed with fur-bearing animals" and then went on to a description of the human landscape of indigenous and diasporic peoples. He divides the two centuries of active trade into three historical periods: French from 1634 to 1763, English from 1763 to 1814, and American from 1814 to 1834.[33] It was first during the French period and then, to a lesser extent, the English period in which a culturally and politically distinctive social status emerged in the form of what some people referred to as the mixed bloods. With their more racially oriented view of human diversity, it would be the Americans who would bring the term "half-breeds" to this social imaginary.

Turner draws on the mid-seventeenth-century writing of Pierre Radisson describing the trade and concludes, "This early commerce was carried on under the fiction of an exchange of presents." And here he is indexing the significance of the quality and texture of the social relationships that were to make the exchange of material goods and services possible, a point that I will return to shortly. He adds that the *coureurs de bois* had formed a distinct class by 1660, "were entirely at home upon our lakes,"[34] and were in violation of the law in moving into these lands west of Lakes Michigan and Superior. This point was later elaborated by Frank Ross, who noted that "they mated with Indian women in such numbers that by the close of the French regime it is stated that most of the white inhabitants of western Canada were related to the savages by birth, marriage, or other ties."[35] The observation points to the weakness of the commitment of these entrepreneurial pioneers to their own ostensibly civilized origins, a fact that would predispose them—and more so their children—to assimilation to indigenous society and polity.

By the late eighteenth century, the voyageurs and their mixed-blood descendants had been assimilated to what Michael Witgen describes as "*Anishinaabewaki* . . . a sophisticated composite social world with important cosmopolitan population centers" and elsewhere, as one of several indigenous "multipolar social formations, not single Indian nations."[36] A hundred years earlier, there were "literally hundreds of such coureurs" despite the French government's various efforts to try to manage this interface.[37]

Competition between the English and French for global hegemony destabilized the Great Lakes region in the seventeenth century, and it only restabilized in the early eighteenth. With the conclusion of the Fox Wars, the general tribal demography had been established. And with the transfer of sovereignty from the French to the British in 1763, the western Great Lakes region would retain its status as a largely Indian-controlled and ethnically French-managed hunting ground because of the value of the trade to the British crown. The Northwest Company organized the trade with Montreal as the headquarters and Detroit, Mackinaw, Sault Ste. Marie and Grand Portage as its emporiums. Turner describes the men at the interface between indigenous production and British consumption as "a picturesque crew in their gaudy turbans, or hats adorned with plumes and tinsel, their brilliant handkerchiefs tied sailor-fashion about swarthy necks, their calico shirts, and their flaming worsted belts."[38] His description reveals the extent to which employees of the NW Company had assimilated the aesthetic norms of indigenous society. They would assimilate more than just sartorial taste.

The Americans would not assert effective control over the region until the mid-teens of the nineteenth century with the emergence of the American Fur Company, the garrisoning of Green Bay and Prairie du Chien, and the establishment of government trading posts in those locations. There the goods that were availed to Indian people included chiefly blankets, coarse cloths, cheap jewelry and trinkets (including strings of wampum), fancy goods (like ribbons, shawls, etc.), kettles, knives, hatchets, guns, powder, tobacco, and liquor.

Indigenizing Fur-Trade Interpretations

From the foregoing description by Turner, the reader can appreciate the general outline of the order of exchanges and the likely demographic consequences of this engagement. Stepping out of our second-nature economistic disposition for a moment, consider how indigenous people appeared to understand this world-historical process and transformation. To call the material exchanges that took place between indigenous people and the Europeans who came amongst them "trade" is to impose the European understanding of exchange upon interaction that was more complex because the exchange was subject to the understanding of another of approximate equal power. Here we follow Richard White's lead—inspired by the anthropologist Marshall Sahlins—and reiterate conclusions he draws from his detailed study of the Great Lakes region in the seventeenth through the early nineteenth centuries wherein he introduced the idea of "the middle ground," useful here especially since the concept has been nuanced by Michael Witgen and critiqued by Michael McDonnell.[39]

The middle ground is the idea that the French and the Natives had to constantly negotiate the terms of their relationship because neither group had the power to impose its definition of any situation on the other. In doing so, each also sought to appeal to the other in what it took to be the other's understanding of its own motivations and desires, thus generating innovative social and cultural forms in this reflexive process. Both brought models of exchange that shaped the improvisational negotiation of their relationships. These were models that were different from each other and necessarily had to be accommodated by the other. The French increasingly embraced market values and regarded the price to be a matter of negotiation, for example. In turn, indigenous people thought and acted in terms of reciprocity, and spoke of *besoins*, needs, and were averse to negotiating price.[40]

Indian people lived in decentralized societies, were without markets as means of distribution, and were without a state as means of enforcement and regulation. By contrast, exchange was organized in terms of the perceived and represented *needs* of each party. As importantly, an antecedent relationship between buyer and seller needed to precede actual exchange.[41] For the French, the market was growing more and more independent of other social spheres as it grew in importance as the site for the allocation of limited goods and services. The trading tribes, by contrast, organized by kinship and reciprocity, were without such institutional differentiation. They were what Sahlins referred to as the "original affluent societies," their members disposed to acting as if Nature was more than adequate to satisfy man's needs and wants,[42] hence their expectation that the French would respond to statements of need, especially since local people now stood in a kinship relationship to the French king.

The necessity of antecedent relationship for tribal people entailed the transformation of indigenous societies to include the offspring of native mothers and European fathers. Even Frederick Jackson Turner took some recognition of this outcome though casting it in negative and racial terms: "By intermarriages with the French traders, the purity of the stock was destroyed and a mixed race produced."[43] By contrast, Sylvia Van Kirk foregrounds Indian agency in this matter pointing out that "Indians initially encouraged the formation of marriage alliances between their women and European traders" because they "regarded mixed blood children as having superior physical attributes which made them better hunters and bolder warriors."[44] Moreover, Jennifer Brown writes that "economic relations were largely coterminous with actual or potential kinship links, and the establishment of marital ties with their white associates was a natural priority."[45] This criteria then organized exchange and tended to push the relationship in the direction of gift exchange. This included considerations of honor and prestige, obligation, power, and the creation, perpetuation, and validation of social relationships and status. This would be acceptable to the French as they saw their trade with the Algonquians as necessary to maintain the alliances they needed vis à vis their adversary, the English, and their alliances with the various tribes of Iroquois.[46]

Non-Indian traders were assimilated using a version of the same practice and for similar reasons. In the same way that the offspring of captives assumed legitimate places in the indigenous social order, so too did the children that issued from the unions between European men and Indian women, though James Clifton finds that for northern hunters and gatherers organized by patriliny, not having an indigenous father marked individuals as less than full members. He writes that these offspring were not counted as Anishinaabeg but were regarded as "affinal kinfolk who lived on the fringes of Indian society. . . . a new people of ambiguous status."[47] This may be true for some period of time in the first generation; however, over the course of decades, most of these individuals appear to have been assimilated to indigenous society as it transformed. For example, the patriclan system was flexible enough to improvise the Wolf dodem for the offspring of Anishinaabeg men and Dakota women as well as Eagle for those with American fathers. And I point out here, the offspring of French and Indian women called for no such social organizational improvisation. These unions were apparently not a problem with this relatively weak form of clanship likely being conferred by the men in the woman's group upon the child of an indigenous mother and a European father.

Bruce White shows how indigenous people attempted with various amounts of success to assimilate Europeans to their own order of value by requiring gifts as a condition for trade.[48] Europeans would need to be integrated into the local sphere of *generalized* reciprocity as a condition of exchanges in the register of *balanced* reciprocities wherein items of equal value could be exchanged. Generalized reciprocity is characterized by love, that is "enduring, diffuse solidarity"[49] in anthropologist David Schneider's terms. Indeed, in illustrating the importance of gifts for the Ojibwe generally, Bruce White's very first example comes from Johann Georg Kohl, who traveled in the region of Lake Superior among the Ojibwe in the 1850s and linked love with gift giving and food sharing: "If you say to one of them 'I love thee,'" wrote Kohl, "have a present ready to hand, to prove your love clearly. You will lose in their sight if a present, or some tangible politeness, does not follow on such an assurance."[50]

Eric Wolf concludes his chapter on the fur trade in *Europe and the People without History* recognizing that economics was subsumed to politics such that "the exchange of goods and services between Indians and Europeans resembled the giving of gifts more than an exchange of commodities, signaling relations that transcended the merely material."[51] As a result, I would suggest, they were relations that would transform the very sociopolitical entities that were doing the exchanging. Hence Michael Witgen's argument that a new indigenous world came about as the result of the engagement with Europeans, and for a long time, its history unfolded with indigenous people's agendas the major driving force, as Michael McDonnell has also claimed for the region focusing on Anishinaabeg people who came to be known to themselves and others as the Ottawa.[52] It was all that was entailed with exchange that transformed this indigenous world.

This effort to model exchange as gift giving was facilitated by the ecological and technical aspects of the so-called trade. The traders brought both capital goods needed to hunt and the domestic wares well in advance of the Indian hunters trapping the game that would repay the traders. We, as Westerners, are embedded in a social formation that defaults to contract and balanced reciprocity, so we might regard the temporal distance between trader's donation and hunter's response as credit. That temporal duration, however, is assimilable to an indigenous order of value and the exchanges construable as gift giving as a result.

Beyond the extended family, the Ojibwe—and we might add, the other tribal groups in the Great Lakes region as well—were organized into clans wherein kinship informed relationships with members addressing each other and interacting as brothers and sisters. The language of kinship also organized the relationship between such social entities with groups regarding each other as siblings or descendants of each other. For example, the Ojibwe, Ottawa, and Potawatomi regarded each other as eldest, middle, and younger brother respectively. Many Algonquian groups honored the Lenape (Delaware), calling them grandfathers. We might say that kinship was even extended to the animals that they hunted[53] as well as to spiritual beings and the relationship constituted in and as gift exchange. Or, alternatively, the entire cosmos of corporeal and incorporeal beings was organized by kinship, human society being the sector of that totality that was uniquely and demonstrably conscious of the reality of relatedness.[54]

Bruce White notes that intermarriage bound groups to each other as well,[55] each drawing the other into the sphere of generalized reciprocity as "marriage prestations are of course the classical form of exchange as social compact." [56] Anthropologist James Clifton argues that daughters and sisters were exchanged by men to establish new or reinforce old alliances, converting outsiders into brothers-in-law and indebted those outside groups, including the French.[57]

This patriarchal view of indigenous exchange has been critiqued, specifically addressing the agency of women in this culturally hybrid fur-trade society, and here the work of Jacqueline Peterson (1978, 1981, 1985, 2012), Sylvia Van Kirk (1983), Jennifer Brown (1980), Lucy Eldersveld Murphy (2014), and Susan Sleeper-Smith (2001, 2009, 2018) has revised earlier understandings. Though the different groups that made up Anishinaabewaki are often described as patrilineal, women controlled the production of two essential foodstuffs, wild rice and maple sugar, thus giving them a political standing in their communities that was more robust that women in the European agricultural societies at the time. The journals of fur traders François Malhiot and Michel Curot from early nineteenth century Wisconsin, for example, index women's political standing as they include references to women with their own trading accounts. Melissa Meyer also pointed out that by the eighteenth century, patriliny was giving way to bilaterality.[58] This reflects the incorporation of the children of non-Indian fathers as members of the community *pace* James Clifton's judgment that these people retained an ambiguous and marginal status, a conclusion that is contradicted by the presence of so many mixed-blood political leaders over the course of the nineteenth century.

In his study of mixed bloods throughout the United States, for example, Thomas Ingersoll lists the factors favoring racial intermarriage on the frontier east of the Mississippi river and all of which apply to the Lake Superior Ojibwe: "Indian openness of marrying out; the greater mutuality and attractiveness of marriage because of the Indian's relative gender equality; the significant frontier production and other cultural skills women brought to a match with a white man, who might or might not become a permanent member of the tribe and a responsible father."[59]

In the diplomatic register, these considerations resulted in the Algonquians and the French coming to agree that their relationship was understandable in a kinship idiom with the former as the children of the latter, though the proportions of obedience, authority, and love that were the substance of that relationship were themselves subject to negotiation. The kinship idiom did, however, provide the parameters for such negotiation. And the practice took place in the villages wherein individual traders also "established the symbolic ties of kinship"[60] as well as physical ones via intermarriage albeit in the fashion of the country, that is, without ceremonial validation recognized by non-Indians. Nonetheless, because the Ojibwe kinship system regarded parallel cousins—same sex parent's children—are brothers and sisters, a man marrying an indigenous woman acquired all her "brothers" and "sisters" as siblings-in-law as well as their parents as mothers- and fathers-in-law, and they acquired him with the attendant expectations of exchange.

Exchange took place in multiple bodily registers and attendant emotional valences. Relationships were realized in and as the actual and symbolic practice of the exchange of bodily fluids, for example, such as the Ojibwe asking the French for mother's milk, a euphemism for rum, or Ojibwe leaders shedding their tears and rubbing them onto the bodies of the earliest French visitors.[61] Corelatively, Bruce White points out that implicit rules for the exchange of alcohol, food, and tobacco—all substances that enter the body, thus constituting sameness among communicants—were different than the rules for the exchange of the capital goods like guns, kettles, and cloth.[62] The complicated relations the Ojibwe had with the Dakota included the exchange of persons, usually daughters and sisters as wives, as well as arrows and later bullets fired into each other's bodies, and then body parts in the form of scalps that would have personlike presences in each other's villages. It is noteworthy that diplomacy was made possible with the exchange of personal items of used clothing, that is, clothing that had been in contact with the body. These practices of entering each other's bodies, in Maurice Bloch's terms, are modes of constituting kinship, "mutuality of being," in Marshall Sahlins terms in his recent study of the concept of kinship.[63]

A Mythopoetic Account of the Fur Trade

Fur-trade scholarship can be arrayed on a continuum with formalist economics at one pole and substantivist at the other, with the former foregrounding individual human rationality, choice, and the presumption of alternative ends and limited means. The latter is oriented toward how groups actually organize subsistence embedding exchange in culturally specific social relations with all of their complexity and idiosyncrasy. Because we are most interested in the status of so-called mixed bloods from an indigenous perspective, an examination of an indigenous account of the origins of fur trade that comes from the Lake Superior Ojibwe provides insights into how Ojibwe people were imagining the world and the relationships between themselves and others, and the place of goods in constituting that world.

The text comes from William Whipple Warren, himself the child of an American father, Lyman Warren, working for the American Fur Company, and an indigenous mixed-blood mother, Marie, eldest daughter of the trader Michel Cadotte and granddaughter of Waub-ij-e-juak, chief of the Crane Clan in the Chequamegon area. High born on both sides of his family, William was bilingual and had the confidence of the indigenous political leadership to undertake a history of the Ojibwe people in the late 1850s and then produce what Matt Hooley argues is a "metropolitan autoethnography" characterized by "an insider's outsidedness—a view of Ojibwe cultural life as seen from the colonial city."[64] The account of the origin of the trade appears in his *History of the Ojibway People* published in 1885. Because trade began several centuries before this story was collected, its value as a reliable history of the origin of the relationship between Europeans and indigenous groups is at least questionable. Nonetheless, the story is very valuable as the mythopoetic manner in which the relationship between Ojibwes and Europeans or even Euro-Americans was thought about during the treaty period of the mid-nineteenth century, the moment at which the indigenous polity was growing more structurally elaborate. Warren offers this internal view of first contact between his people and the Europeans and the exchange that took place:

> While still living on their large and central town on the Island of La Pointe, a principal and leading Me-da-we priest, whose name was Ma-se-wa-pe-ga [Whole Ribs], dreamed a dream wherein he beheld spirits in the form of men, but possessing white skins and having their heads covered. They approached him with hands extended and with smiles on their faces. This singular dream he related to the principal men of the Ojibways on the occasion of a grand sacrificial feast of his guardian dream-spirit. He informed them that the white spirits who had thus appeared to him, resided toward the rising sun, and that he would go and search for them. His people tried to dissuade him from undertaking what they termed a foolish journey, but firm in his belief, and strong in his determination, he was occupied a whole year in making preparations for his intended journey. He built a strong canoe of birch bark, and cedar wood; he hunted and cured plenty of meat for his provisions; and early in the spring when the ice had left the Great Lakes, and he had completed his preparations, Ma-se-wa-pe-ga, with only his wife for a companion, started on his travels

in quest of the white spirits whom he had seen in his dream.

He paddled eastward to the Great Lakes in the route of the former migration of his tribe, till he entered into a large river which flowed in the direction of the rising sun. Undiscovered he passed through the hostile tribes of the Naud-o-ways. At last when the river on which he floated, had become wide and like a lake, he discovered on the banks, a hut made of logs and he noticed the stumps of large trees which had been cut by sharper instruments than the rude stone axes used by the Indians.

The signs were apparently two winters old, but satisfied that it was the work of the sprits for whom he was in search, Ma-se-wa-pe-ga proceeded on his journey, and he soon came to another hut and a clearing, which though deserted, had been built and occupied during the previous winter. Much encouraged, he paddled on downstream till he discovered another hut from the top of which arose a smoke. It was occupied by the "white spirits," who, on his landing, cordially welcomed him with a shake of the hand.

When about to depart to return home, presents of a steel axe, knife, beads, and a small strip of scarlet cloth were given him, which carefully depositing in his medicine bag, as sacred articles, he brought safely home to his people at La Pointe. Ma-se-wa-pe-ga again collected the principal men of his tribe in council, and displaying his curious presents, he gave a full narrative of his successful journey and the fulfillment of his dream. The following spring a large number of his people followed him on his second visit to the supposed "white spirits." They carried with them many skins of the beaver, and they returned home late in the fall with the dread fire-arm, which was to give them power over their much feared enemies. It is on this occasion also, that they first procured the fire-water which was to prove the most dreadful scourge and curse of their race.[65]

Warren begins the story by writing that Ma-se-wa-pe-ga was a Me-da-we (Midewiwin) priest living in the "large and central town" on the island of LaPointe, thus indicating that the Ojibwe historical sociology links the Midewiwin with town life, likely referring to the refugee village at Chequamegon almost two centuries earlier. Representing the Midewiwin as a precondition of the trade is a way to express the understanding that Ojibwe ontology, spiritual values, and practice encompass and motivate the so-called trade in a time before their spiritual practice was objectified on the discursive "middle ground" and referred to as "Me-da-we" in Warren's orthographic practice. The indigenous conception of exchange was substantivist. Importantly, a preponderance of the gifts that were exchanged in the context of the Midewiwin were of European origin, a sign of Ojibwe capacity to attract wealth from beyond the borders of their own society. And though those gifts had a utilitarian value, the wealth being produced by the Medicine Lodge ritual in which they were exchanged was in the form of social relationships that made for the "long life" that practitioners sought.

A related point is made with the whites appearing in a stylized dream account before they are made to appear in historical fact, announcing the presence of a total cultural system in which all events and relationships have mythological precedents. Realities first appear as dreams, gifts of the spirits, and then as material forms, implicating and indexing the virtue of the dreamer/actor. And it is a relationship again, as signified by the white (non-Indian) sign of relationship, the shaking of hands, that in turn, is made concrete by goods. Those goods were given at the end of the visit as tokens of that relationship. Two of the items are in the category of capital goods: the steel axe and the knife, and two are decorative, the beads and the cloth, both worn on the body and indexical of social status. Furthermore, Ma-se-wa-pe-ga put them in his medicine bag as they were "sacred articles [which] he brought safely home to his people at LaPointe." These objects are capable of reproducing and transforming the most valued indigenous relationships and conditions as all sacred objects are always wont to do. And just like any sacred object, the possession of which validates one's social status as an actor in the reproduction of social relations, those objects typically originate from well beyond the borders of one's mundane socioterrestrial world.

The presence of goods at feasts within the context of the Midewiwin, which Warren says was practiced in its "purest form" in the "large and central town," was a sign of a relationship with another world now annexed through Ojibwe effort and virtue, and explicitly understood in spiritual terms. The very capacity to have such a relationship was a sign of health and wealth as traditionally imagined. It represents the deployment of exotic, albeit useful, wealth objects toward indigenous ends. Use values were transformed into exchange values in a new and larger sphere of social relations. A man's ability, inclination, and responsibility to hunt and trap yielded goods that could be given away, effectively in exchange for esoteric knowledge and healing skills, making him and his family healthy and rich and part of an elite by virtue of a validated capacity to constitute and reproduce both human and extrahuman relationships.

Bruce White pointed out that trade goods "could increase the prestige and power of the person who owned them or gave them away in religious and political ceremonies."[66] Here I extend the implications of that observation. In the Midewiwin ceremonies via the fur trade, the bodies of animals were transformed into the wealth that was both a sign of distinction and productive of distinction. The very capacity to take animals and accumulate furs itself was a sign of spiritual power so that we might think of the Midewiwin initiation being as validating as it was creative. In this sense, the presence and interest of the Europeans in animal skins in the form of the trade was given meaning in the context of a ceremony whose ostensible purpose was to prolong collective life by increasing and distributing spiritual power. One of the outcomes was to reconfigure social relationships in the direction of the creation of hierarchies.

All of these relations are rehearsed in the migration story wherein the Ojibwe see themselves as coming from the East and moving to the West and is symbolized in the repeated appearance, disappearance, and reappearance of the *megis* (cowrie) shell on the landscape.[67] This is a historical metaphor of a total social process as it was the presence of European wealth that catalyzed the emergence of the Ojibwe as ethnic group. The shell itself is associated with the generative power of the Underwater Manito but comes to Ojibwe people via the trade with the whites because cowries are ultimately from the Indian Ocean and were used as money by many different peoples for millennia.[68] They were introduced by the Hudson Bay Company to barter for furs.[69] But they also came from the East via the French. It is not insignificant that exotic shell money from very far away would be assimilated to an indigenous order of value conferring upon it the capacity to humanize whole landscapes with the presence of the Anishinaabe upon them.

The relationship is implied by Christopher Vecsey in his study of Ojibwe religion, and he is quite correct when he suggests that "the history of Ojibwa contacts with whites and the history of Midewiwin's development were congruent, if not synonymous."[70] This is to say that religious practice does not only reflect sociopolitical realities but actually constitutes them. The process requires a mechanism that must be grounded in Ojibwe metaphysics and praxis. More than a relationship between an essentialized indigenous ethnic group and a developing ceremonial complex, Ojibwe sacred history references the migration of an ethnogenetic locus, objectified as the ethnonymic "Ojibwe" and realized in the Midewiwin.

Ojibwe ethnicity is the outcome of the interaction between local Algonquian language-speaking communities and access to European wealth. The eighteen named Algonquian-speaking communities identified by Dablon and Allouez in the *Jesuit Relations*[71] reimagined and made themselves into the historic Ojibwe by deploying European interest in fur bearers via the exchanges of goods for spiritual power in the Midewiwin in a historically unprecedented realization of *pimadazawin*,[72] the good life indigenously imagined. The Midewiwin is the traditional religion of the Ojibwe in this sense and the sense in which these communities transformed, coalesced, and authored themselves as Ojibwes, elaborating their healing practices and ritual life as they appropriated European interest in both political alliance and the fur-bearers in their domain. It was, indeed, becoming a new indigenous world in large part due an inherent indigenous capacity and inclination to resignify both European trade goods and the offspring of European and indigenous amorous liaisons.

This chapter explores the ethnogenesis of an indigenous ethnicity and extends the concept of Anishinaabewaki, as a complex, evolving, and culturally heterogeneous, hybrid, indigenous sociopolitical formation. Groups within this formation have a characteristic mode of reproducing themselves and relating to social and political entities beyond their borders. Both foreign objects and persons, via the fur trade, were assimilated to a total order of value and practices, while changing that order even as the order reproduced itself. Indigenous groups experienced a period of developman wherein their culture and society effervesced, creating new social categories of indigenous people.

Perhaps the most mundane icon of this transformation also works as an icon of my general argument. The French greeting "Bon jour," now rendered as "Boozhoo" in current orthographic practice,[73] was assimilated in the late eighteenth and early nineteenth centuries by a number of Algonquian-speaking indigenous peoples. Exchanging a verbal token of their emerging commonality suggests a reconception of their belonging in the face of an internal structural transformation that generated new social categories. We turn now to an extended analysis of one of those categories, the "mixed bloods, belonging to the Chippewa of Lake Superior."

2

Descent Ideology, Sociality, and the Transformation of Indigenous Society

It is souls, not shared blood, that create the ties that bind.[1]

"Mixed bloods," "half-breeds," "Métis" originate as ideological terms posing as descriptive terms among the indigenous peoples of the western Great Lakes. Here I deal with only the first two since the history of Métis is beyond the geographic scope of this project. All three of these terms are European and Euro-American folk categories. The use of these terms represents a political project first on the parts of Euro-Americans, and then Indian people, and only finally the parts of persons so designated, and then only for a relatively short time.

In her recent masterful study of Wisconsin's historical development, Bethel Saler writes that "the very meddlesome category 'mixed-blood' represented another awkward expedient in American endeavors to organize and incorporate the Wisconsin region according to a racially defined matrix."[2] Theresa Schenck writes that the so-called mixed bloods were a solution to the Indian problem: give them land to cultivate and they will be good examples to their full-blood kin.[3] Patrick Wolfe sees the terms as intended to reduce the numbers of people with claims to land as well as a means of exclusion from the privileges of whiteness.[4] Writing about the full-blood/mixed-blood opposition in the early twentieth century at the White Earth Ojibwe Reservation in Minnesota, Jill Doerfler shows how the categorization was both resisted and manipulated because even though whites in power were quite certain that this difference made a difference, according to the residents of the community, biological ancestry was not a significant factor in an individual's identity. The categories were new, fluid, and open to interpretation as they could reference physical appearance, cultural disposition, economic orientation, ancestry, language preference, clothing style, or religious affiliation, and these traits did not co-vary.[5]

The term "half-breed" only begins to gain currency in the 1790s when Americans begin to grow anxious about the advances Indian people were making, especially in the Southeast, where matrilineal, agricultural societies were actively assimilating non-Indians. "Very suddenly, after 1795" observes Thomas Ingersoll, "whites began to regard mixed bloods as a peculiar 'people,' even though these Indians never deliberately formed a distinct group." They were both threatening and a potential political tool.[6] The term would appear in the writings of Fathers Richard and Crevier at Prairie du Chien in 1823 when American settler anxiety began to increase over the loyalty of the formerly British-allied tribes.[7] In the 1837 and 1842 treaties with the Chippewa, they were "half-breeds." By 1847, they had become "half or mixed bloods." In the 1854 treaty, they were "mixed bloods." By the 1870s, when Reverend Baraga assembled his *Dictionary of the Ojibwe Language*, he would be able to collect the term *aiabitâwisid* for half-breed, *wissâkodëwiwinini* for half-breed man and *wissâkodéwikwe* for half-breed woman. The reference was to half-burnt wood[8] and represented a direct translation of the English and French terms. The terms were neologisms, an appropriation of an alien category since there was no indigenous analog. It was now a new social category.

Race, Indians, and Mixed Bloods

"Half-breed" and "mixed blood" are racial terms. And race, as a way of thinking about and enacting belonging and difference, was on the ascent during the early nineteenth century displacing the Enlightenment consensus that regarded differences between groups of humans as not reducible to an independent, internal characteristic of individual human bodies. Enlightenment thinkers were also interested in taxonomy, however. As a result, along with the emergence of the idea of the species came the idea of varieties within species and debates about the immutability of both.

The critique of the authority of Holy Writ that the Enlightenment represented undermined confidence in the idea of the unity of mankind. The emergence of polygenesis contributed to the immutability of intrahuman variation and crystalized in the concept of race. By the early nineteenth century, the idea that humans were organized into a definite, if debatable, number of physically distinguishable, discrete, and rankable groups established by Nature or God, with membership determined by inheritance, and most importantly, that those physical differences correlated with mental, emotional, moral, and cultural dispositions and capacities, was therefore becoming "common sense," if not good sense. Techniques were invented to measure differences in all these dimensions with the effect of increasing confidence in the original presumption of locating fundamental differences between groups within individual human bodies themselves.[9]

Nineteenth-century scholars such as Josiah Nott and Samuel Morton were prominent in arguing for the immutability of races and locating the cause of the difference between groups of humans within the individual humans themselves. Morton transmitted Blumenbach's five-race paradigm and measured the internal volume of brain cases on the theory that physical volume set the parameters for intellectual and moral capacity. Morton concluded that though Indians had been exposed to civilization for up to two centuries at that point, they were rejecting it due to their mental shortcomings. Importantly, Henry Schoolcraft, who had been US Indian agent at Sault Ste. Marie in Chippewa country, then superintendent of Indian affairs for the Northern Department, corresponded with Morton[10] and was sympathetic to his views, though he would denounce Nott and Glidden's scientific racist tract, *Types of Mankind* in 1854.[11] Schoolcraft was married to a mixed-blood Anishinaabeg woman, the daughter of a Scots fur trader and an important indigenous political leader.

Robert Bieder examined the implications of the emerging concept of race for mixed bloods because in the early nineteenth century they were looked upon as agents of progress. Over the course of the nineteenth century, as some scientists gravitated toward polygenism—the notion that we were not, in fact, a single species—these same scientists grew more and more pessimistic about the assimilability of mixed bloods. By the middle of the nineteenth century, a mixed blood was seen as no different from an Indian and incapable of fully embracing civilization, at least within the scientific community.[12] Yet they were distinguished from "Indians" in many treaties at the time.

The eminent historian Francis Paul Prucha came to the conclusion that racial thinking did not play a determinate role in Indian policy in the nineteenth century, carefully laying out his argument in a 1981 essay.[13] The combination of Enlightenment ideas about the perfectibility of man and evangelical Christianity's commitment to the unity of mankind were more formidable than the appeal of polygenic science to the people who crafted Indian policy. Drawing upon reports made to the Senate by several commissioners of Indian affairs and the provisions of treaties made at the time, Prucha makes it clear that the policy makers believed that education, especially in the hands of the churches, was the solution to the cultural differences between Indians and whites. Nonetheless, many different groups of indigenous American people would assimilate the idea of race—especially the tribes in the Southeast.[14]

The cultural difference of greatest consequence between the settling Europeans and Indian people was the role of kinship in the organization of society and the role of parentage in determining social identity. Not only did kinship play a much larger and extensive role in organizing Indian societies than it did in European societies, but kinship included many other-than-human persons such as Thunderbirds and bears.[15]

Parentage also determined identity and group membership in a less flexible way for Europeans than it did for Indians. For Europeans, identity could fractionate with half of one's substance imagined to come from the mother and half from the father, membership, and rights allocated accordingly. In contrast, the children of an Indian mother and a European father were presumptively Indian—or could easily be made so—for both matrilineal and patrilineal groups. Even where patrilineal clanship rules presumptively excluded the children of non-Indian fathers, communities created new clans, thereby conferring rights and obligations upon the progeny of such a relationship. The nearby Menominee, for example, improvised the Prairie Chicken and Hog clans to assimilate the children of Indian women and non-Indian men.[16] For Ojibwe, children of such marriages were assigned to the Eagle clan.[17] In these societies that were largely organized by kinship, there were several mechanisms for assimilating persons to the fold. Generally, Natives were far less interested in what the Europeans came to regard as biological inheritance in favor of commitment to social and cultural inheritance. In Heidi Bohaker's terms "It is souls, not shared blood, that create the ties that bind."[18]

Reflecting the ascendancy of racial ideology, Thomas Ingersoll argues that Europeans "believed that to conquer the land they had to create reasonable facsimiles of European society, in which they preserved whites' class structure, civilized ways, and religion from adulteration,"[19] hence the concern for purity and inclination to fractionate. And though racial intermixture took place in the hinterland, it was frowned upon by fur-trade-company officials, government officials, and missionaries. When white women made their way to the frontier, it became "the occasion for white people of both sexes from the upper class to adopt more explicit, exclusive social rules that created a true racial regime for the first time, one intended to protect the specially delegated dignity of white women, and thereby, the purity of the white race."[20] Perhaps the best measure of this long-standing desire and intention is Ingersoll's observation that "the central fact of American history is that today's basic racial groups exist—rather than a single brown 'race' because white American legally structured them based on morphological differences, phenotypes that whites selected to signify fundamental differences in social relations."[21]

In Canada, by contrast, "a single 'brown' race" did emerge as a distinct ethnic group—the Métis—in the Red River Valley, and to a lesser extent among the Central Siouans. However, the "mixed bloods belonging to the Lake Superior Chippewa," as they were referred to in the treaties, did not represent a separate ethnic group but a social category in the development and transformation of an indigenous polity. With the Ojibwe in mind, ethnohistorian Theresa Schenck states the matter clearly: "In the United States, there had been no special recognition of people of mixed Indian and European descent. This was not to deny their existence, but they did not develop as, nor were they seen as, a separate people. From the Indian viewpoint, identity was simply a matter of lifestyle. Those who lived as Indians were Indians; no distinction between Indian and halfbreed was made."[22]

Included in the "lifestyle," of course, were the social relationships with people more unambiguously indigenous in everyone's eyes.

In his essay "Of Totemism and Ethnicity," John Comaroff makes several points that inform this inquiry and the position I am taking on, including the so-called mixed bloods as members of evolving indigenous polities and societies. Comaroff's first point is that ethnicity has its origin in structural and cultural historical forces.[23] For those taking the position that "a new people" came onto the scene as a reflex of the mode of producing furs in Native North American, this first point is easily agreed to. Second, ethnicity describes a set of relations and mode of consciousness,[24] and here the fact that these people "belonging to the Chippewa of Lake Superior" did not refer to themselves with a special term is critical. Mixed bloods were typically referred to by Indian people as "our relatives" in response to their being designated as separate by Europeans and to a far greater extent by Euro-Americans. The terms listed above are ideological in the sense that it was a European American political project to reshape conceptions of the indigenous human landscape, casting it in the recently emerged racial terms.

Comaroff's third proposition is that ethnicity "has its origins in the asymmetric incorporation of structurally dissimilar groupings into a single political economy."[25] It is well established that the fur trade represented a "single political economy" with large sectors of North Americans being assimilated to the world system. To what extent were dissimilar groupings asymmetrically incorporated into this sector of the world system? Clearly, a new self-conscious sociocultural formation emerged during the first century or so of European/indigenous engagement. The Ottawa are often pointed to as the prime example of this phenomenon as the ethnonym derives from *adaawe*, meaning "to trade," and "was the generic French name for any western Indian who traveled east to trade with the French."[26] A similar process accounts for the ethnonym "Ojibwe," wherein the name of a single prestigious community was appropriated by several groups of culturally similar communities, according to ethnohistorian Theresa Schenck.[27]

To what extent were the people whom European-Americans referred to as "half-breeds" or "mixed bloods," and indigenous people referred to as "our relatives," a "dissimilar grouping"? Only after they had been separately designated in the treaties does it makes sense to talk about mixed bloods as "a dissimilar grouping," and then only for a relatively short time insofar as they would be reassimilated into the evolving indigenous formation as Indians, or in fewer cases assimilated to the dominant society as white.

In writing about concentrations of mixed bloods even at places such as Sault Ste. Marie, Michilimackinac, or Green Bay, Harriet Gorham makes the point that "the mixed-blood people of the Great Lakes region never developed a sense of shared ethnic identity comparable to that expressed as the Métis as the New Nation after 1816." They "appear to have functioned as a disparate collection of individuals rather than as a cohesive group."[28] The people with whom we are concerned in this study were hardly "a disparate collection of individuals," but rather members of unambiguously indigenous extended families and settlements, even *dodems*.

In the same way that tribal family law made the children of indigenous women and French men into indigenous people, so too it was federal Indian law in the form of treaties that made these people into "half-breeds" and "mixed bloods," terms that were also used by teachers and missionaries, therefore making schools important infrastructural sites in the production of identity. Both the letters of the Catholic Reverend Frederic Baraga and his Protestant competitors, such as the Reverends Hall, Boutwell, Wheeler, and Ely, all written from the region in the 1830s and 1840s, are full of references to "half-breeds." It was at this point that a structural dissimilarity might obtain insofar as different rights and capacities were granted and attributed to a class of indigenous person, and again, on the grounds of an ascendant and imposed racial theory of belonging and difference that had been alien to indigenous people and that created the class in the first place. With the signing of the treaties, this class of people were now recognized to be in possession of distinctive property, a separate status, and it was in their interest to acquiesce in that designation.

Racial designations shape life trajectories in profound ways. In rather the same way that designating a person "Negro" by virtue of their having a single dark-skinned great-grandparent permits some social and political options and excludes others—no matter who the person is now related to or looks like—designating an indigenous person, or designating oneself as a "mixed blood" in the middle of the nineteenth century qualified them for options controlled by Euro-Americans that their relatives without this designation did not enjoy. This is not to say that these relatives did not have claims upon them. The designation of "mixed blood" or "half-breed" also largely excluded that person from full membership in the dominant settler society, though the value of such blood was nuanced by class with some mixed-blood people, such as the wife of Henry Schoolcraft, enjoying the benefits of white society while retaining ties to the indigenous.

Scholars have addressed the emergence and presence of mixed-blood people in the region. Jacqueline Peterson's pioneering dissertation on "The People in Between" emerged out of an interest in early Chicago and led to her study of the "genesis, florescence, and sudden death of a numerous people of mixed race who inhabited the Great Lakes region of the United States between 1680 and 1830."[29] Peterson's dissertation and subsequent work is largely concerned with the people of mixed parentage who lived in fur-trade entrepôts such as Detroit, Michilimackinac, Sault Ste. Marie, Prairie du Chien, Vincennes, or Green Bay who did not have a term of self-reference. In fact, she describes the subjects of her study, these mixed bloods, as "a sizeable and influential body *within* tribal society, coerced and pandered to by treaty commissioners."[30] In her essay "Many Roads to Red River," Peterson writes of the cultural and social distinctiveness of these people despite the fact that they have no term of reference that would distinguish themselves from indigenous people and the settlers. Recently, Peterson has revised her thinking and has persuasively argued that the métis identity only emerged in the Red River Valley.[31]

In turn, Lucy Eldersveld Murphy writes about mixed people in Prairie du Chien, one of the entrepôts identified by Petersen. This, too, was a very different social and cultural formation from that the Lake Superior Ojibwe mixed bloods because of the presence of mixed people from several of the regional polities and the independence of that settlement from any of those indigenous polities. Prairie du Chien, as well as a number of other towns where a Creole population emerged in Wisconsin, was established by non-Indian fur traders, unlike the indigenous settlements in the region.

The difference might be understandable in terms of the directionality of the exchange of persons: the fur-trading entrepôts took indigenous women for wives, and the indigenous settlements took French men for husbands. Furthermore, the Creoles in places like Prairie du Chien or Green Bay largely avoided being racialized as nonwhite[32] unlike the mixed bloods in the hinterland. Indeed, as we will see, they will become painfully aware of this when US law fails to take jurisdiction over a famous murder in the 1830s.

Petersen gives us a sense of how it was that these settlements came into existence: "These people were neither adjunct relative-members of the tribal villages nor the standard bearers of European civilization in the wilderness. *Increasingly*, they stood apart, or more precisely in between. By the end of the last struggle for empire in 1815, their *towns*, which were visually, ethnically and culturally distinct from neighboring Indian villages and "white towns" along the eastern seaboard, stretched from Detroit and Michilimackinac at the east to the Red River at the northwest."[33] I have italicized what I take to be the key words in this passage. The visual, ethnic, and cultural distinctiveness of the larger mixed-blood settlements is not contestable, although in the late eighteenth century, as those places were developing, they were less distinct than they had become by the second decade of the nineteenth century. This is far less true of the "mixed-bloods belonging to the Lake Superior Chippewa," who didn't live in dense enough concentrations to be regarded as towns since they moved seasonally from one area of resources to another in association with their "Indian" relatives.

Peterson uses the term "jack-knife posts" and "trading hamlets" to refer to the late eighteenth-century communities at Lac du Flambeau, Lac Courte Oreilles, Lac Vieux Desert, and communities along the Chippewa River.[34] By the mid-nineteenth century, three generations later, the mixed bloods were living throughout the territory politically controlled by the Ojibwa and were integrated into the evolving indigenous society and polity. The people that whites recognized as Indians were adamant about the so-called mixed-blood people being "our relations."

In her book, *The White Earth Tragedy: Ethnicity and Dispossession at a Minnesota Anishinaabe Reservation 1889–1920*, a brilliant study of a single reservation community at a critical time in its history, Melissa Meyer made a good case for what I will concede is the *beginning* of the emergence of "a unique metis society throughout the western Great Lakes region" in the late eighteenth and early nineteenth centuries, but not a full emergence. She writes that "individuals of mixed descent . . . formed a society of their own," sharing "a predominantly French heritage and maintained close affiliations with their Indian relations." However, upon the creation of the White Earth Reservation, these people "emphasized their ties with various Anishinaabe bands to secure the right to move to the White Earth Reservation" because "mixed-bloods who actually lived among the Anishinaabe on one of the reservations were eligible for benefits in the 1867 treaty." They were so well articulated with indigenous communities that prominent chief Hole-in-the-Day regarded these people as his own sons, as they called him their chief, so he added them to the annuity rolls.[35] It was a single bicultural society.

The claim that there was a cultural difference and therefore an ethnic difference between mixed bloods and Anishinaabe people all living on the White Earth Reservation and members of the same polity is a valuable insight. Mixed bloods were "a bicultural class"[36] but nonetheless they were Indians largely because of the magnitude of forces emanating from the settler state, especially race.

Ethnohistorian Rebecca Kugel also takes recognition of the force of race writing that "Americans refused to recognize the Métis as a distinct ethnic or cultural group defining them instead as 'half-breed Indians.'" Here Kugel is effectively asserting that they had already accomplished such distinction, though they didn't call themselves "Métis" at the time. In fact, its pejorative connotations aside, they called themselves "half-breeds,"[37] explicitly including themselves within indigenous polities. Meyer and Kugel show that this group may have begun the process of ethnogenesis as they aspired to distinction, but with the exception of the Red River Valley, they remained Indian. In addition to the force of the racial ideology, the reservation policy sought to separate and concentrate peoples of all manner of indigenous descent in special enclaves so the conditions for the emergence of a separate indigenous ethnicity were no longer present.

Ethnic groups have names for themselves. Notably, the terms that mixed bloods used to refer to themselves were not actually ethnic. Calling the class of culturally different Indians "Métis" well after the fact obscures the particularity of the way in which belonging and difference were being figured at the time. For example, I note that Meyer refers to Gus Beaulieu, editor of *The Tomahawk* at White Earth in the early twentieth century as a métis, as she begins her argument that métis were a separate ethnic group, albeit within the White Earth polity. To her credit, she also identifies him as "Franco-Anishinaabe" even though Beaulieu identified himself as "Chippewa" on the Indian-only registration list for the meeting of the Society of American Indians in Madison in 1914.[38] I think it would have been news to him to be regarded as métis.

Both Theresa Schenck and Michael Witgen spoke directly to the issue of the relationship between the so-called mixed bloods and Indian people as noted earlier. Schenck writes that "the designation 'mixed-blood' or 'half-breed' [was] imposed upon the native inhabitants" by the government, as Indian communities had been "accepting outsiders into their communities since the first *coureur de bois* found his way into their midst."[39] When a small segment of this population, mostly males, were educated and their ties with their mother's people attenuated, they became designatable as a separate group by government officials. This created a continuum with mixed bloods who were fully integrated into Native society at one pole, and mixed bloods were oriented toward settler society at the other. Clearly, there would be far more people in the former category.

In Witgen's recent study of the indigenous Great Lakes region, he argues that the fundamental social categories in this Native New World were not racial. *Inawemaagen* (relatives) and *meuyaagizid* (strangers or foreigners) indexed the depth and extent of one's relationships in the community.[40] Relatives could be made by birth, by adoption, by capture, or through ceremonial exchanges. Presumably, there were mixed bloods who were more and less committed to their *inawemaagen,* often determined by class but not always

The issue of the nature of similarities and differences between Anglo, Ojibwe, and Métis cultural dispositions was directly addressed by Keith R.

Widder in *Battle for the Soul: Metis Children Encounter Evangelical Protestants at Mackinaw Mission, 1823–37,* and they have a lot to do with class and gender. In the very title of the book, Widder reproduces a colonial distinction using the anachronistic "Métis," even though the people to whom he will apply it do not refer to themselves as such or with any other special term.[41]

Widder observes that fur-trade society was stratified by class with the traders and clerks toward the top and the voyageurs or *coureur de bois* toward the bottom. Cultural dispositions were generally co-ordinate with this hierarchy. The traders who took Indian wives or mates were inclined to try to draw their mixed-blood sons toward French culture and society. Their mixed-blood daughters, however, gravitated more toward their Indian mothers. As one moved down the class hierarchy, the draw of Indian society grew more powerful, perhaps as access to resources in the European society diminished. The lower-class voyageur men tended to live closer to their Indian relatives. Less affluent than clerks and traders, they could not afford to send their sons back East to be educated, so lower-class mixed-blood sons were not able to distinguish themselves from their full-blood cousins as thoroughly. Mixed-blood daughters of these men were even closer to their mothers and their mothers' people than the daughters of higher-class mixed bloods. When these lower-class mixed marriages broke up, "their children were usually absorbed into the other's extended family,"[42] that is, their indigenous mothers', according to Jennifer Brown and Laura Peers.

So-called Métis settlements were also ordered within a hierarchy. Corporate trading towns like Green Bay, Prairie du Chien, and Sault Ste Marie were geographically determined and more socially complex than "métis hamlets," which were attached to Chippewa villages such as Lac du Flambeau, Lac Courte Oreilles, Yellow River, Snake River, Sandy Lake, Leech Lake, and Red Lake.[43] There were even "numerous smaller villages" to which mixed-blood employees of the fur trade were attached.

Widder's book examines schools. And here I would ask to what extent did the schools actually create this Métis identity? He points out that the missionaries "had trouble categorizing and understanding the Métis," usually referring to them as "Indians," "half-breeds," or "ignorant Frenchmen," saying that "the documentary record tells little about how the Métis perceived themselves."[44] One would think that writing this sentence would give one pause: Widder is asserting that they are Métis though confessing that we don't know how they perceived themselves. Groups of people who have a sense of themselves as separate from others don't have this problem.

He then recites an anecdote from the writings of Johann Georg Kohl, who, upon encountering a mixed-blood man, was shown the man's seal ring, which bore both his Indian totem and a French coat of arms and concludes that he was identified with both heritages.[45] That anecdote, originally from Georg Kohl's book about the Lake Superior Chippewa, whom he visited in the mid-1850s, actually includes a term of self-reference: "chicot" referring to half-burnt wood.[46] Though this anecdote has been repeated several times in the mixed-blood scholarly literature, no one has yet raised the question as to how this man had a totem at all insofar as totems are said to be inherited patrilineally. In order to address this, we have to reconsider totems.

Theresa Schenk argues that totems are originally references to villages and not the same as clans. She cites Keating, a member of the 1823 Long expedition, who writes that the totem "appears to belong to every member of a family, whether male or female . . . [and] . . . appears to serve no other purpose than that of distinguishing families,"[47] which is I why I earlier referred to clanship as relatively weak. It seems reasonable to conclude that one of this chicot's mother's male relatives must have given him his totem. The result is that he would be more integrated into indigenous society than use of the term "Métis" would suggest. Again, class would matter here. Widder's claim that mixed-blood boys "learned much about Chippewa ways from their mother and her family, their fathers would not allow them to be fully incorporated into Chippewa family or social structures"[48] The sample of children of mixed parentage in the school was skewed. There were, no doubt, many more less affluent or well-connected mixed children in the hinterland who were far more integrated into tribal society at the time.

The same could be said for what the children were taught with higher-class mixed-blood boys more likely to fill their father's shoes and move more freely and often between indigenous and settler worlds. In contrast, their lower-class fellows' fathers spent more time living in greater proximity to their wife's people. So, too, with regard to foods: the diets of the traders included more European foods than the diets of the voyageurs.[49]

In the register of religion, Widder is confident that though "the practice of Catholicism distinguished Métis children from their Chippewa cousins, French-Métis youth syncretized Roman Catholic teachings and Chippewa beliefs."[50] But it looks to me that Christianity has been indigenized. Here, it is difficult to resist a near contemporaneous characterization of this so-called syncretic practice, although it happens to come from the region northwest of Lake Superior:

> The religion of the half-breed is the creed of superstition. Roman Catholic in the main, he adds to its formulas a shadowy belief in the Great Spirit. . . . When he dies, he hopes to be carried to the bosom of the saints; yet he feels that his shade will linger four nights round the place of his decease taking its flight to the village

> of the dead. He believes in signs and omens to some extent and ties a number of feathers to his horse's tail, or paints rude emblems on his bark canoe, to increase their speed. Nevertheless, he yields implicit obedience to his priest, and obeys, in his volatile way, the traditions of his church; but, overall, cherishes a dim faith in the shades of the shadow-land.[51]

This syncretism or indigenization was not only characteristic of people with mixed parentage. Peers and Schenck comment in a footnote that "Voyageurs absorbed Native spiritual beliefs and religious practices from their Native wives and acquaintances."[52] If the voyageurs absorbed them, the children they had with indigenous women certainly expressed them.

The Métis believed in the magical properties of certain objects and took action to stay in proper relationship with the *manitus* (spiritual forces). Here both Catholicism and indigenous religion value ritual action as more efficacious than the personal testimony that is so important to the Protestants. Thus, from an analytical perspective, they practiced both monotheism and polytheism simultaneously apparently without much concern for theology or dogma and the outcome is an indigenized Christianity. Indeed, Widder will later concede that "traders and clerks retained a stronger sense of their French-Canadian identity, especially Catholicism, than did the voyageurs, who adopted more Indian customs and manners" and "whose children's behavior more closely resembled that of tribal Chippewa youngsters."[53]

In general, the Euro-American category of "mixed blood" was genealogically unambiguous—some Indian and some European "blood"—but was culturally quite heterogeneous, including people who were fully integrated into Indian society and those who were "in between" or even somewhat welcome in white society in that Métis were socially excluded and ridiculed by Americans,[54] thus strengthening the ethnic boundary between Americans and all other brown-skinned people no matter their imagined racial homogeneity. Furthermore, according to Ingersoll, "most mixed bloods did not seek acceptance by whites, they instead sought a place in Indian society, specifically in their mother's tribes."[55]

Both the schools and the prayer groups at Mackinac actively produced the social distinctions in that "Indians and French métis" were banned from the prayer meetings.[56] In the school itself, the students continued to speak French and Ojibwe.[57] In discussing the ways in which the curriculum and school culture generally were alien to the children, Widder rarely distinguishes Métis from Indian children, which I consider to be quite appropriate as most of them were members of the same society and shared many cultural practices.

Of all the Métis and Indian children who attend the school at Mackinac in the 1830s, "none began to think and act as a New Englander."[58] The project failed to civilize these children in that "these students would incorporate new elements into their lives without necessarily rejecting their existing world."[59] The fact points to competing centripetal social and cultural forces with indigenous and "civilized" life pulling individuals in different directions and the indigenous appearing to do better in the contest.

Still there were undercurrents of race. William Boutwell came from Boston to La Pointe and established a mission and a school in the 1830s. He will distinguish between Indians and half-breeds routinely in his writing, noting for example that the mixed-blood children were attending the school more regularly than the Indian kids as the former group had parents involved in the fur trade and had greater stability. In his manuscript on Sherman Hall, Hurd notes that Hall had opinions about fellow missionary Boutwell's marriage to the "half-breed daughter" of Ramsay Crooks, as he put it. It is notable that this is a prominent family in the region, Crooks being the new head of the American Fur Company. Hall officiated at the ceremony and made comments in his private letters "indicating that he was not truly happy about it."[60] Hurd speculates that he may have had the same thoughts about Lyman Warren's marriage to a mixed-blood woman. These are subtle reminders of an undercurrent of the rise of racial consciousness on a landscape that figured difference and belonging far more in terms of actual social behavior entailing exchanges in several registers of communication.

Widder writes that it was American schools that widened the gap between the two groups within the indigenous society. I would suggest that the schools transformed consciousness of belonging and difference such that speaking in terms of different indigenous social categories began to make sense, not that a new group was emerging. This transformation was co-ordinate with the power of law in the form of treaties wherein different social groups of indigenous people were named and distinguished by being granted different legal rights. If the mixed bloods can be designated as "a distinct ethnic group in the nineteenth century," as Thomas Ingersoll argues,[61] it was American settler colonialism that produced this effect, and largely in the minds of white Americans.

I think that Widder begs the question when he describes the fate of "Métis identity or nationalism in the Western Great Lakes region,"[62] contrasting it to what transpired in the Red River Valley. Though Anglos made a distinction between indigenous people who had two indigenous parents and those who had only one, these indigenous people did not make that distinction, in that they regarded themselves as all related to different and manipulable degrees and part of the transforming indigenous community.

Widder writes that after the demise of the Mackinac mission, "Metis families from the Lake Superior region lived in the relative safety of the woods and lakes of northern Wisconsin and Minnesota, where for another twenty or thirty years they continued to live their traditional lifestyles."[63] Excluded from full participation in American society, many Métis moved closer to their Chippewa kin, who were even more alienated from the Americans. This is hardly evidence for the existence of Métis ethnic identity or consciousness, aspirational nationalism, or a separate society. This formulation smuggles in the ascendant and hegemonic racialist conception of belonging and difference. Despite this, Widder regards it is a "mistake" on the parts of nineteenth-century Americans to view "Metis and tribal Indians as a single entity."[64] There may have been a potential for this indigenizing population to become "a distinct group of people," but the combination of the indigenous centripetal force of inclusion and Anglo-American centrifugal force of exclusion prevented the emergence of a tripartite social and cultural landscape in the hinterland of Great Lakes trading towns.

It appears that in places like Mackinac, or Green Bay in the 1820s and '30s, the indigenous sector of society was more diverse with people of mixed parentage of different socioeconomic classes who were more and less integrated into native society. Indeed, Widder states clearly, "Technically, socially and economically, life at Mackinac was far more complex than at LaPointe, Fond du Lac, or Sandy Lake, or at a winter hunting camp."[65] American elites excluded these people from their social affairs, and, instead, people of mixed heritage maintained ties with their native kin, thus contributing to the maintenance of a most consequential border between the two societies.

The hundreds of so-called mixed bloods living in proximity to their "Indian" relations may have been a separate social category *in* themselves insofar as each individual person in that category had something in common with others in it. They all had parents from different ethnic groups. However, it would not be until several decades into the nineteenth century that mixed bloods in this tribal hinterland would be made into a group *for* themselves, conscious of this difference, distinguished by virtue of it, and acting politically upon it. As such, they would come to resemble the concentrations of these people at Green Bay, Mackinac, or Prairie du Chien, sites identified by Jacqueline Petersen as mixed-blood settlements, although more intimately articulated with their relatives who were less mixed.

As Richard Jenkins observes, if "a group is an explicitly self-conscious collectivity," mixed-blood self-consciousness would only be created by Anglo-Americans in the early nineteenth century, that is, more than a century, four or five generations, after which the process of producing such people had begun. Mixed bloods was a category for whites "defined according to a criteria or criterion that its members share in the eye of the external beholder, without their recognizing the fact, it is thus definitively non-members who know about categorical identity."[66] For Jenkins, the "boundaries and contents of human groups have always been . . . flexible, changeable, negotiable, anything but definite."[67]

Rebecca Kugel focusses on women in her 2008 article, "Reworking Ethnicity: Gender, Work Roles, and Contending Redefinitions of the Great Lakes Métis, 1820–42." Here she reveals that women with mixed parentage actively resisted the racialization being imposed by the Protestant missionaries at the time. They thought of themselves in social and cultural terms, that is, in how they were related to each other and their communities. She writes that these women "dressed much the same as native women, wearing moccasins, elaboratively decorated leggings, and knee-length skirts," though they didn't go in for the vermillion powder and wore fewer earrings,[68] thus distinguishing themselves from Native *women*, but not from Native *people*, I would suggest. Though they may have resisted being *racially* designated as Indians, they clearly embraced a *cultural and social* identification with Indians.

The missionaries thought these women would play an important brokerage role, but they also attributed their shortcomings to their Indian blood, so "increasingly, the missionaries collapsed Métis and Indian identity into one," Kugel writes. And as long as "Métis" designates a social category within indigenous society and not a separate ethnicity, I would agree. She also notes that "as the missionaries struggled to impose a bipolar racial order on the upper Great Lakes, Métis men were being identified as Indians."[69] However, these people didn't call themselves "Métis" and maintained extensive commitments to whom the whites called Indians.

This indigenous resistance to the imposition of race as a means of figuring belonging and difference is perhaps best revealed in the ways in which members of the Bonga family were incorporated into indigenous society. The son of manumitted African slaves, Pierre Bonga was living in a Chippewa village of fourteen lodges on the St. Louis River when the Cass expedition passed through in 1820.[70] The settlement was part of what James Doty would call "the Fond du Lac Ojibwe band" and was constituted of forty-five men, sixty women, and two hundred and forty children. He wrote, "There are about thirty half-breeds, and three freemen, who have families."[71] An interpreter and later boatman in the employ of both North West and American Fur Companies, Bonga was the first of his line to be integrated into indigenous society. Pierre Bonga had five children with his likely Leech Lake Ojibwe wife. One of the three sons had an Ojibwe name, while both daughters had only Ojibwe names.[72] His son George, literate and trilingual like his father, rose through the ranks of the company and distinguished himself by arresting the murderer of a prominent man's son. Mattie Harper, Anishinaabeg tribal member and Bonga descendant, whose dissertation on the Bonga family I draw upon, points out that he, too, was regarded as a "half-breed," and "mixed-blood,"[73] and all three sons married Ojibwe women in this world where distinctions were drawn along the lines of cultural traits.[74] Both George and his brother Stephen Bonga worked as interpreters and guides for both federal officials and missionaries. The Bonga name appears on the tribal rolls of many of the Lake Superior and Mississippi Chippewa bands to the present day.

Tanis Thorne's history of the Central Siouan mixed-blood communities is also instructive for describing society and polity in the region south and west of Lake Superior in the first half of the nineteenth century. Her effort to decolonize the political imagination is similar to the way in which Witgen calls us to do with his conception of Anishinaabewaki. Thorne wrote that the Central Siouan mixed bloods were patrilineal and patrilocal and that there was continuity of occupation, biculturalism, and bilingualism facilitating work as go-betweens from generation to generation. Furthermore, endogamous marriages among mixed bloods of different tribes of Central Siouans was the rule. All of these factors contributed to distinguish the culture of the French-Indians from that of the full-bloods.[75]

To what extent did these conditions exist among the mixed bloods south and west of Lake Superior? The Algonquian—or particularly Ojibwe—patrilineality is not as strong as that of the Central Siouan groups. There was more matrilocality among the Ojibwe mixed bloods. On this topic, Jennifer Brown cites the work of Charles Bishop and Shepard Krech and evokes the idea of "matriorganization . . . [which] reinforced women's centrality among their kin."[76] And though there was likely as much mixed-blood endogamy, it was not with different tribal ethnic groups but mostly only with Ojibwes; consequently, the culture of the "mixed bloods belonging to the Lake Superior Chippewa" Indians was less socially and politically distinct from the so-called full bloods.

Whether a mixed blood was an Indian or not was litigated in 1837 in the first criminal case under territorial law in Wisconsin. The mixed-blood son of the trader William Aitken was killed by Che-ge-wais-cum, a Chippewa Indian,[77] and though the drunken judge found him guilty because the victim was "brought up and educated as a white man," the jury's verdict that mixed bloods were Indians was left to stand.[78] The shock of the verdict caused the mixed bloods to convene a council and write to the Superintendent. They wrote that since they were not subject to the laws of the United States for purposes of being protected by such laws, they would assert jurisdiction over the case and take the accused's life by applying "the Indian law—blood for blood" in the words of "Jean B. DuBay, half-breed Chippewa" as recorded by Henry Dodge, superintendent of Indian affairs. The subagent acquiesces in their decision and adds, "The decision of the Court in this case, if correct, is a virtual acknowledgement of your title to the Indian land in common with the Indians, and I see no other way for you to obtain satisfaction than to enforce the Indian law."[79]

The Indian agent later counseled restraint and indicated that their cooperation would speed the delivery of the $100,000 they were owed under the treaty signed a year earlier being members of the indigenous polity that signed the treaty.[80] The mixed bloods wrote a formal letter to the sub-agent at LaPointe complaining of their ambiguous legal status, as they had been recently regarded as citizens for purposes of voting in Michigan, yet not eligible for protection and recompense in the recent murder case. They refer to themselves as "half Breeds," as well as members of *this Tribe of Indians*.[81]

The incident and series of exchanges were a watershed moment for these mixed bloods in their own understanding of the complexity of the political landscape and how it had come to be shaped by the emergent concept of race for the ascendant power in the region, the United States. They were not going to be permitted to join the dominant society as citizens.

A measure of its importance comes in a biography and an account of a trial of the Menominee mixed blood Jean Baptiste DuBuy written a century later. Merton E. Krug spent several pages on this Menominee mixed bloods' "leadership among the Chippewa half-breeds as a *Chippewa half-breed*" (italics in the original), in giving an account of DuBay's intervention in this legal and political process. On the way to his conclusion that these "half-breeds" lost their cause, and citing oddly bibliographed Indian Office documents, he points out that there were "two classes of half-breeds . . . the educated and business men—these the Indians regard as whites; the second, comprising the boatmen, the hunters, the trappers &c who live as Indians, &c are treated as such."[82] This foreshadowed the importance of class, occupation, and residence in determining community membership.

More than a year earlier, in March of 1838, 167 of this same group describing themselves aspirationally as "Chippewa Half-Breeds citizens of the United States" petitioned the president of United States to distribute their payment under the recent treaty at LaPointe and "not subject them to a long and costly journey" to some other location. They positioned themselves vis à vis the signatories to the treaty as "Half-Breed brothers."[83] In October, Governor Dodge endorsed the petition in a letter to the commissioner of Indian affairs, adding, "The half-breeds always exercise treaty influence over the minds of the Indians."[84] These cases illustrate competing conceptions of an evolving indigenous polity and of the racial ideology of the ascendant Americans, but not the emergence of a mediating ethnic group.

The articulated expectation of being protected by the laws of the United States and at the same time retain their membership as a distinct class of Indian people is clear and speaks to their own conception of their political status. The group also debated the criterion of their own membership when it came time to receive payment under the land cession Treaty of 1837: "The sum of one hundred thousand dollars shall be paid by the United States, to the *half-breeds of the Chippewa nation*, under the direction of the President. It is the wish of the Indians that their two sub-agents Daniel P. Bushnell, and Miles M. Vineyard, superintend the distribution of this money among their half-breed relations."[85]

Lucius Lyon was commissioned to determine who was eligible to receive a share of this money. He investigated claims at Michilimackinac, Sault Ste. Marie, and LaPointe. Theresa Schenck summarizes the internal debate: "The half-breeds themselves were at odds over who should be admitted, many of them wanting to exclude all those living outside of the ceded country, even if they had been born in it and retained ties to their relative there. Others believed that all those born outside the ceded country should be admitted, as long as they had relatives living there."[86]

Ojibwe society at this time was an evolving polity organized in relationship to other polities using the indigenous understanding of kinship. It was now undergoing a fundamental transformation because of the political force of American conceptions of indigenous society in terms of race, manifested in a discourse of blood. Over the long run, that conception will be assimilated and appropriated by indigenous people but not as a criterion of membership.

The social category of mixed blood was inherently heterogeneous. Not only did mixed bloods have different degrees of "Indian blood," but they were also socioeconomically diverse. For the Ojibwe, and perhaps for the Menominee and Ho-Chunk to a lesser extent, the recognition of being of mixed blood began the transformation into tribes of what had been band-level societies with their engagement with the fur trade. That is, societies that had been nearly exclusively organized by kinship into formally and structurally similar units were generating a class of persons that cross-cut the different bands and articulated the bands with each other in a new way. Not only were mixed-blood people individually integrated into kinship groups, but they were becoming a self-conscious social category known to themselves and others as "half-breeds." In fact, the account of DuBay's 1838 speech above included a line that indicated that the tribal borders themselves were porous, though, of course, they always had been. DuBay said, "The Half-breeds muster strong in the Northwestern frontier and we know no distinction of tribes."[87] He may have been referring to different Ojibwe bands as tribes, or the fact that he was a Menominee mixed blood in the company of Ojibwe mixed bloods.

Theresa Schenk points out that many of the men who appeared on Lucius Lyon's list of mixed bloods potentially eligible for a share of the $100,000 that was stipulated in the Treaty of 1837 "had established themselves in their wives' communities,"[88] pointing to their integration into indigenous polities.

The claim that the mixed bloods represented a class within indigenous society is not new. Helen Hornbeck Tanner documented the life of one Joseph La France, a mid-eighteenth-century *coureur de bois*, son of an Indian mother and a French father. She concluded noting that the first generation of *coureur de bois* were French, but subsequent generations were Métis, and most of this "class" collected around trading locations such as La Pointe, Green Bay, Prairie du Chien, and others. She notes that in Canada, Métis became distinct, but in the United States, they were absorbed into the settler population or the tribes and speculates that LaFrance left family in the Western Great Lakes since the name occurs among the Turtle Mountain Ojibwe.[89] Harriet Gorham also argues that the absence of self-consciousness as a group, despite their declining economic fortunes, disqualifies mixed bloods from being regarded as an ethnic group. They "might better be described as an economic class, subdivided into traders and *voyageurs*,"[90] with the latter rather deeply entailed in the lives of their Indian relatives.

Not only did new ethnicities such as the Odawa and Ojibwe come into existence as the result of the contact between Europeans and indigenous Americans, but these new sociocultural formations were undergoing transformations themselves. With such groups apparently in mind, Morton Fried writes that over time egalitarian societies "based upon hunting, trapping and fishing" typically "fragment and reconstitute." However, he points out that if you "subvert this setup with an external market for furs and [then] substantial basis for stratification has been laid."[91] Here the stratification took place in the form of the emergence of the class of mixed bloods with their differential accumulation of social capital. The transformation viewed from the perspective of the Americans—a competing stratified regime predicated in part on an ideology of racism—the change in indigenous society was misapprehended as the emergence of intermediate *racial* category.

The mixed bloods belonged to the Chippewa Indians, to paraphrase how they appear in the 1854 treaty, because collective indigenous virtue attracted the wealth-bearing Europeans and then domesticated the living channels of this wealth via the reproductive powers vested in women. That is, Indian women married French men. And here, the Ojibwe history of assimilating external sources of power that make society possible consists in the repeated reenactment of events that never took place—to paraphrase Nigel Davies characterization of Mexican history[92]—or more charitably, took place mythologically. The story "The Woman Who Married a Beaver" is particularly apropos in this context as the human is enriched by the interspecific liaison. On a fast, a woman encounters a man whom she marries and who supplies her with food and material riches such as "kettles and bowls, knives, tobacco. . . . Now, the woman knew that she had married a beaver."[93] Such stories of women marrying the animals that make human cultural life possible are the prototype of this mode of appropriation.

Were it not for European desire to identify with and socially distinguish themselves from each other by wearing furs or their products in the form of felt hats, there would be no fur trade and probably no mixed bloods. So I will end this chapter with several anecdotes about Indian people manipulating their social identities in the register of dress, which is an index of location in the matrix of variables that constituted one's status. The first comes from Minnesota in 1857 and reveals the likely depth and breadth of this discourse in the period as the categories of "mixed blood" and "Indian" were conflating, and both opposed to white, in the latter's sociological imagination.

Ethnohistorian Bruce White recounts that Henry Sibley, the state's first governor, was assisted by the votes that came from the largely mixed-blood Cass and Pembina districts in the election of 1857. And though the legislature had enfranchised mixed bloods "who shall have adopted the habits and customs of civilized men," the loser in the election alleged that the mixed bloods passed a single pair of pants amongst themselves, donning them to vote and returning to the blanket and breech clout when finished.[94] The joke indexes the dissembling that took place on everyone's part in manipulating the symbols of belonging and difference with the *sotto voce* presumption that the newly enfranchised mixed bloods were far more Indian than white.

The second story comes from the journal of Reverend Hall, Sept 11, 1832, describing a trip from La Pointe to Lac du Flambeau:

> This morning as soon as it was sufficiently light to follow the path, we arrose and prepared to recommence our march. My man dressed himself in the bait of a voyageur, that is, a short shirt, a red woolen cap, a pair of deer skin leggings which reach from the ancles a little above the knees, and are held up by a string secured to a belt about the waist, the azion of the Indians, and a pair of deer skin moccasin without stockings on the foot. The thighs are left bare. This is the dress of voyageurs in summer and winters, and is *substantially the common dress of the Indians.*[95]

Finally, in the mid-1840s, in his memoir written more than three decades later, Alfred Brunson, the subagent at LaPointe for a short period of time, elaborates on what we might call diffusion, cultural flow, appropriation, or assimilation, depending on our social location, and all implicating belonging and difference:

> I soon learned that the eldest son of this (Buffalo) chief, who was the heir apparent to the chiefship, had, previous to this, adopted civilized habits; had built himself a comfortable cabin house, both he and his wife dressing and living like the whites, and perhaps half of the band had done the same. And before a year rolled round, by and with the consent of all the chiefs in council, a new band was organized of this class with this young chief at their head, and were called the "Pantaloon Band," all of whom, men and women, dressed and worked like the whites.

And again from Brunson, "Among the voyageurs were Frenchmen, half-breeds [which means any degree of mixed Indian and white blood], and full-blooded Indians who had donned the hat or cap with coat and pants, the insignia of civilization, who had the same pay and performed the same work as white men."[96]

I have argued in this chapter that because the so-called mixed bloods in the region of western Lake Superior only began to refer to themselves as "half-breeds" toward the middle of the nineteenth century, and then regarded themselves and were regarded by others as belonging to the Lake Superior Chippewa, they are not properly thought about as a separate ethnicity but rather as a class formation within a structurally evolving indigenous society. This is the New Native World, in Michael's Witgen's terms. These people of mixed parentage did not so much embrace the emergent racial ideology of the time as they acquiesced in and manipulated it. For the most part, they retained their social relationships predominantly with what the whites regarded as "Indians" and were regarded by those same whites as Indians. In chapter 4, we will see how "mixed bloods" were thought about by "Indians," but in the interim, we will examine their status in the treaties of the time.

3

Ojibwe Treaties, the Emerging Paradigm of Race, and Allotting Mixed Bloods

> The half or mixed-bloods of the Chippewas residing with them shall be considered Chippewa Indians.[1]

From the 1830s through the 1850s in Wisconsin, the lumber and mining industries lobbied the federal government to buy out the fur-trading interests using the mechanism of treaties.[2] Pressured by commercial interest in Indian lands, there were nearly twenty separate land cessions during this era. Tribal members were often indebted to traders and in need of income, and this provided an incentive to participate in the transfer. Bethel Saler writes of the "treaty economy" and the "treaty polity" in describing the political and economic realities that obtained in the Wisconsin Territory during this period. The treaties "as a group . . . created what was, in effect, a directed, transitional economy between the former fur trading and the future American agrarian economies." Treaties worked "to establish the central and sovereign authority of the American government and formally move Indian land into the land tenure system of the Republic."[3] Decades before, President Jefferson hoped for just such a solution to the problem of the tribal presence in the western and southern sectors of the growing nation.[4] Robert Keller asserts that the nearly four dozen treaties with tribes in the Great Lakes "had economic origins and effects."[5] Rhonda Gilman regards them as an "elaborate charade" that subsidized the fur companies for facilitating land transfers.[6]

One of these elaborate charades in particular—the 1854 treaty with the Chippewa—stands out as a watershed moment in upper Great Lakes history because it included a provision that was written and interpreted in such a manner that permitted scores of eighty-acre mixed-blood land patents to be easily alienated because they were issued "in the usual form." As we will see, "the usual form" of patents granted to mixed bloods were highly restricted to prevent such alienation. This aspect of the charade would play an outsized role in the history of the peoples and land of this region because it lay at the origin of the corporate mining phase of Wisconsin's economic history.

Ojibwe Land Cession Treaties

The first direct negotiation between Ojibwe Indians in the western part of the Lake Superior region took place in 1826[7] wherein the Chippewa Tribe upon Lake Superior was assembled for the US government commissioners to explain the stipulations of the Treaty of 1825[8] that established the boundaries between a number of tribes in the region of the western Great Lakes. Apropos of Keller's assessment of such treaties, Article III of that treaty granted the United States the right "to search for, and carry away, any metals or minerals from any part of their country." A discussion of this treaty noting the mineral provision is the last event discussed in the final chapter of William Warren's *History of the Ojibway,* written in the 1850s,[9] a chapter dealing with three incidents that "seem to represent the waning years of Ojibwe political independence."[10] The first land-cession treaty with the Ojibwe in 1836 was similar. It ceded the western half of Michigan and the Upper Peninsula, and though motivated by the fur traders' desire, it was valuable for the fisheries, pineries, and water power.[11]

In 1837, a treaty was negotiated with the Ojibwe of Lake Superior that ceded about one-quarter of what would become the state of Wisconsin eleven years later, and it was motivated by the lumber industry's interest in expanding its operations with growing markets in the Mississippi River Valley.[12] Ojibwe people explicitly stipulated for the right to continue to occupy and subsist upon the land ceded so that hunting, fishing, and gathering would be augmented by access to federally funded blacksmiths, farmers, and substantial payments of cash for the next twenty years.

In 1842, the lands between the 1837 treaty cession and Lake Superior were ceded in a structurally identical agreement motivated by industry's desire to extract copper.[13] It was Douglas Houghton's geological surveys beginning in the 1830s that led to the 1842 treaty,[14] the same year that the American Fur Trade Company declared bankruptcy. The region had been known for its copper deposits since the early French colonial era.

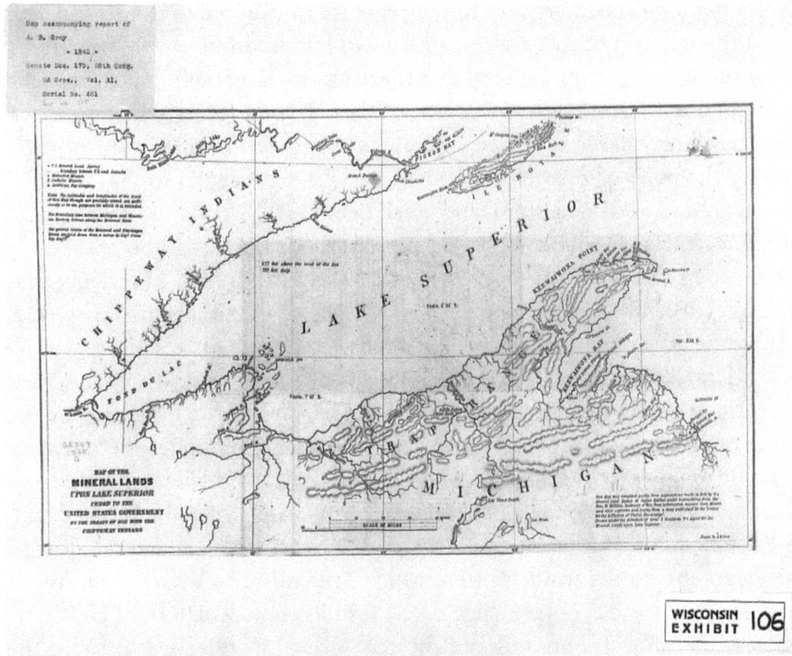

Map 3.1. Map of the Mineral Lands upon Lake Superior Ceded to the United States by the Treaty of 1842 with the Chippeway Indians. Andrew Belcher Gray, 1845. Image #116582. Courtesy of the Wisconsin Historical Society.

The pseudonymous "Explorer," in an 1845 publication, wrote that "in the latter part of the fall of 1843, or early in the succeeding winter, a knowledge of the vast and concealed resources of this region . . . was conveyed to persons in high authority in Washington."[15] In 1847, Congress created the Chippewa Land District in what was about to become northern Wisconsin, transferring jurisdiction of these public lands from the War Department to the Department of the Treasury, and instructing and authorizing the latter to survey and study these lands.[16] Hence, in 1848, David Dale Owen's detailed report on the Chippewa District of Wisconsin was received by the Thirtieth Congress, first session. In his introduction, Owen writes: "It has been ascertained that there extend into Wisconsin two if not three trap ranges, similar in their character to ranges in Michigan, and that these, in some places, afford ores which hold out a prospect of productiveness."[17]

Later in the report, a certain Mr. A. Randall, who assisted Owen in his geological study, followed the fourth principal meridian, south from

Lake Superior, called attention to the presence of iron ore in the region, and wrote the following: "At an elevation of two-hundred feet above the general elevation of the country, on section 3 township 45, is an outburst of magnetic iron and trap bearing northeast and southwest. It is dark colored, fine grained and exceedingly hard. At this point there is remarkable magnetic disturbance, causing the poles of the needle to turn nearly at right angles to the course of the range, and to deviate from true north nearly 50°."[18] Congress ordered that two thousand copies of the report be printed. We do not know how extensively these copies circulated in the area, but I surmise that such knowledge was widespread in the region as the *Superior Chronicle* (Wisconsin) ran several front-page articles about the geology of the region in the 1850s.

Charles Whittlesey, head of Owen's subcorps, contributed a comprehensively titled "Geological Report on that portion of Wisconsin bordering on the South Shore of Lake Superior surveyed in the year 1849 under the direction of David Dale Owen, United States Geologist," in which he wrote: "There is a continuous chain from the Montreal River to Bladder Lake, the prolongation of the Porcupine Mountains in Michigan. I have called it the *Penokie* Range, this being the Indian word for iron, which is found in its westerly portion in great force . . . The Penokie Range is visible in its entire length from La Pointe, or from the water twenty miles offshore."[19] In fact, he intended to call it the "Pewabic Range," thus more accurately reflecting the indigenous language's term for metal, *biwâbik*, but apparently his handwriting left something to be desired in the eyes of the typesetter, and we are left with "Penokee."[20]

Two failed attempts to remove the Lake Superior Ojibwe in 1850 and 1851[21] followed as mineral exploration of the region continued. The efforts were not so much to remove Indians *from* where they were living but *into* Minnesota so that businessmen and traders could benefit from the treaty annuities that would flow into the local economy.[22] Ethnohistorian Charles Cleland points out that the payments made to Indian people as stipulated in their treaties "were the only real source of hard cash on the early 19th century Great Lakes frontier."[23] Indeed, ethnohistorian Bruce White quotes territorial governor Alexander Ramsey's address to the Minnesota legislature in 1851, saying: "The payments of the Indian annuities supply much the larger portion of our current currency, and through the various channels of trade contribute greatly to our prosperity."[24]

With minerals on the minds of congressmen and geological scientists as well as hundreds of non-Indians in the region who had been issued permits to locate mineral lands as of 1846 by the War Department, we find the Indian agent at La Pointe on Lake Superior writing of rich mineral deposits on the *north* shore of Lake Superior and suggesting yet another land cession treaty.[25] Soon a treaty conference would be convened.

Treaty commissioner Gilbert estimated that four thousand Ojibwe people attended the negotiations in September of 1854 at La Pointe. The gathered Ojibwe ceded the desired mineral lands north and west of Lake Superior; however, they extracted a number of stipulations in the process. Deeply disturbed about the recent attempts to remove them across the Mississippi to Minnesota onto lands that were yet to be ceded, Ojibwes negotiated for the right to continue to live within the lands that had been ceded in 1837 and 1842 in the form of collectively held as well as individually held reservations. Absent this provision, the Arrowhead region of Minnesota northwest of Lake Superior would not have been ceded, and the Mesabi Iron Range's discovery would have been delayed.[26]

The establishment of collectively held reservations in the 1850s represented a change in federal Indian policy that had previously sought to solve "the Indian problem," as it was called, by removing communities west of the Mississippi River. Though the new policy was motivated by the presence of powerful tribes in possession of lands west of the river,[27] the Indian communities not already removed in Wisconsin were able to benefit from the policy change and stay in place. The change was made by George Manypenny, the new commissioner of Indian affairs who took up his post in 1853 after the election of Democrat Franklin Pierce. Manypenny was also opposed to the policy of paying Indians for their land with annuities, seeing the practice as delaying their integration into American society as Christians committed to agriculture and the market economy. As this would require permanent homes, he would acquiesce in the idea of reserving estates with the caveat that the lands would be allotted in severalty at some future date under the direction of the president. Manypenny negotiated fifty-two treaties in his five-year tenure—no commissioner before or after him would negotiate more—and many would have such land tenure provisions within them. He thought the annuity system worked "to cripple Indian tribes," preventing them from becoming civilized. The Indian needed to "settle himself in a fixed habitation and commence the cultivation of the soil."[28]

He would write of the 1854 treaty with the Chippewa: "An important feature in this treaty, is the setting apart of certain designated tracts of land for the occupancy of various bands of these people, with a view to the cultivation of the soil, and prospectively, of the transfer of the same to them in severalty."[29]

George Manypenny negotiated more than a dozen treaties in 1854 alone, and more than half of them contained a provision for allotting land on the newly created reservations, the provision in the Omaha treaty becoming a boilerplate. It gave the president the discretion to "survey the land, set it off in lots, assign the lots in specific amounts" to all willing Indians. "There were to be regulations for bequeathing the land and restrictions on its lease and sale"[30] and only rescindable by positive action of both Congress and a state legislature.[31]

The Ojibwe retained the rights to hunt, fish, and gather on the lands within the new cession as they had also retained usufructuary rights within the cessions of the 1837 and 1842 treaties. They were also paid cash and a variety of other services only useful to a population that all parties understood were intending to stay in their present locations. As another measure of the degree to which the mixed bloods were understood to be an important class of persons within the Ojibwe polities, "the mixed bloods of said nation" were to receive $6,000 "in agricultural implements, household furniture, and cooking utensils to be distributed at the next annuity payment"[32] in 1855. As this was a one-time payment, we can think of this provision worth $184,000 in 2020 dollars as the federal government capitalizing a mixed-blood cultural transformation that was intended for its demonstration effects upon the balance of the tribal population. They would be settled on their allotments in short order.

At the same time, the mixed bloods were quite explicitly thought of as part of the Chippewa people. Mixed bloods appeared in the legislation introduced into the US House of Representatives in the spring of 1854 (but only passed after the treaty itself had been negotiated). Reading in part, "All the benefits and privileges granted to said Indians shall be extended to and enjoyed by the mixed bloods belonging to or connected with the tribe, and who shall permanently reside on the ceded lands."[33] This legislation also envisioned that the heads of the families of *all* the members of the polity would receive eighty-acre allotments with restrictions placed on alienation.

For the purposes of the present inquiry, however, the most important provision of this treaty appeared in Article II. Significantly, the provision was within the section of the treaty that created the collectively-held Ojibwe reservations in Wisconsin and Minnesota. The seventh paragraph read as follows: "Each head of a family, or single person over twenty-one years of age at the present time of the mixed-bloods, belonging to the Chippewas of Lake Superior, shall be entitled to eighty acres of land, to be selected by them under the direction of the President, and which shall be secured to them by patent in the usual form."[34]

In reporting the proceedings of the treaty and general success of the negotiations to the commissioner of Indians affairs, two weeks after the treaty had been signed, Agent Gilbert wrote of the mixed-blood provision: "The provision going to each Half Breed family 80 acres of land was most strenuously insisted upon by the Indians. There are about 200 such families on my payroll and allowing as many more to the Interior Indians, which is a very liberal estimate, the amount of land required will be about 32,000 acres."[35]

There is no evidence in the correspondence preceding this treaty that this provision was anticipated, although the tone of his writing indicates that it was not extraordinary that some kind of compensation for the so-called mixed bloods was expected. According to Benjamin Armstrong, aka Shaw-bwaw-skung, an interpreter, friend, and son-in-law of Chief Buffalo (the principal chief of the Lake Superior Ojibwe for the first half of the nineteenth century) and author of a memoir written several decades later, the issue of land for the mixed bloods was discussed among the Native leaders negotiating the treaty the day before the provision was adopted:

> That night the subject of providing homes for their half-breed relations who lived in different parts of the country was brought up and discussed and all were in favor of making such a provision in the treaty. I proposed to them that as we had made provisions for ourselves and our children it would be only fair that an arrangement should be made in the treaty whereby the government should provide for *our mixed-blood relations* by giving to each person the head of a family or to each single person twenty-one years a piece of land containing at least eighty acres which would provide homes for those now living and in the future there would be ample room on the reservations for their children, where all could live happily together.[36]

Here the term "the reservations" does not refer to what would become the six collectively held tribal estates enumerated in Article II, but to the parcels that would be availed to the mixed bloods. The "provisions that we had made for ourselves and our children" refers to Chief Buffalo's insistence that his adopted son, Armstrong, receive a parcel of land and "that it should be patented directly to me by the government without any restrictions."[37] This hope for an unrestricted patent was fulfilled, and Armstrong would come to own a parcel of land upon which the city of Duluth would come to be sited.[38]

But others received unrestricted patents as well, which would have the effect of dispossessing most of the mixed-blood members of their eighty-acre allotments.

Armstrong's specific desire for an unrestricted patent may have been shared by mixed bloods belonging to the Lake Superior Chippewa. The historian J. P. Kinney writes of mixed-blood desire regarding land mostly in the Southeast: "The records of the period beginning with the election of James Monroe in 1816 indicate a marked tendency on the part of the more progressive Indians, and especially of the mixed-bloods, to seek for themselves a security of title to particular tracts of land analogous to the tenure under which their white neighbors held their lands."[39]

This does not mean that the same "progressive Indians" or "mixed-bloods" were also interested in socially separating themselves from their relatives. Indeed, historian Rebecca Kugel has shown that the tribes in Indiana used similar provisions in treaties as a land-retention strategy by identifying sites of tribal significance and having individuals receive patents for them on the group's behalf.[40] There is some evidence that the same strategy was employed by the Lake Superior Ojibwe as some of the mixed-blood allotments in the region are not contiguous with others and may be located on ecologically and culturally significant sites.

Article X of the treaty of 1854 provided for "missionaries, and teachers, and other persons of full age . . . to enter the land occupied by them at the minimum price," not quite the gift Buffalo apparently intended in Armstrong's memory, but significant in that such parcels would implicitly be held in *fee simple*, the ordinary way in which private citizens hold land, which includes the unrestricted right to transfer ownership to another.

There are two important points to draw from Armstrong's memory: Armstrong was not an Ojibwe mixed blood, and his memory of the purpose of the provision was for the land's *use* value, not its *exchange* value. That is, the eighty-acre parcels were for "our relations . . . [to] . . . live happily together," on those lands, a goal that was shared by the commissioners and the Congress that ratified the treaty. As it would turn out in the early 1870s, Congress undertook an investigation into the abuses of this treaty provision. And though the focus was on the period well after the early Wisconsin mining companies had been capitalized, the recollection of the intent of this provision was explicit: "We find it was made part of the treaty at the instigation of some of the most intelligent of these mixed-bloods, *who hoped that all of their class might be thus induced to abandon their roving lives and settle permanently upon their own farms, and so come directly under the influence of Christianity and civilization*."[41]

Recall also that the fur trade, which created the class of mixed-blood people over the course of eighteenth century, was on the decline at this time, and that they, therefore, had begun to seek to diversify their subsistence activities.[42] We may wonder here whether or not "some of the most intelligent of these mixed-bloods," some of whom who were traders or clerks in the upper echelons of the local declining fur-trade economy, advocated for unrestricted land patents with an eye toward those patents' exchange value rather than their use value, thus inadvertently contributing to the general dispossession that would take place.

The possession of alienable property was and still is a sign of whiteness so that mixed bloods aspiring to inclusion in the dominant society would find this avenue attractive. The historical record does not provide this level of detail, and we must acknowledge that the mixed-blood class was anything but culturally homogeneous.[43] Melissa Meyer's study of the history of the White Earth Reservation in Minnesota reveals the diversity of the mixed-blood sector in that community several decades later. She indicates that some Lake Superior mixed bloods used their treaty right to acquire an eighty-acre parcel to speculate in the Crow Wing Area.[44]

Returning to Agent Gilbert's letter, however, his use of the phrase "strenuously insisted upon" is significant in describing how the Indian treaty negotiators apparently felt about accommodating the interests of their mixed-blood relatives. This indicates that even though this provision would align nicely with Commissioner of Indian Affairs George Manypenny's goals, this provision was not drafted before the negotiations. Moreover, it indicates something else.

In his account of the 1836 treaty in Michigan, Charles Cleland points out that because Indian people were indebted to the traders who agitated for a treaty not only to be reimbursed by the federal government for money they were owed by the Indians, but also "hoped to pressure the chiefs to request land grants or payments in lieu of land grants for their mixed-blood children."[45] As indicated earlier, Jacqueline Petersen describes these mixed bloods as "a sizeable and influential body *within tribal society*, coerced and pandered to by treaty commissioners."[46]

Relationships between traders and tribal members were close, and they were often in-laws, with the traders as structurally wife-takers vis à vis the indigenous polity. As such, they owe a debt for the reproductive services of the daughters they received as wives. The debt would be repaid in brokerage services delivered by self-described "half-breeds" such as Jean Batise Roy, Vincent Roy, and Alec Corbin. In fact, when Jean Batise Roy wrote for the La Pointe Indians to Governor Ramsey, he referred to William Whipple Warren as "their halfbreed to interpret for them for we all know that he can talk good English and good Indian." Roy would sign the letter, "I their halfbreed, Jean Batise Roy"[47] The designation "halfbreed," though originating in a racial ideology, evokes the idea of a new official status clearly within the tribal polity, and the third-person possessive "their" suggests obligation. Similarly, Rebecca Kugel refers to "their literate Métis kinfolk" dictating letters of protest over a treaty negotiated in 1863.[48]

Of the fifty-five claims made by traders pursuant to the fourth article of the 1842 treaty that settled the debts of the traders, twenty-nine of the claims were made by men with French surnames and are individually identifiable as mixed-blood members of the La Pointe community. And of those twenty-nine, ten were issued scrip redeemable for a land patent under the 1854 treaty. The "strenuous insistence," therefore, clearly speaks to an alliance of interest between the "half-breeds" and the contradistinguished Indians. The lion's share of $51,000 of the $75,000 allocated for such debts, however, went to the American Fur Company and John Jacob Astor indexing, therefore, the non-Indian corporate interest that played the largest role in driving these proceedings.

Furthermore, note that some two hundred mixed-blood families were represented by Agent Gilbert as on his "payroll," and another two hundred anticipated, meaning they had been receiving treaty annuities. Indeed, these people were explicitly enfranchised as members of the indigenous polity in a treaty with the Chippewa in 1847, a point which I will elaborate below. They also received payments as *de facto* members in the 1837 treaty. In his brief account "Chippewa Halfbreed Scrip" William Watts Folwell appends to his *A History of Minnesota*, that this provision of the treaty was provided "to secure their (mixed-blood) desirable assistance in gaining the consent of the Indians to the treaty, or at least to prevent their possible opposition."[49]

Note the magnitude of the contemplated reservation of allotments for mixed bloods and the implications of this for the relationship between the goals of the policy and the actual outcome. Agent Gilbert's "very liberal estimate" of 400 eighty-acre parcels for a total of 32,000 acres seems to be presented to Commissioner Manypenny to assure him that despite this either routine or unanticipated contingency, the specific goals of the treaty had been realized. As it would turn out, by 1870, 1,168 scrip certificates for such parcels would be issued[50]—three times the original estimate—and a congressional investigation was undertaken to identify the nature and the extent of the fraud that produced this entirely unanticipated and unwelcome result.

Finally, I will also point out here and explore later that the specific phrase "*shall be secured to them by patent in the usual form*" does not appear in any other of the 371 treaties with Indian tribes ratified by the United States between 1778 and 1871. However, a year later, in 1855, a similar provision would be written into the treaties with the Winnebago and the Chippewa. That same year, another treaty with the Wyandotte abolished tribal bands and made the Indians into citizens. It also granted unrestricted fee simple patents unless they were designated "not so competent."[51] The treaty made with the Chippewa in Minnesota in 1855, though it has language that works to nearly the same effect, includes a critical difference. In this treaty, mixed-blood heads of family were also granted patents in fee simple to eighty-acre parcels, *but to lands upon which they were already living and had made improvements.*[52] The

1854 mixed-blood language has no such stipulation, and therefore represented a significant departure from the language used in similar treaty provisions that described mixed-blood land tenure rights to that point and afterward. As I will show, the "usual form" of patents issued to mixed bloods belonging to Indian polities restricted their alienation, although, of course, the phrase "patent in the usual form" was by this time a term of legal art and referred to a patent in fee, unrestricted and fully transferable.[53]

Alienability of Land in Treaty Land Provisions for Mixed Bloods

In the first few decades of the nineteenth century, before racialist thought had become hegemonic, there was a consensus among policy makers that Indians could be detribalized and assimilated to the dominant society and body politic. They would need to be convinced that "the plow" was superior to "the chase," as the difference between these modes of production were expressed at the time; that Christianity was superior to their tribal religious practices; that republican forms of government were superior to their radical democracies; and most importantly and fundamentally, that holding land in severalty was superior to holding land collectively, although this last presumption was contested and Congress would typically restrict the alienability of lands held both collectively and individually.[54] As a result, a number of treaties negotiated at this time included allotment provisions for mixed bloods pursuant to this objective. They are dealt with most systematically by Paul Wallace Gates in his essay "On Indian Allotments Preceding the Dawes Act." Gates asserts that the purpose of allotting land to mixed bloods can be best read from the consequences of that practice: "That the allotments when patented quickly fell into the hands of traders and agents who had written provision into the treaties providing for them is a clear indication of the purpose for which they were granted."[55]

I find this kind of historical functionalism to be rather cynical, especially in light of the detailed history of the policy of granting land to mixed bloods that Tanis Thorne undertook in her dissertation research on the mixed-blood families living in the lower Missouri River Valley. In a long footnote,[56] Thorne reviews Gates's conclusion and how it has been used by others. She then concludes her analysis by distinguishing her own interest in the intentions and the effects of the policy from Gates's interest strictly in the policy's *consequences*. The following is a summary of her argument.

For different reasons, government agents, missionaries, humanitarians, and fur traders came to see mixed-blood people as the means to achieving their different goals. An aversion for war, a desire for land cessions, and the assimilation of Indian people to the settler cultural order motivated the development of a *de facto* "mixed-blood allotment policy" that sought "to reinforce mixed-blood's cultural and kinship ties with whites."[57]

I would point out here again, as elaborated in the previous chapter, that the very identification and designation of a sector of the indigenous polity as "mixed blood" was a political project that was based upon reigning and ascendant racial theories of belonging and difference. According to Patrick Wolfe, "mixed-bloodedness operated as a synonym for—or, at least, conduit to—a wider cultural political assimilation whose achievement would amount to the dissolution of Indianness."[58]

The distinction between "mixed" and "full," or homogenous and heterogeneous parentage, was not a distinction that indigenous people made much of, according to Theda Perdue. In fact, in her own study of "mixed bloods" in the Southeast, she uses those scare quotes in the title of the book to foreground the problematic nature of this category. [59] This is concordant with Michael Witgen's understanding of Anishinaabewaki discussed earlier. Furthermore, according to historian Rebecca Kugel, native peoples of northwest Ohio regarded adoptive and in-married kin as full members of families. The Miamis explicitly contested American negotiators' efforts to designate their polity as made up of "Indians" and "mixed-bloods," arguing for "Miamis by birth" and "their heirs" in an effort to dispense with blood ideology in favor of kin and family terms.[60] Nonetheless, according to Thorne, it was Secretary of War William Crawford in 1816 who recommended that Indians be permitted to live on their ceded lands, but only under the condition that they would hold the land in severalty initiating this *de facto* mixed-blood policy.[61]

It would be Lewis Cass, governor of the Michigan Territory from 1813 to 1831 who took up Crawford's recommendation in negotiating treaties with several Great Lakes groups that included granting allotments to individuals.[62] Cass recognized the "political expedience of granting what in effect were preemption rights to French mixed-blood fur-trade families."[63] He would rely upon traders and mixed bloods as go-betweens in an effort to win large cessions of land from the tribal leaders, and because the full texts of treaties were printed in the newspapers at the time, the practice came to be expected.[64] Furthermore, in their evolutionary view of culture, policy makers interpreted the Euro-American aspects of evolving indigenous culture as evidence of a disposition for civilization. As a result, they allotted mixed bloods but were very attentive to the problem of alienation as the following case shows so clearly.

Although Tanis Thorne describes several treaties as "granting Native Americans fee-simple allotments,"[65] restrictions were placed on the alienation of these allotments in all these cases, thus strengthening her argument that the intentions of the treaty were betrayed rather than revealed in their consequences *contra* Paul Gates and supporting the argument made here that the 1854 mixed-blood treaty provision represents the beginning of a new policy—and breaks with past practice.

A review of the treaty provisions applying to mixed bloods and their land tenure is in order. An 1817 treaty with the Wyandot, Seneca, and Shawnee granted land in fee simple to nearly forty named individuals, however, the Senate amended the treaty, noting that the provision

> was unprecedented by any former treaty, and at variance with the general principles on which intercourse with the Indian tribes has been conducted. The laws . . . have also prohibited any sale of their lands, except made in public council, and to authorized agents of the Government, thus presuming their incapacity to transact business, and assuming on the part of the Government a superintending concern and guardianship over their interests in order to protect them from the impositions of civilized men, more enlightened than they, but too often less just.[66]

A subsequent treaty in 1818 with the same group amended the 1817 treaty to include an article that stipulated that the lands granted in the previous treaty "shall never be conveyed, by them or their heirs, without the permission of the President of the United States."[67] This interdiction would last for decades.

Historian Rebecca Kugel discusses these two treaties as efforts on tribal people's part to attempt to use the new system of land tenure that came with American jurisdiction in an effort to preserve tribal community and natural resources. The tribes sought to place individually held life estates in fee simple in mostly mixed-blood hands, thus preserving village sites, subsistence resources, rivers, and lake shores. As full members of the indigenous communities, with kinship ties and attendant obligations, the tribe was attempting to make individual tribal members stewards of community resources in holding the land privately.[68] Similarly, in Michigan in the 1830s, the tribal leadership sought to hold land in fee as they "saw land ownership as a defense against removal because he understood that, for Americans, possession of real property established a claim to citizenship."[69] The land provisions in subsequent treaties should be read as the outcome of negotiations: between tribal leaders seeking to conserve land and community, and American negotiators seeking either removal or assimilation.

Article IV of the 1818 Treaty with the Potawatomi provided eight named individuals full sections of land, adding, "but the land so granted shall never be conveyed by either of the said persons, or their heirs, unless by the consent of the President of the United States."[70] In a land-cession treaty also made in 1818 with the Saginaw Chippewa, lands were "reserved, for the use of the Chippewa nation of Indians" and "for the use of persons hereinafter mentioned and their heirs, which persons are all Indians by descent."[71] Insofar as the same language "for the use of" is employed for both collectively and individually held land, the same standard of alienability applies to both, namely, congressional or presidential action.

In the same year, Article III of the treaty made with the Wea provided two individuals single sections of land with the identical language restricting alienation.[72] Several years later, Article III in the 1826 treaty with the Miami granted about twenty people parcels of land and "the tracts of land therein designated; but the land so granted shall never be conveyed without the consent of the President of the United States."[73]

Article IV in the aforementioned 1826 treaty with the Chippewa tacitly recognized the kinship link between "half-breeds" and "the Chippewa tribe" and motivated the land grant in a theory of the power of property held in severalty to demonstrate the putative value of civilization:

> It being deemed important that the half-breeds, scattered through this extensive country, should be stimulated to exertion and improvement by the possession of permanent property and fixed residences, the Chippewa tribe, in consideration of the affection they bear to these persons, and of the interest which they feel in their welfare, grant to each of the persons described in the schedule hereunto annexed, being half-breeds and Chippewas by descent, and it being understood that the schedule includes all of this description who are attached to the Government of the United States, six hundred and forty acres of land, to be located, under the direction of the President of the United States, upon the islands and shore of the St. Mary's river, wherever good land enough for this purpose can be found.[74]

And though it stipulated that "the grants be surveyed in the ancient French manner, bounding not less than six arpens, nor more than ten, upon the river, and running back for quantity," it also stipulated that "persons to whom grants are made shall not have the privilege of conveying the same, without the permission of the President."[75]

Another example is Article III of a treaty with the Potawatomi in 1828 granted between one-half and two sections of land to eighteen individuals stipulating "nor shall the tracts there granted be conveyed by the grantees, without the consent of the President of the United States."[76] Similar provisions appeared in treaties with United Chippewa, Ottawa, and Potawatomi in 1829,[77] and in 1830 the treaty with Sauk and Fox and several other tribes, declaring that mixed bloods are legally Indians for purposes of alienation. To wit: "they holding by the same title, and in the same manner that other Indian Titles are held." [78]

Article V of the 1829 Treaty with the Winnebago, now called Ho-Chunk, just to the southwest of the Lake Superior Ojibwe, granted forty-three named Ho-Chunk mixed bloods parcels of land. The grants were designated as inalienable as the treaty article concluded that "all which aforesaid grants are not to be leased or sold by said grantees to any person or persons whatever, without the permission of the President of the United States."[79] Holding their property "without the full rights of title enjoyed by White American property holders and citizens" is a "stipulation common to Indian allotments and one that effectively placed these 'mixed-blood' reserves, like their Indian kin, under the guardianship of the national government" according to historian Bethel Saler.[80] This was a manifestation of the trust responsibility assumed by the federal government as compensation for constraining the sovereignty of these indigenous communities, wherein persons and communities would be protected from the ravenous inclinations of the ever-increasing population of non-Indian settler neighbors.

Provisions to protect those who were allotted parcels of land continued even when the Jackson administration (1829–1837) brought an emphasis on removal of Indian people living east of the Mississippi to the west of the river as a solution to the so-called Indian problem. The Chickasaw Treaty of 1834, for example, allotted parcels between 320 and 2,560 acres to individuals that could only be alienated subject to the approval of two specified tribal community leaders and a federal official.[81] This practice continued into the next administration. The treaty made with the Wyandot in 1842 granted patents in fee simple to thirty-five tribal leaders "and their heirs all of whom are Wyandotts by blood or adoption." However, the lands were "never to be conveyed by them or their heirs without the permission of the President of the United States."[82]

Less than twenty years before the treaty of 1854 was negotiated, the issue of the power of mixed-bloods to alienate lands had emerged in the context of the Treaty of 1830 with the Sauk and Fox, and several bands of Sioux, as well as Omahas, Ioways, Ottoes, and Missourias. The half-breed reservation that was created for the Sac-Fox was surveyed in 1832, and then Congress granted the allottees the right to alienate their property two years later. Land speculators would persuade the majority to sell their lands. Those who did not sell asked the War Department to rescind Congress's decision, which it did, but could not enforce its ruling. The District Court of Iowa confused matters and left those matters unresolved for a long time.[83] The case illustrates how "political expediency and bureaucratic inefficiency must be considered the chief causes of the faulty design and ineffective implementation of the half-breed allotment policy." Thorne adds that an accumulation of ad hoc decisions added to administrative confusion, and "this well-intentioned and ambitious plan" failed and resulted in serving "the baser motive of land speculators and politicians."[84] The next chapter details just how such a plan unfolded for the Ojibwe mixed bloods of Lake Superior.

These mixed-blood allotment provisions were rationalized by Lewis Cass and Thomas McKenney upon completing treaty negotiations with the Chippewa at Fond du Lac on August 5, 1826. They wrote Secretary of War Thomas Barbour on September 11, 1826, transmitting the treaty for Senate ratification. The letter reports that peace was achieved between the Sioux and the Chippewa; that the right to procure copper on the southern coast of Lake Superior was secured; that those responsible for "the atrocious murder perpetrated on lake Pepin in 1824" were brought to account; and that these proceedings had a salutary effect in displaying our judicial methods, contrasting them to "their own arbitrary customs" of taking scalps for revenge. These issues were all anticipated. Dealing with the mixed bloods, however, apparently was not, so they were carefully articulated. I quote at length because this paragraph established the rationale for what Tanis Thorne refers to as "the mixed blood allotment policy."

> It is important that some provisions should be made for the half-breeds who are scattered through that country. They are principally the descendants of the French *voyageurs*, who have for many years been engaged in the laborious duties of the Indian trade. It would be equally polite and humane to collect these people into one neighborhood, and induce them to become agriculturalists. Situated as they now are, they have neither fixed residence, certain employments, nor such habits as regular business would give them. They form no inconsiderable force of the country, and the moral force they could exert upon the Indians is still stronger. To secure their permanent attachment to our Government is an important object; and by locating them along the St. Mary's river, they would occupy a position most favorable for any operations, offensive or defensive, which future circumstances may deem necessary, while the grants they receive, unalienable as they are, would insure their fidelity.

> And to these considerations is to be added another, little less important. It seems worse than useless to provide the means of education for this class of people, without also making provision for the practical application of the knowledge and habits they may acquire. If, after passing through the missionary school, they are to be thrown back *into the society of their Indian relatives*, there to seek the means of support, hopeless in deed will be their condition; but if they are placed upon land of their own, on the confines of civilization, they will have stimulus for exertion, and means of employment, they will become an intermediate link between our own citizens and our wandering neighbors, softening the shades of each, and enjoying the confidence of both. Their example will produce a most salutary and permanent effect. Many of the grantees are now at school at Michilimackinac, of different ages; some having just entered, and some being about to leave the establishment. It is our firm conviction that upon the immediate fate of these persons depends the issue of all the experiments upon this subject which we are making in this quarter.[85]

This is not so much a moment in the *recognition* of a distinct group of indigenized and indigenizing people as it is the *creation* of that category. The authors admit that these people are more like Indians than anyone else as they "have neither fixed residence, certain employments, nor such fixed habits as regular business would give them." Yet there is hope for them to change. Made into agriculturalists, segregated, and concentrated on the border between the United States and the British, mixed bloods will act as a "moral force" vis à vis Indians and we will have "secur(ed) their permanent attachment to our Government." Granted "unalienable" lands, "on the confines of civilization, . . . they will become an intermediate link between our own citizens and our wandering neighbors"—that is to say, they were not yet such a link being far more integrated into native society. Cass and McKenney conclude that the so-called "half-breeds" are the key to the Indian problem in the Northwest, promising a satisfactory outcome to "all the experiments upon this subject which we are making in this quarter." The account continues and indicates that these principles underlay practice in five previous treaties in the Northwest region.

In his extensive study of mixed bloods, Thomas Ingersoll argues that the culturally hybrid network of French mixed-blood settlements in the area west of the Great Lakes, "scattered throughout that country," was perceived to be a threat to the Americanization of the region in the eyes of policy makers inclined to remove Indians. The settlements were effectively presenting a "social alternative." Policy makers "were concerned about the expanding mixed-blood population; they were Indians, some were adapting bourgeois values, and all defended Indian land claims."[86] Their numbers were a source of anxiety, so an effort was made to segregate them and end the threat of their proliferation. Ingersoll argues that part of the Jacksonian removal strategy was to separate the mixed bloods from the rest of the tribal population because they were disproportionately leaders of resistance. As a result, the special provisions for land for mixed bloods were included in the treaties to placate and co-opt them. Tribes that were being removed acquiesced in these provisions because the provisions did not diminish the size of the promised estates in the West, and they also expected that the mixed bloods would remain invested in the political future of the tribe.[87]

Though Ingersoll's analysis of the circumstances of the mixed bloods draws heavily on the experience of the southeastern tribes, some of his insights are valuable for understanding the experience of the Ojibwe in the Northwest. If part of the motivation for setting aside individual reserves for the mixed-blood Ojibwe was the general reputation that mixed bloods had acquired as politically astute, the policy makers would not have had to look beyond the Midwest for models of what competent ethnonationalistic mixed-blood leaders could accomplish. Billy Caldwell and Alexander Robinson, both Potawatomi mixed-blood leaders—Waukon Decora of the Ho-Chunk, Jean-Baptiste Richardville of the Miami, and Joseph Renville among the Dakota in Minnesota—all won important concessions from the government in its effort to remove them.[88]

After 1854, allotments continued to be made to mixed bloods, and those patents were also restricted. For example, the treaty with the Sauk and Foxes in 1859 provided for mixed-blood people and stipulated that the "lands granted in this article shall remain inalienable except to the United States or members of the tribe."[89] Even so, Commissioner of Indian Affairs George Manypenny would later bemoan the inadequacy of laws to protect the newly-allotted and quickly dispossessed Indian people.[90]

The Mixed-Blood Provisions in the Chippewa Treaties

The treaties of 1837, 1842, and 1854 with the Chippewa of Lake Superior explicitly retained hunting and fishing rights on the lands they ceded to the federal government, though the president retained the right to revoke those privileges. Linguist John Nichols finds it unlikely that this stipulation to revoke those retained rights would have been translated and therefore communicated to the Ojibwe treaty negotiators.[91] As such, the treaties cannot be considered as removal treaties. Both 1837 and 1854 had considerations for the Ojibwe mixed-blood relatives. Article III of the 1837 treaty, in full, read as follows: "The sum of one hundred thousand dollars shall be paid by the United States, to the *half-breeds of the Chippewa nation*, under the direction of the President. It is the wish of the Indians that their two sub-agents Daniel P. Bushnell, and Miles M. Vineyard, superintend the distribution of this money among their half-breed relations."[92]

Jennifer Brown and Theresa Schenck write that the "chiefs in council decided who of 879 applicants should be accepted based on ancestry and residence." They would designate 392 persons "as belonging to the nations in the area ceded in the treaty,"[93] clearly indicating the political status of their so-called "half-breeds" as well as foreshadowing the political problems that were to come when tribal membership criteria would be reduced to blood quantum.

The Treaty of 1842 also explicitly enfranchised the mixed-blood class within the tribal community. "Whereas the Indians have expressed a strong desire to have some provision made for *their half breed relatives*, therefore it is agreed, that fifteen thousand (15,000) dollars shall be paid to said Indians, next year, as a present, to be disposed of, as they, together with their agent, shall determine in council."[94]

The year 1847 brings another treaty that once again explicitly enfranchises the mixed bloods as within the Ojibwe polity. The treaty with the Chippewa throughout the ceded territories, as well as a treaty in 1847 at Fond du Lac, ceded a portion of their remaining estate in Minnesota. Not only did six individuals identified as chiefs and warriors, "Half-breeds- La Pointe Band" sign the treaty—along with Julius Ombrian (sic), that is "Austrian," as one of several witnesses, who will soon come to play an important role in this story—Article IV specified the legal and political status of those "half or mixed-bloods": "It is stipulated that the half or mixed-bloods of the Chippewas residing with them *shall be considered Chippewa Indians*, and shall, as such, be allowed to participate in all annuities which shall hereafter be paid to the Chippewas of the Mississippi and Lake Superior, due them by this treaty, and by the treaties heretofore made and ratified."[95]

A version of this same sociopolitical process had been taking place south and west of the Lake Superior basin with Dakota mixed bloods on the Mississippi River. The aforenoted 1830 treaty with the Sauk, Fox, Dakota, and others established a mixed-blood reservation that would be held collectively "in the same manner that Indian titles are held."[96] Implementing the provision raised constitutional issues and so subsequent negotiations resulted in the passage of a law by Congress in July of 1854 that exchanged the Dakota mixed bloods' right to a 640-acre parcel *within* the reservation designated in that treaty for scrip certificates for the same amount of land to be located elsewhere.[97] Several of those certificates would be redeemed for parcels in the Penokees beginning in 1859 adjacent to Chippewa mixed-bloods' parcels, and in short order, come to capitalize the Wisconsin and Lake Superior Mining and Smelting Company, though this company had begun to consolidate those same lands using the Pre-Emption Act already in 1856.[98]

This chapter offers further evidence that indigenous polities of the Western Great Lakes region were changing in no small way by virtue of their having generated a class of people of mixed parentage who were both bound to their relatives and playing important economic roles within the communities as links to white communities and markets. Seen as leaders of Indian opinion, they were given special consideration in several treaties, a practice that was as generative of their status as it was reflective. When Indian negotiators stipulated for reserved lands for members of this class of people, those individual reservations were typically and explicitly protected from alienation as an exercise of the federal government's obligation to protect all Indian people—so-called full and mixed blood alike—under the developing trust doctrine. The cases reviewed reveal that the ways in which alienation of land was restricted depended upon the particulars of the sociohistorical contexts. We now turn to the specific shape of that evolving indigenous polity in the southwestern sector of Anishinaabewaki.

4

"Mixed Bloods" in the Southwest Sector of Anishinaabewaki

They grow from my side. My blood flows in their veins.[1]

How were "mixed bloods" or "half-breeds" integrated into indigenous polities in the region of northern Wisconsin, and what is the best evidence for determining the character of that integration? From an Ojibwe perspective, they were *inawemaagen* (relatives) and not *meuyaagizid* (strangers or foreigners), "indigenous in origin . . . [and] . . . a part of Anishinaabewaki," according to historian Michael Witgen, and *aibitawsid*, "half-breed man or woman" according to Bishop Baraga.[2] I first take up the issue of the apparent social texture and fabric of these communities and then turn to the contemporaneous writings of a sympathetic federal official as a way to understand indigenous ways of figuring belonging and difference.

In a short section of his pioneering 2005 law review article, "A Legal History of Blood Quantum in Federal Indian Law to 1935," Paul Spruhan sketches a history of mixed-blood treaty provisions to show the role that blood quantum played during a phase of the treaty period, specifically, 1817 to 1865. He concludes a long footnote with the following: "There is surely a wealth of material to be discovered concerning the tribal understanding and use of terms like half-breed and mixed blood that may have informed the language of treaties. *As such is beyond the scope of this paper, the author can only encourage others to explore these issues.*"[3]

I would like to take up that challenge and argue that mixed bloods or "half-breeds" were an integral part of the indigenous polities in the region. The treaties the Ojibwe signed between 1837 and 1854 may give a different impression because of the connotations of "half-breed" and "mixed blood." But as I have shown earlier, indigenous practices of adoption and incorporation produced kinship relations with full membership, rights, responsibilities, and obligations and these mixed bloods were kin. Although terms such as "mixed blood" or "half-breed" came to have some standing in the communities over time, they appear to have been used to recognize and exacerbate a *social* difference within the indigenous polity for less than salutary reasons at the same time that indigenous political power fell to its nadir at the turn of the twentieth century.

There were no tribes nor nations in the Great Lakes region in the seventeenth century. And though he titles his book *An Infinity of Nations*, Michael Witgen is quoting a French source who was imagining the indigenous New World using a term from his own conceptual inventory. Rather this was "a world of bands, clans, villages and peoples, . . . a multipolar social formation" capable of shape-shifting, through "a process of encounter and transformation." Anishinaabewaki was "a dynamic and evolving world," that included all of what the French called the Algonquians, "the Odawa, Boodewaadamii, Mississagua as well as numerous small groups living in the interior north of Lake Superior and west of Hudson Bay."[4] Much the same could be said about the Dakota, Nakota, and Lakota-speaking communities west of Anishinaabewaki, imagined as the Oceti Sakowin, or of Commancheria or Apacheria to the southwest.[5] Anishinaabewaki was organized or imagined in terms of kinship. Actors within it were seeking to expand it, as they characteristically sought to incorporate persons, largely indifferent to those individuals' ultimate origins. Social growth was desirable and a sign of virtue. The literature on captivity narratives is certainly testimony to this widely shared disposition.[6]

The geographer, geologist, ethnographer, and Indian agent Henry Rowe Schoolcraft traveled throughout the region between Lake Superior and the Mississippi, between June and September in 1831, covering 2,300 miles. He was investigating the on-going hostilities between the Chippewa and the Sioux, depositing American flags, presidential medals, and gifts to political leaders in several villages along the way. He detailed the geography and demography as well, noting that there were trading posts associated with most of the settlements. He indicates that there was a population of just over 3,000 Chippewas in twenty-seven different villages in the region.

We get the strong sense that this was a society on the ascent consistent with Michael Witgen's appraisal of the period as one of expansion and consolidation. "The population was enterprising and warlike. They have the means of subsistence in *comparative* abundance. They are increasing in numbers."[7] Consistent with this, mixed bloods were mentioned only once by Schoolcraft. The mixed bloods were victims of a raid. Kapamappa, chief of a village on the Yellow River, told him that the Sioux violated the recent peace by making an attack the previous year "on a band of Chippewas and half-breeds, and the murder of four persons."[8] The phrasing is telling: the band had two classes of persons within it, yet implicitly all of the members were acting in concert in all the different ways in which bands produce a life for themselves.

The locations of some of these villages Schoolcraft visited also appear in the testimonies collected by Lucius Lyon undertaken for purposes of implementing the mixed-blood provision of the 1837 treaty, and soon to be treated herein in greater detail. I indicated earlier that many of the male mixed bloods had established themselves in their wives' communities,[9] such as Lac Courte Oreilles, Lac du Flambeau, Sandy Lake, Leech Lake, La Pointe, Fond du Lac, Red Cedar Lake (near Mille Lac), Crow Island, Gull Lake, Saint Peter, Mackinac, Grand River, Keeweenaw, Red Lake, St Croix River, St. Croix Lake, Yellow Lake on the Yellow River, Lake Winnipic, Isle Royale, Grand Portage, Pine River in the Iowa Territory, Folleavoine (in the region of Yellow Lake), Wisconsin River, Pointe St. Ignace.

What was this human landscape like? How were people being incorporated into indigenous society? What was the status of the distinction that non-Indians made between "Indian" and "mixed bloods" in the eyes of those people so designated? We can look to the writing of Alfred Brunson, an Indian Office subagent, highly sympathetic to his charges, for insight into how this evolving indigenous polity was organized and imagined by people within it.

When Alfred Brunson was seven years old, his family moved from Danbury, Connecticut, to Sing Sing, New York, where his father ran a ferry on the Hudson River. Several years later, during a violent gale, the young Alfred watched from shore as his rheumatic father fell into the water. With a man to row for him, the boy reached out only to have the wet hair of his drowning father slip through his fingers as "he saw his father sink for the last time . . . [T]he incident made the lad into a man."[10] Appraising his character, that author—whom I assume to be his granddaughter or a niece—described him as "a plain honest man who loved justice and fair dealing . . . Loyalty was a deep and fixed principle of his conduct . . . woe to the perverter of truth, the traitor, or the inhumane for them he had at his command severe language, and in his denunciation of crime or injustice never minced words."[11] Not an unsurprising character appraisal on the part of a descendent, to be sure, but the rest of his biography provides support for the claims. A veteran of the War of 1812, Brunson became a missionary and found his way to Wisconsin. He would go on to be admitted to the bar and served in the territorial legislature. In 1842, Brunson accepted a commission as the subagent for the Indian Office at La Pointe in charge of the Lake Superior Chippewa Indians of the region.

As an old man reflecting on his life thirty years later, Brunson wrote of his tenure at that post in his memoir, *A Western Pioneer*: "I concluded that, if in holding an office under government I must be accessory to palpable fraud, I would hold no such office, and sent in my resignation, having held the office about a year, traveled about two thousand miles, and disbursed in money and goods about one hundred thousand dollars."[12]

Brunson arrived at a subagency that was very poorly equipped to do the business of the government on behalf of the Chippewa Indians in its care. All of the account books were in the possession of the previous subagent who would hold on to them for the entire duration of Brunson's year-long tenure. Worse, he was getting conflicting instructions from Robert Stuart, the Indian agent in Detroit and James Doty, the superintendent of Indian affairs for the Territory of Wisconsin. The fraud he refers to was the matter of Superintendent Robert Stuart's claim that Isle Royale in Lake Superior was included in the 1842 treaty cession although the Pigeon River Ojibwe, who were recognized as owners of that island, did not attend the treaty proceedings. The band was quite adamant about their sovereignty over the island even as non-Indian copper miners began to descend upon it. Although Stuart negotiated that treaty, Brunson wrote that Stuart's ambition blinded him to what transpired vis à vis Isle Royale. Brunson believed Indian people and he would pay dearly for it.

Brunson's integrity as an advocate for Indian people—full blood and half-breed alike—comes through in his correspondence. And although he supported their removal from the lands they had ceded, he did so because he saw this option as protecting them from the whiskey-selling traders who exploited the ambiguous jurisdictional status of ceded lands.

Brunson is painfully eloquent when writing about the terrible effects of alcohol on the Indians. He was also quite honestly concerned about his charges' spiritual condition, thinking that their conversion to Christianity was necessary for them to take up civilized habits and therefore survive the tide of settlement that was creating such havoc in their lives. We may no longer be sympathetic to such a position today, but it is clear that at the time, he saw their conversion as the means of saving Indian people from destruction.

Having read his entire official two-hundred-plus-page hand-written correspondence[13] while he was subagent over the course of a couple of days in the Wisconsin Historical Society's archives, I would argue that the effect of his sympathy was a tacit agency capture—and in this case, subagency capture—a concept that we tend to associate with the corporate practice of coming to control the governmental regulatory agencies that regulate them. Brunson's writing about the Indians' circumstances, and particularly the relationship between Indians and "mixed bloods" or "half-breeds," as he would call them,

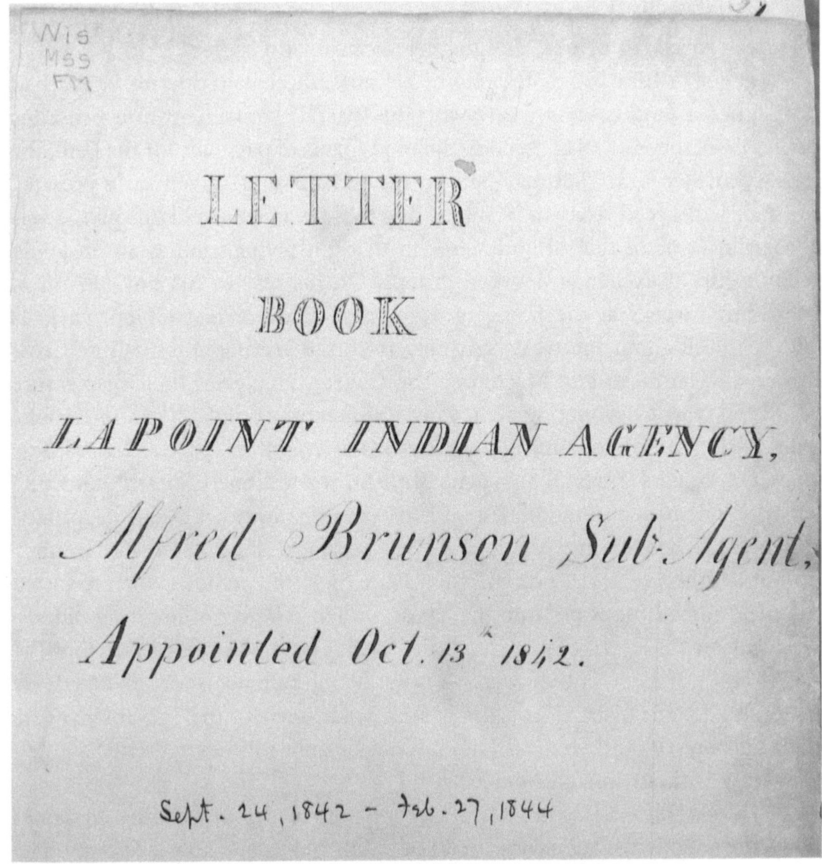

Wis
Mss
FM

LETTER

BOOK

LAPOINT INDIAN AGENCY,

Alfred Brunson, Sub-Agent,

Appointed Oct. 13 1842.

Sept. 24, 1842 - Feb. 27, 1844

Figure 4.1. The frontispiece of Alfred Brunson's leather-bound Letter Book at the State Historical Society of Wisconsin. Photo courtesy of the author.

might as well be the voices of the Indians and mixed bloods themselves. In fact, as we will see, he often quotes them directly, or at least appears to do his very best to translate and reconstruct what they said to him.

Foreshadowing twentieth-century ethnographic practice, Brunson spent a great deal of time with Indian people—his reference to travelling about two thousand miles—was written in a letter to James Doty on July 20, 1843, adding that he had been "travelling through this country as I do, conversing with them in their lodges." Here I offer a close reading of his letters in an ethnosociological effort to deliver what Jennifer Brown called for in her article, "Linguistic Solitudes and Changing Social Categories," which directly addresses this issue: "We need to come to grips with the question of how to use and interpret the 'natives' own categories,"[14] the most consequential of these categories, of course, designating social relationships.

When Alfred Brunson came to his post, the Lake Superior bands had just signed a land cession treaty with the federal government a few months earlier in October of 1842. Among different forms of payment for the land, the treaty provided a $15,000 payment to the Indians to be given as "a present" to "their half-breed relatives."[15] Interesting that the language of gift-giving was chosen in favor of that of commerce in that gift-giving implies an on-going relationship of exchange between groups. On his way to his post, Brunson spent three weeks at the home of the Lyman Warren near Chippewa Falls and heard all about the treaty, learning from the visiting chiefs White Crow of Lac du Flambeau and Marten of Lac Courte Oreilles of their displeasure about the recent negotiations. He would hear more complaints from Buffalo, chief of the La Pointe band upon Brunson's arrival at his post at La Pointe.[16]

On January 5, 1843, Subagent Brunson wrote Robert Stuart, the acting superintendent of Indian affairs, and the commissioner who had negotiated the recent treaty, about what he had been hearing. "The Indians declare they do not consider it a sale, nor will they abide by it, nor remove when required to unless something is put into the hands of their relatives," the mixed bloods. He went on to describe how the "half-breeds" were planning to disrupt the next treaty payment as they were so upset about being so short-changed. He ended his letter writing, "You know with what tenacity the Indians hang to their half-breeds, and you was [sic] not out of sight till they regretted signing the treaty without this allowance."

He would write a nineteen-page version of the same letter to James Doty the following day saying that the failure to more fully accommodate the half-breeds "was displeasing to the Indians and highly offensive to their half breed relatives, some six or seven hundred in number, and from letters and speeches, copies of which are herewith enclosed, it appears that this dissatisfaction is very general."

Brunson articulated the Indians' argument for the full enfranchisement of the mixed bloods and based it on their common occupancy of the same lands:

> The claim of the mixed bloods, in this case, is based as before said, upon the connection of blood with the people acknowledged to have the right of occupancy and control of the soil, and upon their having been born upon and occupying the soil in common with other occupants. If the Indians have the right of occupancy because they occupy it, which is admitted by our laws and treaties made with their relatives to this latter, the right of the half breeds must be admitted upon the same principle. And if the law

> of nations holds good, that by becoming civilized the occupant strengthens his claims then the half breeds and several hundred whole bloods who have adopted civilized habits in this nation, have a still higher claim upon the soil they occupy and cultivate. Their claim is still further based upon services rendered the original Lords as well as occupants of the soil in feeding, clothing, counseling and instructing them in the arts of civilization. The Indians appreciate these services and wish either to given them a stipulated sum, in consideration of relinquishing their rights to the soil, or to have them share in common with the nation in the payment received. But as their friends are civilized and likely to hold property, not in common, but in individuality they prefer to receive their portion of the payment separately.

Here Brunson transmits the sentiments of both mixed bloods and Indians and the different ways in which the groups are entailed with each other: kinship, residency, and reciprocal exchange of services: "They were born and reared upon the soil and having by degrees introduced habits of civilization, they have greatly changed the savage character of their relatives of deeper blood." This is the local theory of hybridity. The whites see this as progress in the direction of becoming civilized. However, Indians, half- and full-blood, as it were, probably do not, as they appear to recognize an intra-societal cultural difference with respect to holding property. Brunson is also making the argument for the mixed bloods being useful for demonstration and educational purposes, in that they have *already* been doing this. Paying mixed bloods is recognition and incentive to continue. From an Indian perspective, the "half-breeds" receiving benefits facilitates and recognizes indigenous control over the mode of sociocultural change. Brunson adds that they have helped out with introducing missionaries to the country. He refers to the theory of a Mr. Crawford [commissioner of Indian affairs] about the value of the presence of white blood. It "seems to predispose him to civilization. And when but one fourth of Indian blood remains their color seldom indicates any taint of 'cast' [sic]."

In making an argument for a bigger payment, Brunson puts a cash value on indigenous production of furs, sugar, wild rice, canoe-building materials, fish, and game. The presumption seems to be that both the Indians and the "half-breeds" are doing the same subsistence round, so by implication they also share these central subsistence practices. To this point, Leonard Wheeler, the Congregational Presbyterian minister who had come to La Pointe in 1841, wrote a very detailed description of a maple sugar production camp in the area of Bad River in 1844. It is notable for the presence of "Indians, French and half-breeds,"[17] leaving Madeline Island all together, using the same technology and building the same temporary homes and living for a few weeks in the same area. This gives all appearances of being a single community with internal social distinctions of little overall significance to its members.

Brunson will boldly write of the mixed bloods that "they at present hold the balance of power with the Indians on these Lakes" and that unlike the stereotype, the mixed bloods are not rich, so they are deserving of consideration. He ends the letter suggesting that the treaty be amended to provide more for mixed bloods to forestall the need for military force, but appends to it a series of affidavits from the chiefs and headmen.

Each affidavit was labeled with uppercase alphabetic letters in shadow script A–E. The first was from Buffalo, dated October 29, 1842, very shortly after the treaty negotiations where Buffalo blamed the other chiefs and wrote, "I am ashamed of my treaty; all white people and the half breeds laugh at me." The document marked B was from White Crow, dated December 18, 1842, when he visited Brunson at the Warren family. He was an important regional leader of Lac du Flambeau and a signatory of both the 1837 and 1842 treaties. His comment suggests what Indian leaders generally thought about their relationship to the people called by the whites "half-breeds," or "mixed bloods," and I note that he does not use these terms in his remarks, but White Crow refers to them as "my relations of Indian blood":

> I did not want to sell any more of my lands, but I was told it made no difference whether I did or not, if the majority of the chiefs signed, our grandfather* would take the land. But I did not agree to remove, nor to sell unless my relations of Indian blood were provided for. But I am told since the treaty I must remove when my grandfather wants me to, and yet that no provisions is made for my relations (Raising his voice) I speak louder to my grandfather, that I do not consider my land sold unless something is put into the hands of my relations, and what I say is the voice of all my people. [He represents Flambeau, Wiskonsin and Vieux Desert bands].
>
> *The word usually rendered great father is litterally (sic) grandfather, father of a father.

Affidavit C, also dated December 19, was from Marten, head chief of the Ottawa, or Lac Courte Oreilles, bands and represented Ottawa Lake, Chippewa River, and the Lac Chetak Bands.

Marten said:

> My father: what my brother chief has said, is true, and we will stand to it. We were told by the commissioner that our grandfather wanted our lands for the sake of the mines, but that we might remain on these as long as our grandfather sees fit. But I and my brother chiefs refused to touch the pen *unless our half breed relations were provided for* and we should be permitted to live on the land as along as we behave well and peaceable with our grandfather and his white children. I was not at St Peters in 1837 and never touched the pen to sell my lands until last fall, and when I touched the pen it was *on the condition that my relations were provided for*, that we should remain on the land as long as we are peaceable. We have no objection to the white mans working the mines and the timber and making farms, but we reserve the birchbark and cedar, for canoes, the rice and sugar tree and the privilege of hunting without being disturbed by the whites. *Our half breeds must be paid if we give our own pay*. But our grandfather can better afford to pay them than we can. He is rich and has plenty of money. Let him give the half breeds $200,000 and we will be satisfied. Tell our grandfather this [They mean by half breeds, all of blood mixed with Indian of any degree]. (italic emphasis added)

Buffalo would add another affidavit on the same day that Brunson wrote his original letter to Superintendent Stuart.

> Affidavit D. In council at LaPointe Jan 5, 1843. Buffalo, head chief of this band. Says the provision in the treaty at Prairie du Chien that transferred title to minerals is not legitimate. "I shall now say a few words to you in regard to my half breeds. *They grow from my side. My blood flows in their veins.* I pity them, for in this treaty nothing is given to them. My grandfather gives them nothing, my heart aches on their account . . . I wished after I saw the course of the treaty, *to take my child, the half breed*, by the hand and go and plead for him with my grandfather at his own seat, but in this thing I was repulsed, and these are the reasons that my heart aches within me."
>
> La Grand, second chief, said My father: I have but a few words to say. The treaty is finished and we are too feeble to break

> it. Our half breeds get nothing. But I speak the mind of these my chiefs and young men present, when I say, that if we have failed in our duty to *our half breed children* in one instance, we shall not fail in another. The payment for these lands shall be theirs. I wish my grandfather to know it. (Italic emphasis added)

The final affidavit was a letter written to Michael Cadotte at La Pointe by a fellow mixed blood, one Ki-chi-saw-bau-dis, writing from Sault Ste. Marie, and it is telling that he uses his Anishinaabe name. At the time of this writing, Michael Cadotte was fifty-five years old. A veteran of the War of 1812, he led a group of Ojibwe warriors in the capture of Mackinac by the British. He was licensed to trade at several locations south of Lake Superior.[18] In her essay on five generations of Cadotte men, all of whom married Ojibwe women, Theresa Schenck concludes that "they stayed with their people. They are still there today—at Lac Courte Oreilles, L'Anse, Red Cliff, Bad River, and Bay Mills—for unlike the white fur traders, they were not there to exploit the Native people, but to share their life."[19] The italic highlighted section of the letter speaks eloquently to how so-called half-breeds thought about their relationship with their "red brethren."

> Affidavit E. Sault Ste Marie, 19 October 1842
> To the half-breeds,
> Michael Cadotte, Dear Sir.
>
> It is with a high state of feeling we address you these lines. We find ourselves almost destitute of that confidence we once had in our red brethren and we call your attention to the subject, to ask your opinion upon it. Was it right that we should be disinherited and robbed of our constitutional rights? No human being with a knowledge of the rights of man could have done such a thing, as our relations did in their late treaty. Consider the cause why we complain. Did not our fathers support these [unclear] men in their time of need? Did they not suffer, themselves and families, to help them by hundreds in time of War, in sickness, in hunger, and in all their troubles? Did they not help them, both old and young, infants, fathers, mothers, brothers, sisters, widows and orphans? And did they not even loose [sic] their precious lives for them? And at the present do we not help them in all their trouble?
>
> *Can a half breed eat a piece of bread and not offer or give a piece of it to his own blood? No. And don't we claim half of their blood, which they cannot deny before the face of heaven and earth?*

> *And don't we justly claim half of the lands they have sold when our fore fathers are buried? Don't we have their blood curing to their children for vengeance tho' the voice of the loved ones is gone for a season?* I might show a great many more causes for complaint. But at present I am in great haste. The vessel is about to leave. But I hope to see the day when I shall meet our friends, and unbosom [?] myself to them. You can share this to the half breeds if you choose. We are all well and hope you are the same. It is hard times at the Sault. Yours most truly Ac Ac.
>
> Ki-chi-saw-bau-dis

The author refers to "our red brethren," also known to him as "our relations," and "constitutional rights," suggesting an indigenous political model wherein "half-breeds" are a class within this transforming polity. He cites as examples the reciprocal help in bad times and good. The relationship is one of both blood and necropolitan soil. In a letter dated July 14, 1843, to Major Dearborn at Fort Snelling requesting troops to protect the annuity payment from the threatened seizure by the mixed bloods, Brunson echoes this model referring to "the half breeds of the Nation," that is, the Ojibwe nation. He will later refer to Joseph Default and John McGillies, as "both half breeds of the nation" a few days later.

Subsequently, the commissioner of Indian affairs wrote to Brunson on April 3, 1843, indicating his own apparent acceptance of this political model in commenting on the issue of the size of the payment. He wrote: "The Senate and the country at large complained seriously of the evils which have heretofore resulted from large allowances to *this class of Indians*" (emphasis added). Yet on March 10, when Robert Stuart writes a letter upbraiding Brunson for being taken in by the half breeds, he explicitly distinguishes mixed bloods from the Indians. "The lands belong to the Indians, and when they sell, they have a right either to withhold, or give a portion to the half breeds."

These are competing models of indigenous society and polity with some American officials insisting on a bigger difference than indigenous people appear to countenance in describing sociopolitical formations. Indians were imagining Anishinaabewaki, a complex, evolving, and culturally heterogeneous, hybrid, indigenous sociopolitical process and entity. Robert Stuart took the position that the mixed bloods are manipulating the rest of the indigenous community, which is distinguishable from those mixed bloods. In her own account of these interactions for purposes of foregrounding the self-described "quarterblood" William Whipple Warren's work as an interpreter, ethnohistorian Theresa Schenk expresses the judgment that the Indians were quite sincere about their interest in accommodating the mixed bloods. She asserts that the accusation that the mixed bloods were manipulating the Indians "is an insult to deny native people the faculty to make their own decisions."[20] Her allegation critiques the ascendant and official, simplistic and racialized conception of sociopolitical organization in the face of its apparent evolution.

Although sincere about accommodating their "half-breeds," the limits of the polity were also debated in that November of 1842 when Brunson convened a group of chiefs pursuant to the treaty provision regarding "the present" of $15,000, "to be disposed of, as they, together with their agent, shall determine in council,"[21] quoting the treaty. The issue was which "half-breeds" were going to be included in the payment. Hole-in-the-Day affirmed the group's decision against the strangers who "came from a far country to get their money, and care no more for them." I expect the "them" referred to were those Indian people and "half-breeds" still resident in the area as opposed to those who have gone off to those denser concentrations of mixed bloods such as Sault Ste. Marie or Michilimackinac. By contrast, Big Wind describes them as pigeons: "They come and they fly away and I see them no more. Those who are among us go inland in the Winter and help us." And here we see that the criteria for inclusion is kinship, sustained relations of generalized reciprocity, co-residence, the enduring diffuse solidarity that forms the grounds of inclusion and belonging.

At that same meeting, David King, chief at Keeweenaw, spoke in favor of enfranchising those "half-breeds" who have never received annuities before and justifies his right by appealing to his understanding of American federalism. "You Americans are in states, all are brethren, but no one has a right to go into another state and control its affairs. We wish for our proportion of the half breeds money, to do as we please with." Blackbird of La Pointe disagrees with the emerging consensus, speaking of his relatives at Sault Ste. Marie as "my nephews," likely imagined as sister's sons. The warriors interrupt the debate and proclaim, "It is only those who stay with us, we admit to the payment," requiring a residence requirement that implicitly entails reciprocal relations. And with this the group had apparently reached consensus.

Alfred Brunson would not last in his position as subagent at La Pointe. He had angered Robert Stuart, the acting superintendent for Indian affairs in Michigan with accusations that his boss had bargained in bad faith when he made the treaty of 1842. Not only had Stuart underpaid the "half-breeds" in Brunson's opinion, listening to the chiefs, Stuart had also committed what Brunson called a "gross and palpable fraud" in claiming that Isle Royale was ceded although Isle Royale was not brought up in the negotiations, and the Indians adamantly denied that it was part of the land cession.

Brunson's correspondence does reveal the intimate connection between what the whites were calling "the Indians" and who they were calling "half-breeds" and "mixed bloods." Indigenous society was transforming even as it reproduced itself via the traditional means of intermarriage. A class of persons had emerged that belonged to the traditional polity. They were relatives of each other, and kinship was the coin of the realm, the essential means of constituting society and polity.

In consideration of a more complicated sociopolitical organization, one seen more from within, with kinship as the central organizational feature rather than race, we now turn to an account of how the mixed-blood provision of the 1854 treaty was implemented in an improvised administrative process. That process both ignored and directly engaged the fact that there was no specific language in the treaty to deter the alienation of land once it was allotted and patented to mixed bloods belonging to the Lake Superior Chippewa Indians.

5

Implementing the Mixed-Blood Provision of the 1854 Treaty of La Pointe

> Yet still Indians . . . not citizens of the United States, but domestic subjects.[1]

The treaty of 1854 was mainly motivated by the desire to acquire the mineral lands north and west of Lake Superior. The bands of Ojibwe acquiesced in this land cession but stipulated for the continued right to hunt, fish, and gather on the ceded lands, a measure of their intention to stay in the area. An even more telling measure of their desire to remain, they stipulated for having six tracts of land ceded in two earlier treaties for their use be "set apart and withheld from sale." This treaty article creating reservations under the new federal Indian policy, also included a seventh paragraph that created individually held reservations for the mixed bloods: "Each head of a family, or single person over twenty-one years of age at the present time of the mixed-bloods, belonging to the Chippewas of Lake Superior, shall be entitled to eighty acres of land, to be selected by them under the direction of the President, and which shall be secured to them by patent in the usual form" (Article II, paragraph 7, Treaty of September 30, 1854).

Implementing this provision of the treaty proved to be complicated and would have long-term effects. It was also consequential for the particular constitution of the indigenous polities now in possession of collectively held land bases because mixed bloods would now be marked by the potential possession of landed property, unlike the members of the polity, who were not mixed bloods. And although there was a great deal of concern among federal officials about the potential for fraudulent transfer of the right to that property, the phrase "secured to them by patent in the usual form" would make for their dispossession and the subsequent capitalization of the first iron-mining companies in northern Wisconsin.

Mixed bloods were structurally liminal—that is, they were Indians for purposes of inclusion in the treaty proceedings but non-Indians for purposes of the right to hold patents "in the usual form." Therefore, they were vulnerable to non-Indians who were able to secure powers of attorney over them which interfered with the land allocation process. The provision also created a great deal of conflict between mixed bloods and Euro-American settlers who were mobilizing the Pre-emption Act of 1841 to secure land. These two modes of land acquisition were emblematic of the different legal status of the two groups.

The Treaty of La Pointe containing the mixed-blood provision under examination was ratified by the Senate on January 10, 1855, about three weeks after the bill authorizing the extinguishment of the lands ceded actually passed the Congress—the bill having been introduced in the spring well before the negotiations. Three months later, in April, the commissioner of Indian affairs, George Manypenny, received a letter from Julius Austrian, a German-born businessman who had been trading with Indian people—mostly at La Pointe—since the early 1840s, when he joined the trading post that had been established by the Leopold brothers earlier that year.[2] Austrian had just purchased much of the town of La Pointe in 1853, "a small village of cabins, warehouses, houses, churches and wigwams at the price of one dollar and twenty-five cents per acre,"[3] perhaps a good index of his commercial aspirations.

For the most part, Austrian appears to have been on good terms with federal officials. When the commissioner of Indian affairs instructed Agent Gilbert at Detroit to work with Major Herriman to negotiate the 1854 treaty, he had advised Gilbert to keep the project confidential but that he should call upon Julius Austrian "commended to me as a faithful man" having "rendered service to this office, in collecting Indians" earlier, "to confide the message to Herriman."[4] There was no mention of mixed bloods in those instructions.

Austrian wrote that he recently had sat down with the half-breeds for "a smoke" wherein the half-breeds asked him to communicate some of the concerns to "theyr (sic) great father" specifically: "The Half breeds wish to know how to proceed to get a legal title to such land as they are entitled by the last Treaty as theyr (sic) is land already surveyed and [in?] market which they would like to enter under the act of Treaty."[5] At the same time, C. W. Rollins and A. W. Burtt wrote a letter to Horatio King, first assistant postmaster general complaining about Austrian, who held the federal contract for carrying the mail at La Pointe. A reference to mixed bloods—here "illiterate Frenchmen"—suggests the quality of his relationships with at least some segment of that population. "Now whenever Mr. Austrian wishes to effect an alteration in mail matters, he goes to these illiterate Frenchmen, gets them to sign something they hardly know what, but he gets their names and these, with his unprincipled misrepresentations, are the instruments and means by which he accomplished his selfish ends."[6]

Photograph 5.1. Julius Austrian. Julius Austrian Papers, Madeline Island Museum, LaPointe, Wisconsin. Image #147229. Courtesy of the Wisconsin Historical Society.

Austrian did not indicate who the "half-breeds" were who wondered about their land titles, but it may be fair to assume that some of the half-breed signatories of the Treaty of 1847 at Fond du Lac were present, because Austrian himself was present at that treaty, although his name was transcribed as "Julius Ombrian," one of the witnesses of the treaty.[7] Of course, it is quite possible that no such "smoke" ever took place at all, and Austrian was merely pointing to his good relations with these people and hoping to move his plans along to acquire their land interests.

Austrian was also in a dispute with the Indian office at the time. His store in Fond du Lac was burned down by tribal members, as the chiefs admitted. The chiefs would not identify who was responsible, which is good evidence for the traditional bifurcation of leadership with the civil chiefs advocating peace and the warriors taking action was well in fact at this time as Rebecca Kugel shows for the Minnesota Ojibwe.[8] The act clearly has all the marks of incendiarism as political act[9] and is a measure of the precarious relationship Austrian had with at least some sector of the regional indigenous community.

Austrian was seeking compensation from the Indian Office for losses that he estimated at over $4,500 and was having trouble getting satisfaction.[10]

Later in the spring, in April of 1855, three La Pointe mixed bloods wrote to Agent Henry Gilbert asking for his intervention, complaining that their claims under the treaty of 1854 had been jumped by strangers. They wrote that "according to the stipulations of the treaty made at La Pointe last fall with the Lake Indians, it was understood that each half breed family were entitled to 80 acres of good farming land."[11] They seem to represent the group of mixed bloods who apparently took the treaty provision seriously on its face desiring the land for its use value.

The letter—and another from the nearby Fond du Lac community referring to mixed bloods having already made locations and improvements,[12] as well as one in September that was notarized at La Pointe[13]—indicates something of the nature of the competition over land at the time. In fact, mixed bloods had been willing to work for St. Paul and Canadian speculators, alternatively thought of by some as "land sharks," as they were called in the pages of the *New York Times*, as preemptors who would squat, improve, prove up, and sell their interests to the speculators. The newspaper article listed Joseph Lamoureax, Joseph Defaut, Joseph Dennis, Joseph Gauthier, Francis Decoteau, John B. Goslin, George D. Morrison, and Levi B. Coffee.

Americans were coming into the area in bigger and bigger numbers, attempting to use the preemption law to secure lands. At the same time, members of the Lake Superior Ojibwe were trying to secure lands using the recently signed treaty. In September 1841, Congress had authorized citizens to settle on ceded lands as preemptors, paying a minimum of $1.25 an acre within either twelve or thirty-three months, depending on survey status of the land. According to the legal historian Nelson Knute, "The law contemplated that the settler should occupy, improve and cultivate the land from the date of first settlement until final proof and payment."[14] Persons on their own initiative as well as persons acting as agents for others were exercising this right in these ceded lands.

In June of 1855, in Detroit, Agent Gilbert issued a public notice[15] addressing the issue of non-Indians attempting to jump the claims of the mixed bloods already settled and making improvements on lands that would soon be patented to them.

The following public notice ran for several issues in the local newspaper:

Office Michigan Indian Agency

DETROIT, June 12, 1855

It having been represented to this office that many of the "mixed-bloods" belonging to the Chippewas of Lake Superior who are

> entitled to eighty acres of land each, under the provision of Art. 2 Sec 7 of the Treaty of September 30, 1854 have made locations and improvements, with a view to claiming the same under said provision, and that such claims are in some cases disregarded and encroached upon by white persons, I am directed by the Commissioner of Indian Affairs to give public notice as follows, to wit:
>
> That the "mixed-bloods" may properly make such locations, under the treaty, upon any lands not previously occupied by other persons who may be entitled to claim the same, and that the "mixed-bloods" who have made, or shall hereafter make, such locations and improvements in good faith, will; be deemed to have acquired rights which will be recognized and protected by the government to the exclusion of any white person who shall afterwards attempt to take possession of the land.
>
> As soon as surveys can be made the "mixed-bloods" will be allowed each the eighty-acre lot on which his improvements may be situated, and all lands will be conveyed only according to the usual legal subdivisions.
>
> Henry C Gilbert, Indian Agent[16]

It would seem that the goals of the provision of the treaty were being met with "many of the mixed-bloods" establishing themselves on the ceded lands at a remove from their tribal relations presumably to begin farming on their own.

The commissioner responded to Gilbert's inquiries regarding eligibility under the provision by advising him to be inclusive, affirming the authority of the tribal leadership in determining who belonged to their community. He would write: "You should submit the list when completed, for the revision of the general council of the Indians, and strike off or add to the names on such list in accordance with the facts therein ascertained. The Indians themselves, in council, by their own traditions and knowledge will doubtless greatly aid in arriving at the facts regarding the ancestry of those who may claim under the provisions for mixed-bloods."[17]

While Agent Henry Gilbert worked on his list of eligible mixed bloods during the summer, Commissioner Manypenny consulted with the General Land Office on the conflicts emerging between Anglo-American preemptors and mixed bloods settled or settling on the recently ceded lands. He began and ended his letter encouraging the office to conduct a survey of the recently acquired mineral lands on the north shore of Lake Superior. "The rush of travel in this direction by the opening of the canal at the Sault St Marie is very great, and with the impression that prevails in relation to the mineral wealth of the country, I am of the opinion that land would be rapidly taken up on the north shore, if it were surveyed." He also registered his concern for the mixed bloods in the face of this "rush" indexing his own apparent understanding of the trust responsibility he had been appointed to discharge in his capacity as commissioner, and wrote: "The Half Breed or Mixed-blood is not generally able to contend with the adventurous white man in relation to his claim or right, and is therefore liable to be wronged."[18]

The designation of the "Half-Breed or Mixed-blood" as *de facto* ward to whom the United States had a duty of protection was also rehearsed in a letter from Charles Mix, the acting commissioner of Indian affairs, to the secretary of the interior later that fall. He sought to clarify the competing claims of mixed bloods and pre-emptors in the newly acquired but yet-to-be-surveyed Minnesota lands. Thomas Hendricks, Commissioner of the General Land Office recommended to the secretary of the interior that the claims of pre-emptors be honored "until the lands to be so selected," by the mixed bloods "shall be indicated"[19] (underlined in original).

We note that Commissioner Mix regarded the mixed bloods as far more Indian than not in this representation. He closes his letter: "However, in consideration of the premises stated by the Commissioner, and to prevent injustice and wrong being practiced upon the *unlettered and simple red man* by the expert, if not heartless speculator, it is respectfully recommended that the respective surveys mentioned in the Commissioner's letter be caused to be made as early as practicable."[20] Again, acting in the capacity as fiduciary, Commissioner Manypenny wrote the head of the Government Land Office (GLO) protesting the issuance of a patent that offended the aforementioned La Pointe mixed blood with the notarized complaint.[21]

Agent Gilbert completed his list of 278 eligible mixed bloods in late November, and in the early winter of 1856 the offices of Indian Affairs, Government Land, and the secretary of the interior worked out how the mixed bloods would be certified for purposes of receiving a patent. On January 7, 1856, Commissioner Manypenny asked Agent Gilbert to specify not only the "names of the reservees, but the specific description of each tract, that may be allowed and approved by the President to them respectively."[22] By late February, Agent Gilbert had drafted the scrip certificates to be presented to the GLO by the mixed bloods in exchange for their land patents.

However, the GLO commissioner responded by expressing his concerns to the secretary of the interior that there was no provision in the treaty or the law for issuing such scrip. Here the GLO effectively anticipated the fraud that would unfold in the administration of this treaty provision if this method were to be adopted. He wrote that "even as a temporary expedient, it seems to me, it would be fraught with many evils in opening the door to speculation, and irregularities by crediting a sort of Indian pre-emption float liable to pass, indirectly if not directly, into other hands leading to disputes in ownership, and liable to conflicts with settlers."[23] The GLO commissioner suggested that the land be located in consultation with the "Indians," clearly meaning the mixed bloods by this designation. And that it should be done under the supervision of the agent who would then contact the General Land Office to secure the issuing of the patent. Apparently, this was his understanding of the clause, "under the direction of the President" in his duty as guardian.

It is very significant that Commissioner Hendricks regards the mixed bloods as "Indians," hence presumptively protected under the trust responsibility that had been articulated in *Cherokee Nation v. Georgia* twenty-five years before, in 1831. Here Hendricks is worried about the mixed bloods losing their property *before* the patent is issued, given its potential value as "a sort of Indian pre-emption float" that would interfere with the patenting process for citizens acting on the provisions of the 1841 Pre-emption Act and creating conflicts. He does not concern himself with the patents' future *after* issue, perhaps because he had already suggested a means by which the patents' mobility would be restricted. He had recommended that "locations to be made through the Indian agent under his responsibility as an officer, *after consultation with the parties claiming* . . . all intervention of outside interested parties should be prevented as much as possible."[24] Despite these cautions, Julius Austrian and others, who represented just the kind of "outside interested parties" the commissioner was worried about, began to intervene either preempting or displacing in "consultation with the parties claiming," and locating parcels of land in the Penokee Hills on the largely agriculturally useless land. This outcome was an explicit contravention of the intent of both the treaty provision and the clause "under the direction of the President."

In response, the Indian Office compromised with the GLO, and the following was cryptically written on the wrapper that contained Gilbert's original letter and Hendrick's response: "Let mem's be given In's as proposed, but with clause expressly and decidedly vs. any transfer, mortgage etc. *Patent be issued to the Indians, not in anywise to inure to the benefit of any one but the Ind. and his heirs.*"[25] "Mem's" (memorials) is a reference to the proposed scrip certificates, I assume, and I highlight in italic to call attention to the use of the word "Indian" again, and to the fact that though "his heirs," might benefit, no "assigns" should benefit from the patent per the usual fee simple formula. However cryptically written, Hendricks is explicitly advocating for a restricted patent.

The commissioner of Indian affairs settled the matter and opted for the original plan of issuing a restricted form of scrip in favor of involving the Indian agent in every location of each eighty-acre parcel. He described the challenge that the demography presented. He wrote, "It is simply impossible for these locations to be made by the Indian Agents; the parties are scattered over a wide extent of country and their locations instead of being confined to the reservations specified in the treaty, as the Commissioner seems to suppose, cannot be made within them at all, but will, undoubtedly be spread over a part of Michigan and Wisconsin."

Of course, what would soon come to be called "full-blood" members of the polity were similarly "scattered over a wide extent of country" as well. Here the commissioner is recognizing that mixed blood parcels will not be within the lands specifically reserved for the Indians themselves, but be spread throughout the region.[26] So, instead of having the agent guarantee that parcels not become a kind of currency by having the agent involved in the location of each eighty-acre parcel, the wording of the scrip certificate would accomplish this goal. As a result, the scrip certificate was quite explicit on the topic of alienation: "It is expressly understood and declared that any sale, transfer, mortgage, assignment or pledge of this certificate, or any rights accruing under it, will not be recognized as valid by the United States; and that *the patent for lands* located by virtue thereof shall be issued directly to the above named reservee or his heirs and *shall in no wise inure to the benefit of any other person or persons*; and that the object and purpose of this certificate is to identify the said above named as one of the persons entitled to the benefit of the provisions of the said 7th clause of the 2nd article of the treaty aforesaid."[27]

Note that the issue of the status of the patent itself is directly addressed in the italicized phrase "the patent for lands located. . . . shall in no wise inure to the benefit of any other person or persons." The scrip certificate is foreshadowing a restricted patent rather along the lines of what had historically been issued to mixed bloods in all previous treaties rather like the patents that would soon be issued to persons allotted on the collectively held reservations themselves.

The leadership of the indigenous communities in the region had been making efforts to resist outside interests in separating the so-called mixed bloods or "half breeds" from the "Indians," in much the same way that the Miamis in Indiana had done several decades before. In fact, Ojibwe leaders succeeded in having that unitary identity recognized in the treaties of 1837 and 1847. Nevertheless, the distinction is clearly drawn here and for purposes of delimiting federal responsibility. Agent Gilbert's assessment in his October 1854 letter[28] reporting on the treaty negotiations—that it was the Indians who were insistent on the mixed bloods being accommodated—indicates that Indian leaders saw their mixed bloods as an asset to their long-term interests and genuinely understood them to be full members of these evolving indigenous polities. They were repeatedly called "our relations."

These mixed bloods had not only worked as interpreters for the tribal leaders, but they also traveled to Washington DC with them. They saw themselves as inextricably entwined with their so-called "full-blood" relatives, representing themselves in correspondence as "their halfbreeds." Insofar as the mixed-blood provision of the treaty "has no connection with the general purpose of the treaty or with the specific reserves," according to the commissioner of Indian affairs, the recognition represents a watershed moment in the legal status of mixed-blood members of the Lake Superior Ojibwes, one that will be reflected in the precise form of the actual patent for those eighty-acre parcels of land.

Documented competition between mixed bloods and Anglo settlers began even before the treaty gave mixed bloods an advantage and would lead to an important legal opinion regarding the status of mixed bloods. And this not only for securing land for *use*, but also in the register of speculating. Vincent Roy, for example, was a prominent nineteenth-century Lake Superior Ojibwe mixed blood. Educated and fluent in Ojibwemowin, French, and English, he worked as an interpreter for the tribal leadership as well as a trader and in the employ of Julius Austrian and his business partner, Louis Leopold, at La Pointe. In August of 1854, before the treaty was negotiated, Roy and a group of other mixed bloods took out a notice in the *Daily Minnesotan*[29] warning

Photograph 5.2 Portrait of French Indians and Vincent Roy, back row, second from the left. Image #39626. Courtesy of the Wisconsin Historical Society.

potential investors that they had pre-empted lands in what would become the city of Superior, Wisconsin. They claimed that they had preempted two lots in Section 13, Township 49, Range 13, but their claim failed in the face of an allegedly earlier claim. Roy and company were clearly playing the speculative game that was being played by so many others in the region at the time.[30]

The controversy made the *New York Times*, whose local correspondent stationed at Superior City offered a comprehensive, clever, and rather opinionated account. He noted that having lost his claim as an American citizen, Vincent Roy attempted to establish his claim using Chippewa scrip.[31] The case was brought to the attention of first one then a succeeding secretary of the interior, who apparently, in turn asked the Attorney General of the United States for an official opinion regarding the legal status of those mixed bloods. He asked whether or not a mixed blood could claim land under the 1841 pre-emption law and receive a patent for it under the provision of the 1854 treaty. In other words, were mixed-bloods citizens? If not, what was their legal status?

The Honorable Caleb Cushing considered the qualifications for citizenship noting that it is not co-extensive with suffrage, that is, that "electorship and citizenship are different things."[32] Furthermore, although Congress had provided rules for naturalization, they applied only to foreign whites. Indians, by contrast, although born here, "are the *subjects* of the United States, and therefore are not, in mere right of home-birth, citizens of the United States" (original italics).[33] And though there are "men of indubitable citizenship, . . . who have aboriginal blood in their veins" they are citizens only by virtue of "some act of recognized legality" that severs their "tribal relations."[34]

One might think that accepting scrip and an unrestricted patent, "of the usual form," might qualify as such an "act of recognized legality," but the Honorable Caleb Cushing opined that mixed bloods who availed themselves of the benefit of this clause of the Treaty of 1854 "declare themselves at that time not citizens, but Indians." Therefore, ". . . a person of mixed-blood, retaining tribal relations, cannot also enjoy at the same time the rights of a citizen of the United States. . . . I think the language of the 7th clause of the 2d article of the treaty with the Chippewas, before me, legally describes persons not citizens of the United States, but, though half bloods, yet still Indians."[35]

Caleb Cushing may have had a motive for his opinion, since he was no stranger to the network of competing mineral and real-estate interests in the region where "half bloods, yet still Indians" continued to live. In 1845, he and two of his wealthy friends, organized the St. Croix and Lake Superior Mining Company, one of dozens of companies that "sprang into existence" after the ratification of the 1842 land cession treaty with the Chippewa.[36] His opinion meant that the mixed bloods could not benefit from the 1841 pre-emption law, but apparently that did not stop them from trying, or more precisely, the opinion of the Attorney General did not stop certain non-Indian parties from hiring mixed bloods to settle upon prospectively valuable tracts of land on the former's behalf having an eye to siting a new city.[37]

This is notable for illustrating the diversity of mixed-blood interests, legal experience, sophistication, and capacity for acting decisively in the emergent settler, social and economic order. But more significantly, these mixed bloods, "though half bloods," are Indians and "declare" their "tribal relations" by mobilizing this provision of the treaty. The only thing that could alter their status as Indians was "the treaty-making or the legislative powers of the Government."[38] Race was now that powerful. This assignment of eighty acres" exercise, in order to fulfill the provision of the treaty had to be taken—and now quoting Attorney General Cushing who in turn quotes the treaty, glossing the significance of a critical phrase—" 'under the direction of the President,' *as guardians of Indians*"[39] as the treaty required. How would the "direction of the President" be realized—in order to avoid the possibility of fraud—and honor the trust responsibility due to these mixed-bloods who were "yet still Indians . . . not citizens of the United States, but domestic subjects?[40]

It would take the rest of 1856 to complete the lists of eligible mixed bloods, issue the scrip certificates, and transmit the information to the Government Land Office in anticipation of the scrip being redeemed throughout northern Michigan, Wisconsin, and Minnesota at local land offices. Conflicts between pre-emptors and mixed bloods continued with Indian leaders calling upon the commissioner of Indian affairs to act on behalf of those mixed bloods, and continuing to refer to them as "our relatives," discursively indexing their desire to keep the evolving polity intact. One of the letters read, "We hope Our Father you will remedy this Evil in such a way that *our relatives* may select themselves *homes near us* before the whole of the land in the neighborhood are all entered by the whites."[41]

Of course, the purpose of this provision of the treaty was apparently common knowledge. Nearly thirty years before, in the Treaty of 1826, Article 4 offered the rationale for such grants: "It being deemed important that the half-breeds, scattered through this extensive country, should be stimulated to exertion and improvement by the possession of permanent property and fixed residences, the Chippewa tribe, in consideration of the affection they bear to these persons, and of the interest which they feel in their welfare . . ."[42] However, these empropertied "domestic subjects" were vulnerable now as the possibilities for commercial mining began to unfold.

First Efforts at Mining the Penokees

The intent of the policy was well known and circulated widely at the time. The mixed-blood article in the treaty appeared in full in a letter written in

October of 1856 from George Johnston to the Indian Agent at Sault Ste. Marie complaining about his relatives being left off the mixed-blood list.[43] Nonetheless, at the very moment that the letter from the La Pointe chiefs to the commissioner of Indian affairs was written, asking for relief from "this Evil," Surveyor Albert Stuntz, working for the General Land Office, signed an affidavit certifying his completion of the surveys Townships 44 North and 45 North, 1 West, 2 West and 3 West in northern Wisconsin just south of the recently created Bad River Reservation. Therein he noted for many parts of the sections, that the land was "Unfit for cultivation," and he noted the presence of the Iron Range.[44] Clearly, well before the lands were *located*—that is, chosen and recorded at the GLO by the mixed bloods or individuals putatively acting on their behalf—it was known to the GLO officials that the lands in the Penokees were largely useless for agricultural purposes, and therefore not well-suited for realizing the intent of the treaty provision.

The lands were, however, potentially valuable to mineral interests.

Photograph 5.3. Studio portrait of geologist Charles Whittlesey dressed for a field trip. 1858. Image #36627. Courtesy of the Wisconsin Historical Society.

Charles Whittlesey had made the first systematic geological survey of northern Wisconsin in 1849 before townships and sections had been surveyed. He produced the first geological map of both the region and the Penokee-Gogebic Iron Range. See map 5.1. After the publication of Owen's *Report of a Geological Survey of Wisconsin, Iowa, and Minnesota* in 1852, he wrote that "the excitement of 1845–46 in reference to copper was repeated in reference to iron. Pre-emptors followed the surveyors, erecting their rude cabins on each quarter-section between the meridian and Lac des Anglais [now English Lake], a distance of 18 or 20 miles."[45] This accounts for the competition for land between the pre-emptors and mixed bloods that appeared in the correspondence between Indian leaders and government officials, as well as government officials with each other.

There was great hope for the Penokees and for the development of the city of Ashland. The self-described speculative settler and teacher at Reverend Wheeler's mission school at Odanah, Edwin Ellis, reflected on the late 1850s twenty years later:

> We had learned through the United States geological surveys of the vast deposits of iron ore, in what is now known as the Penoka Range. Although we had ourselves no actual knowledge of the extent or richness of the ore, still we had entire confidence in

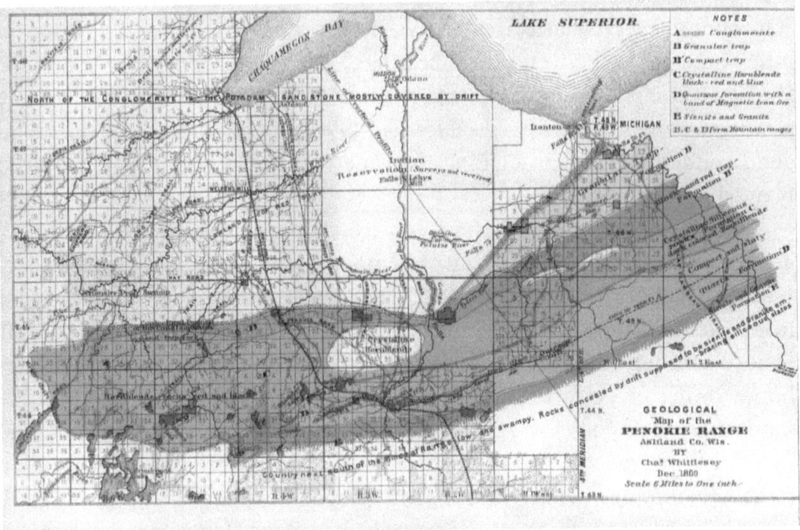

Map 5.1. "Geological Map of the Penokie Range," Charles Whittlesey, Dec. 1860. Geology of Wisconsin. Survey of 1873–1879, Volume III, Plate XX.

> both—a confidence which, through all the doubts and uncertainties of late years—we still entertain. We thought this iron must be used in the coming years, and we had no doubt that would reach the great water highway at Ashland. This trade alone would create a city. The iron trade itself would create a market for the products of the soil in the vicinity, and soon all the country from the bay to the iron mountains would be opened."[46]

Appropos of that great hope for development, and in regard to the matter of the "pre-emptors," we should note that Increase Lapham visited these lands in September 1856 after the ratification of the 1854 treaty but before implementation of the mixed-blood provision. He wrote the following for the Charter and Organization of the Wisconsin and Lake Superior Mining and Smelting Company describing the resources and the squatters: "We find that about nine-tenths of all the trees on the range are sugar maple," [a boon as] "the maple yields one of the best kinds of charcoal with which to smelt the ore."

Lapham continued, "On almost every quarter section we found small log houses, situated in openings or clearings in the woods. In these clearings, some grain and vegetables had been raised which were mostly in good condition, notwithstanding the rude manner in which they had been planted and cultivated."[47]

However, an important phrase was missing from the corporate charter. In the hand-written draft of these sentences in the Lapham papers at the Wisconsin Historical Society, there is another telling phrase, here foregrounded in italics. It had been deleted from the published corporate charter: "On almost every quarter section we found small log houses, situated in little openings in the woods, or "clearings," *intended to secure the title to the land by a compliance with the requirements of the pre-emption law*. In these clearings some grain and vegetables had been raised, which were mostly in good conditions, notwithstanding the rude manner in which they had been planted and cultivated."[48]

Lapham's endorsement of this undertaking was no small thing. In a 1917 article for the *Wisconsin Magazine of History*, titled "Increase Allen Lapham, First Scholar of Wisconsin," Milo Quaife, predicted that "when the future historian shall come to scan the record of the first half century of Wisconsin's history as a territory and state, he will affirm that no man brought greater honor to her or performed more valuable services in her half than did the modest scholar, Increase Allen Lapham." A. N. Winchell points out that Increase Lapham "was one of the first to use the glowing style which was so frequently repeated in later years, luring speculators to the range."[49] Erika Janik describes Increase Lapham as "Wisconsin's first Renaissance man . . . renown as surveyor, engineer, mapmaker, historian, self-taught botanist, geologist, forester, meteorologist and a prescient conservation voice."[50]

Lapham's prestige was valuable to the company. In the General Remarks of the Charter of the Wisconsin and Lake Superior Mining and Smelting Company, the topic of securing the land patents was revisited: "It is, however, only very recently that the Company's title to the valuable lands described, has been perfected and the patents thereof obtained. *The Company has encountered great difficulties in the location, purchase, and procuring of patents for their lands.* These difficulties had all, at last, been triumphantly overcome, and the Company holds a clear and undisputed title to its lands, by patent from the United States."[51]

Those "great difficulties" are further elaborated in an entry in a nineteenth-century vanity publication titled *History of Milwaukee*, a compendium of (a mere) four thousand personal biographies, which narrates the efforts of the same company. The publication was originally cited in the afore-mentioned and acknowledged blog-posted paper authored by Amorin Mello.[52] I quote at length the *History*, and italicize for emphasis, because the account reveals some details about how the title to the land was gained by the companies, and because the account refers to both Indian and mixed-blood people in the area of the Penokees: A certain Lysander Cutler along with,

> Mr. Palmer, the brothers Hercules and Talbot Dousman, Dr. Greaves and others organized the Penokee Mining Company.[53] *The company had a sort of undefined and undefinable title to some parts of the celebrated iron deposits in the Penokee Range* lying some thirty miles inland from Lake Superior at the extreme northern point where at what is now Bayfield County, juts out into the lake. *The title was held by virtue of some Indian script which had been bought from the Sioux Indians, then inhabiting that region,* and was by no means a perfect one, except the land was surveyed and occupied by the company and direct warrants secured from the Government Land Office.[54]

Notice that the author does not distinguish between Indians and mixed bloods in writing that the "script" "had been bought from Sioux Indians," and that they had been "inhabiting that region." If the scrip was purchased at all—and more likely the scrip was redeemed for patents in consultation with non-Indian businessmen with an interest in mining—it was Sioux or Dakota *mixed bloods* who had the right to land under the amended treaty that the Sioux signed in 1830 discussed in Chapter 3. These people had been "inhabiting that region" insofar as they lived in the vicinity of Prairie du Chien on the Mississippi River, "a French-Indian Community" recently described in detail by Lucy Eldersveld Murphy.[55] So they were not inhabiting the region immediately south of Lake Superior.

More detail about squatting in the Penokees comes from John S. Buck who was part of the group that attempted to set up a mining operation in the Penokees at the time. In one of the articles that appeared in a series in the *Ashland Weekly Press* from November of 1877 to January of 1878, there is incidental mention of several "half-breeds" who worked for the entrepreneurs. Big Joe Houle once carried a 200 lb. barrel of pork many miles from Ironton to their mining site. "Old Bateese," described as "an Indian," covered 42 miles in ten hours, half the time carrying a 125 lb. pack. One Joe Le Roy also carried for the crew, and "Little Alie" was the cook. These were not Sioux "then inhabiting the region," but members of the Lake Superior Chippewa.

Many Chippewa mixed-blood men carried the name Jean Baptiste making it impossible to identify "Old Bateese" with any certainty at all. Three different Houles took payment under the treaty of 1837,[56] and a descendant of one of them, Joseph Houle, received a patent for an eighty-acre parcel in January 1859. Four men with the name "Joseph Roy" applied for scrip under the treaty of 1854,[57] and one took a patent for an eighty-acre parcel in 1858. However, of far more significance for the project, one of the group of principals decided to call it quits at one point, and the author of the newspaper article writes, "He left in the fall after the failure of the Sioux scrip plot."[58] This was either intentionally cryptic or a familiar strategy to his readers, and a dicey one requiring mobilizing a treaty provision and all that entailed.

The *History of Milwaukee* narrative continued to hyperbolically describe the deposit, the organizational and social challenge of the proposed operation, and the competition:

> Most brilliant reports had been made of the extent of the deposits and the purity of the ore. There could be no doubt that the development of these immense mineral resources would bring to the owners untold wealth. Mr. Cutler was appointed the managing agent of this prospective Wisconsin bonanza, at a fair salary, to which was added a liberal amount of the stock of the company. His first task was to perfect the title of the company, and the first step toward it was to take a personal view of the situation and the property. It was a somewhat arduous undertaking, not unfraught with danger. Excepting two or three traders or surveyors, who had stock in the company, *the population, which consisted mostly of Indians and half-breeds, viewed this incursion of wealth-hunters from the lower lakes with suspicion and distrust. To add to the*

> *difficulties of the situation, other parties owning Sioux script were endeavoring to acquire a title to the mineral range . . .*
>
> He had ascertained that the immense value of the claim had not been overestimated, and had made a further discovery, less desirable, that the company had no valid title to it, except that they occupied it as actual settlers. It was *determined to organize a colony sufficiently large to cover every section of the territory desired, and squat it out a sufficient time to entitle them to settlers' warrants.* The colony consisted of picked men, some from the state of Maine who entered the employ of the company and built their cabins as fast as the surveyors' stakes were driven. The main cabin which was a depot of supplies, was of importance as it was the center of the town, and as it complied with all the requirements of the law, being organized as a store and a school, it gave the company a claim to a "town plat" of a square mile. . . . *All supplies were packed in on the backs of the squatters of half-breed packers* who sometimes in a surly mood would lay down their burdens and return to the settlement . . . Once during each winter, he [Cutler] made the trip on snow shoes to St. Paul, a distance of over two hundred miles. The claim was at last secured, and a valid title to the land vested in the company.[59]

John S. Buck in his *Ashland Press* series elaborated the strategy:

> Meanwhile, our enemies who had begun to show themselves occasionally—not idle, and from fear of yet losing a part of our land on account of not being able to hold all by pre-emption, we decided to adopt at that point what was known at that time as 'the town site plan' in part. This townsite fever was in full blast from Maine to California, in fact. The whole lakeshore was dotted with them from the Sault to Superior City. Every man had one and as they were supposed to be "sure fire'" they were of course just what we wanted.
>
> Three were accordingly plotted—one at Penoka, one at Lockwood's, and one at the Gorge.[60]

The company would build warehouses and docks at what was then known as Ironton, now Saxon Harbor.

In the final installment, the author reports that they abandoned the range about July 1, 1858, as "The fruits of labors are now enjoyed by others. . . . [that] . . . this whole thing . . . pass[ed] into the hands of those who had not labored for it." Those "who had not labored for it," who succeeded in using

Sioux scrip would incorporate themselves as the Wisconsin and Lake Superior Iron and Smelting Company.

Bruce K. Cox has recently compiled a great deal of the corporate history of 410 mining companies that either mined or explored in the "Pewabic Country of Michigan and Wisconsin," as he refers to it. He used secondary sources as well as county deed books and mortgage books, technical reports, trade publications, and newspapers in an admirable effort. The Wisconsin and Lake Superior Mining and Smelting Company was organized in June of 1857 but began exploring for iron ore two years earlier. Its explorers are the aforementioned "enemies who had begun to show themselves occasionally." Twenty "pre-emption cabins" were built at various locations. The preemptors were to secure possession then transfer title to the company. Quoting from the *Bayfield Press* 8 July 1971: "A few hundred pounds of the Penoka ore was converted into wrought bars, at the works of Messrs. Corning, Winslow and Co at Crown Point in 1858 . . . A parcel of 276 pounds was made into cast steel . . . a piece was used at the Bad River Mission by Mr. Vantassel, the government blacksmith for the Chippeways of Bad River.
The company was dissolved in 1907 with most of the lands eventually conveyed to U.S. Steel Corporation."[61]

John Buck doesn't mention the antagonistic relations between the recently proletarianized mixed bloods and the pre-empting speculators. These "half-breeds" constituted a flexible labor pool now available to speculators mobilizing the pre-emption law of 1841 that required physical presence on the land as well as improvements to qualify for a claim of ownership. Other mixed bloods, especially Vincent Roy, noted earlier, had also caught "townsite fever" pointing to the class differences within the mixed-blood segment of the indigenous population. In both cases, the seventh paragraph of the second article of the treaty of 1854 would provide a more powerful tool to get access to land insofar as the Constitution of the United States holds that "all treaties made . . . shall be the supreme law of the land"[62] and therefore more compelling than the 1841 pre-emption law. Recall Agent Gilbert's Public Notice indicating that mixed-blood claims to particular locations would be protected.

Who exactly would benefit from this legal superiority, however, is a more complicated tale.

Private Interests and the Locating of Mixed-Blood Lands in the Penokees

In his annual report of 1856 to the commissioner of Indian affairs, Agent Henry Gilbert assured the commissioner that scrip certificates had been issued to the mixed bloods belonging to the Chippewas of Lake Superior. Furthermore, that "if the necessary instructions to the several land offices are issued relative to the location of lands selected under those certificates, no further action of this department will be required." He was thus ending the supervision of these people "belonging to the Chippewas of Lake Superior."[63] By mid-December the list of eligible mixed bloods had been sent to the Government Land Office, but no certificates would be redeemed for patents for more than a year, despite apparent mixed-blood interest in receiving them as evidenced in letters continuing to complain about conflicts between mixed bloods and white settlers displacing them.

Almost a year later, in September of 1857, GLO surveyor A. C. Stuntz wrote of Township 44 North Range 2 West in his field notes a general description. "This Township is well Timbered and well watered and is well adapted to Farming and grazing as any Township in the North of Wisconsin. *The Iron Range runs across this Township from Section 1 to Section 18 and is nearly all claimed by Preemption*. Under the South Side of the Iron Range is [sic] a number of lakes well supplied with Fish and Beavers. The SE Corner is well timbered with White Pine. Timber Suitable for Lumber and other purposes."[64]

It is at this moment that private businessman, Julius Austrian, takes decisive and rather consequential action. Born in Bavaria, he had been living in the area since the early 1840s making his living as a trader. As indicated above, he had been a witness at the 1847 treaty and was apparently well-acquainted with many of the indigenous people in the region as he employed Vincent Roy, the well-connected and entrepreneurial mixed blood. Austrian was also, no doubt, well aware of Mr. Stuntz observation that the iron range was full of pre-emptors.[65]

In January 1858, Austrian began to accumulate power-of-attorney documents over mixed bloods who were entitled to eighty-acre parcels of land under the 1854 treaty. In his 1906 MA thesis Gustav Brohough identifies this as the mechanism by which the non-transferability provision in the scrip was evaded and the mixed-blood people dispossessed. The first power of attorney authorized the attorney to enter or locate the lands on behalf of the mixed blood and a second authorized conveyance upon patenting.[66] Historian William Folwell, in his appendix discussing the details of the Sioux scrip, and attentive to the issue of how such a carefully-written certificate restricting transfer of any kind could be subverted, noted that thirty years later President Cleveland's secretary of the interior found that the two powers of attorney could *not* convey title, much to the dismay and surprise of locals who had been receiving favorable rulings in this matter.[67]

Volume II of the Warranty Deeds in Iron County, Wisconsin reveals that Julius Austrian began this undertaking on January 11, 1858 procuring power of attorney over two eighty-acre parcels. First, John Baptiste Roy, originally from Sandy Lake and the son of a long-time fur company employee,[68] and his wife Catherine, identified an eighty-acre parcel on the eastern end of the Penokee Range.[69] Next, Austrian procured the eighty-acre parcel of Joseph Dejadon.[70] A week later he would receive power of attorney over Louis and Charlotte Nah-waw-goo (today, Newago) for, "a certain tract of land which our said attorney now holds the power of attorney to locate for us and in our name, eighty acres of land to which I am entitled according to the treaty of the United States, and with the Chippewa Indians of Lake Superior, September 30, 1854 (Article 2nd Clause 7th) and for which said attorney will receive the patent."

However, the land was not in the township Stuntz had commented upon in his general description. In fact, it was in the adjacent township but it *was* in the newly discovered Iron Range. Julius Austrian would locate the North ½ of the Southwest quarter of Section 24 Township 45 North Range 1 West, the eighty-acre parcel that contains the very middle of the "Top of Iron Range" that the surveyor had identified on his map of the section a decade before.[71]

Ojibwe mixed bloods Michael Bazinet, August Bazinet, Frances Belanger, Joseph Vasseur and Stephen Butterfield would grant powers of attorney to Austrian shortly thereafter.[72] The parcels were obviously located for their value *to mining interests* rather than agricultural value to the mixed bloods. Some of these lands were in the township and sections described by Stuntz above as "nearly all claimed by Preemption," thus indicating Austrian's gamble that mobilizing the mixed-blood provision of the treaty would be a more efficient means to acquire iron-rich land than use of the preemption law.

We might stop the narrative right here and question the legality of a private non-Indian gaining power of attorney and yet acting on behalf of an individual mixed-blood Indian person. These mixed bloods' entitlements are the subjects of treaties, part of the corpus that makes up "the supreme law of the land" according to Article VI of the Constitution. Mixed bloods are explicitly included as members of the Native polity in those treaties. The Attorney General of the United States officially opined that absent a new treaty or act of Congress, these mixed-blood subjects were Indians by virtue of exercising this provision of the treaty.

Laws regarding powers of attorney are state laws, subordinate to federal law. The issue had been explicitly addressed less than twenty years earlier in 1838 and with regard to the neighboring Winnebago. Paul Spruhan quotes from Major E. A. Hitchcock, the military disbursing agent at St. Louis:

> Half-breeds are neither white men nor Indians, as expressed in their name; and the proper treatment of them is neither defined in

> the regulations, nor, perhaps, established by usage. If it is said that they are not Indians, and must therefore be treated as white men, it may more plausibly be said that they are not white men, and ought to be treated as Indians, as they unquestionably have been in almost all treaties containing stipulations in their favor . . . *It is against all knowledge (although there may be exceptions) to suppose the half-breeds are acquainted with the power of attorney* or bills of exchange; and to discuss a question concerning them, upon a presumption of their moral responsibility to our laws and usages, is to my mind, an absurdity.[73]

Orchestrating that "absurdity," again in 1846, the Secretary of War opined that

> paying moneys due Indians on powers of attorney given by them, is wholly inconsistent with the duty of Government to pay over to them, promptly and without abatement, whatever may be due them under any treaty or law, or for any claim whatever to which they may be justly entitled. Agents are appointed and paid by the Government to attend to their business for them, and they should be the medium of all communications with the Government, whether in relation to any claims they may have, or to their wants or wishes upon any other subject . . . The practice therefore should be discountenanced . . .[74]

Despite this opinion in 1838 that it was "against all knowledge to suppose the half-breeds are acquainted with the power of attorney," and despite the efforts made to protect mixed-blood interests, we find evidence that they did sign—or rather made their X's on—power-of-attorney documents. And of all the lands that might be selected, the documents were used to locate land in the iron-rich Penokee hills south of the Bad River Reservation.

Recall that it was George Manypenny, commissioner of Indian affairs at the time, who implemented these treaty provisions for individuals to hold land in severalty, thus effectively enabling the movement of land out of Indian hands. He, too, had an opinion about the use of power of attorney by "combinations," as corporations were referred to at the time, and included his position on the issue in his annual report to the secretary of the interior in 1855. And although the immediate peoples he had in mind were the Potawatomi and the Menominee, everything he wrote applied to the neighboring Ojibwe:

> Combinations of men, too, as powerful as they are unscrupulous, keep constantly on foot systematic and organized plans to deceive

> and corrupt the chiefs and principal men, and thus they often obtain the signatures of these ignorant, deluded, and corrupted people to powers of attorney and other instruments, appropriating and assigning to them and their confederates in such nefarious practices large amounts of the funds of the Indians without any valid consideration therefore. These last named parties have frequently been enabled, with instruments and powers of attorney, obtained by means as degrading to them as injurious, demoralizing, and corrupting to the Indians, to obtain the sanction and approval of Congress and the executive departments, and thus the government, instead of protecting, has, in some instances, been the oppressor of its wards."[75]

In other words, Manypenny identified the means by which Indian people were swindled. The issue of power of attorney was also addressed in the Congressional investigation into the proliferation of fraudulent Lake Superior Half-Breed scrip that took place in the mid-1860s. In 1871, the special commissioners wrote: "We are well satisfied that the mixed-bloods signing said powers of attorney, which was generally done by touching the pen once, even if there were a dozen papers to sign, as a general thing *never had the slightest conception of the nature of and consequences of the act*; and that no explanation was made to them which for a moment would lead them to suppose that they were doing anything that would prevent them from obtaining the possession of their scrip."[76]

It had been both Congress's and Commissioner Manypenny's intention that reserving eighty-acre parcels of land for the mixed bloods would facilitate their settling in a single location to cultivate the soil much as their Indian relatives would soon do *within* the borders of the newly created, collectively held reservations. He reported the following in his 1856 report to secretary of the interior: "Certificates have been issued to all the half-breeds who, by the provisions of the recent treaty, are entitled to land, which, if respected at the land offices, will serve to secure to each of them the quantity to which they are entitled, and which they may designate from any of the public domain otherwise not appropriated."[77]

Manypenny was also quite sure that federal protection must be extended to these mixed-blood Indians. Reporting on developments among the Lake Pepin Sioux and also Kansas half-breed tracts, he wrote: "The larger portion of the half-breed (Kansas) tract is now in the possession of trespassers, who have actually driven from their homes some of the half-breed Indian owners. Such lawless conduct is very disreputable, and can result in no permanent advantage to those engaged in it, as the government must protect the half-breed Kansas Indians in their rights."[78]

The American land policy historian, Paul Wallace Gates, appraised George Manypenny's integrity: "He stands out as one of the few commissioners who truly sought to protect and improve Indian welfare, no matter what the consequences. He held no brief for the usual methods of securing Indian treaties and cessions of land by the tricks of working through the minority chiefs and half-breeds, who would be given special annuities or allotments of land, or through traders who would favor cessions provided their vastly inflated claims were taken care of, or through the use of liquor to soften up intransient leaders."[79]

Two months after the Nah-wah-goos transferred power of attorney to Julius Austrian, on Monday, March 1, 1858, sixty-one mixed-blood people had their eighty-acre parcels entered into the Government Land Office Tract books in Superior, Wisconsin.[80] Although we don't know how many of these land entries were made with power of attorney, we do know that Austrian filed an affidavit against the Eliab Dean, the Receiver at the Land Office, in Superior. Austrian swore that "on the first day of March A.D. 1858, this affiant [Austrian] applied at said Land Office to locate certain Chippewa Half Breed scrip under power of attorney to this affiant from the Half Breeds to whom this scrip was issued,"[81] and that Austrian could only get the land entered if he paid Dean a bribe of $500. How many power-of-attorney documents would Austrian have to have in his possession that a $500 bribe would be credible in that he was paying each mixed-blood scrip holder $100—its minimum value—for their eighty-acre parcel? Quite a few, I would suggest. Maybe even sixty-one.

In a letter written by Joel Allen Barber, surveyor, to his parents, he commented on the recent coup that Austrian and his brother-in-law had accomplished: "Their land grab has proved perfectly successful through out and these Jews own more iron land that all other persons or companies—more than 6000 acres. I want to commence Surveying again soon."[82]

All of the land was in the Penokee Hills and all but 240 acres—three parcels patented to Dakota mixed-blood Emily J. Barrett—were procured using scrip certificates issued to Lake Superior Chippewa mixed bloods. This land entry appears to be an attempt to displace the squatters, who were already being paid to settle in the Penokees by competing aspiring mining entrepreneurs. Indeed, the affidavit was one of several that formed the basis of an investigation into the machinations of Eliab Dean, who also proposed that he and a certain John Howard enter into "a combination." Dean wanted Howard to invest $1,500 for purposes of purchasing half breed scrip, wherein,

"The Half Breed Scrip was to be laid by affiant under power of attorney from Half Breeds on lands in the Superior Land District known as the 'Iron Range' near Ashland, which lands had been filed upon by settlers under a pre-emption law of the United States, that said Dean showed this affiant a list of the persons claiming the said lands by pre-emption, which list was contained in the Register's abstracts of Declaratory statements and told the affiant that these were the lands he proposed to enter with the said scrip."[83]

It appears that Julius Austrian and others used the provision of the treaty as a means for displacing their competitors who were using the 1841 pre-emption law to gain access to the mineral lands. One can only wonder if Austrian played a role in initiating or specifying the language in this treaty provision in the first place, inasmuch as there certainly was some interest within the La Pointe Indian community for eighty-acre individual reserves held in fee. Not only is privately held real property a sign of status and whiteness, there is precedent for mixed-blood tribal members among the Miamis, Delawares, Potawatomis and Weas attempting to secure resource sites for the benefit of the entire tribal community using land patents in fee held by individuals.[84]

But more significantly, laying "the Half Breed Scrip . . . under power of attorney" in the "Iron Range near Ashland" was arguably a violation of the treaty as the relevant provision of the treaty required that the lands be "*selected by them under the direction of the President*." There was no apparent "direction" being exercised by a federal fiduciary. Furthermore, the practice points to the legal plurality of this emerging landscape with the overlap of state and federal law. This condition made the mixed bloods citizens for some purposes, such as granting powers of attorney, and yet, at the same time, dependent wards for other purposes, such as denying them the right to pre-empt land or vote.[85]

Patenting the Mixed Bloods

Having entered the names of sixty-one mixed-blood people and located their eighty-acre parcels in the "Iron Range near Ashland," the next step for the federal government would be to actually issue the patents. As detailed in chapter 3, Congress and the Indian Office had a long history of concern about the mixed bloods losing their lands to unscrupulous non-Indians and so addressed themselves quite directly to the issue of alienability in the treaties by restricting the patents they issued. The problem was also explicitly addressed in administering the mixed-blood provision of the 1854 treaty.

On May 4, 1858, two months after those sixty-one eighty-acre parcels had been located in the Penokees, Thomas Hendricks, Commissioner of the

Government Land Office wrote the commissioner of Indian affairs to ask him about the nature of the restrictions *on the patents* that would be issued pursuant to the seventh clause of this treaty. Hendricks called attention to alienability and quoted from the scrip certificates that had been issued and were now about to be redeemed for patents: "The scrip certificate "expressly declared that any sale, transfer, mortgage, assignment or pledge of this certificate, or of any right accruing under it will not be recognized as valid by the United States *and that the patent for lands located by virtue thereof shall be issued directly to the above named reservee or his heirs, and shall in no wise enure to the benefit of any other person, or persons.*"[86]

This last phrase is an explicit recognition of the need for placing a restriction on the yet-to-be-issued patents. Nonetheless, Commissioner Hendricks' office was ready to issue the actual patents. He asked the commissioner of Indian affairs explicitly, should the patent *itself* be restricted such that it was not transferable? Hendricks insisted that the Indian Office restrict the patents: "At this stage of the proceedings, however, it becomes necessary for this office to be advised as to whether it is the judgment and purpose of the office of Indian affairs that there should be *express clause of interdict inserted in the Patent against transfer* either absolute or with the sanction of the President, and if so, whether the terms of interdict herein before quoted from the aforesaid certificate will be used, or other words expressing a conditional interdict of assignment, and if so, this office desires to be advised thereof.[87]

I have not been able to locate correspondence between the local land office in Superior, Wisconsin, and Washington DC. Nonetheless, the federal agent in Superior had recently entered nearly 5,000 acres of claims in the Penokees—and he knew them to be mixed bloods, and he knew the nature of the private interests that were motivating the locations as he was attempting to profit from the transaction. As a result, it came to the attention of the Commissioner of the General Land Office, who presumably saw fit to exonerate his own office from accusations of failure to exercise the trust responsibility toward Indian people by reminding the commissioner of Indian affairs of his responsibilities. Hendrick's letter concluded: "We take this course in the issuing of the Patent because *the Indian office has the immediate guardianship under the Secretary and the President* of the Indians, and hence necessarily must exercise control over the management of their property."[88]

Recall that less than two years earlier, the attorney General of the United States opined that ". . . a person of mixed-blood, retaining tribal relations, cannot also enjoy at the same time the rights of a citizen of the United States," that they are "not citizens . . . but domestic subjects."[89] Notwithstanding that opinion, the commissioner of Indian affairs responded to his colleague in the GLO on the following day, since the offices were in the same building in

Washington. The commissioner of Indian affairs told Hendricks that he took the issue to their boss, the secretary of the interior and the secretary saw no reason to restrict the patent.

> Sir,
>
> I have to acknowledge receipt of your letter of this date, enclosing the form of a certificate issued to a Chippewa Indian under the 7th clause of the 2nd Article of the treaty of September 30, 1854 which contains an interdict or restriction respecting the issuing of the patent; and in reply to your inquiry as to whether any interdict on the power of alienation should be incorporated into the patent. I would remark that a form of the certificate was approved by the former Secretary of the Interior. I deemed it proper to submit the question to Secretary Thompson, and he is of the opinion that the patent should issue in conformity with the language of the treaty, "in the usual form," *without any restriction or interdict.*
>
> I herewith return the papers which accompanied your letter.[90]

This ended any protection for the mixed bloods. There would be no explicit restriction placed on alienation of the patents. Consequently, this decision made it possible for non-Indians to purchase the land by gaining power of attorney over mixed bloods entitled to eighty-acre parcels. In the congressional investigation that was undertaken in the 1870s into the hundreds of fraudulent scrip certificates that were produced under this treaty after 1864, the commissioners discovered and revealed the scam. It hinged on this disparity between an explicitly restricted scrip certificate and an unrestricted fee patent. A single exchange in that hearing between the investigating commissioner and a purchaser of fraudulent Chippewa half-breed scrip reveals the vested interests, the motives of the different actors, and the contours of the plausible deniability afforded to all of the players:

> Commissioner: "Have you, then, any doubt but that the object of the Department in putting this restriction upon the right to alienate, was to save the half-breed from the loss that would be sustained by making a sale previous to the location and patent?
>
> Answer: I have doubts, because I believe it was well known to the Department [Interior] at the time the certificates were issued that they were bought and sold in the market, and intended so to be bought and sold by the parties who received them, meaning the half-breeds and their agents.[91]

Plausible Deniability and the Dangers of Liminal Legal Status

Of the 371 treaties ratified by Congress in the century-long period that treaties were made with Indian people, the phrase "patent in the usual form" appears in exactly one treaty: the Treaty of 1854, signed at La Pointe with the Lake Superior Chippewa, although similarly unrestricted patents would be issued to Winnebago and Minnesota Chippewa mixed bloods under the authority of treaties signed the following year.[92] The 1854 treaty, then, set a rather short-lived precedent. With the elimination of any restriction on alienability in the patent itself, a mixed blood regarded as a "Chippewa Indian," that is, "a subject," and not a citizen, according to the attorney general of the United States at the time, exchanges a highly restricted certificate for an entirely unrestricted patent and does so, *not* "under the direction of the President." Instead of the president directing this exchange, according to the requirement of the treaty, "in the usual form" results in a private individual directing the exchange with rather explicit and independent interests of his own.

This is the site of the breach of the trust responsibility. As result, most mixed bloods, now dispossessed, would strengthen their ties with their so-called "full-blood" Indian relatives and become tribal members over time. It was also the means by which the ceded lands, which retained their status as federal lands for the time the patents were in the possession of those mixed bloods, were transferred into private corporate hands subject to the newly formed state of Wisconsin's jurisdiction.

The plausible deniability for failure to protect these mixed bloods, belonging to the Lake Superior Chippewa Indians, was afforded to federal officials by the apparent fact that some part of the leadership of this heterogeneous[93] mixed-blood class sought or acquiesced in receiving unrestricted patents. Perhaps they better understood the fungibility of such patents, or perhaps they sought unrestricted ownership as the badge of whiteness that would guarantee their citizenship in the emerging political community of state and nation. Or perhaps, like the Miami, they saw this mechanism as a means of protecting tribal resources and accruing prestige for their generosity to their community. The effect for most of that community, however, was dispossession, and it happened rather quickly.

On June 10, 1858, a month after the secretary had concluded that the patents should be issued "without any restriction or interdict," thirty-one fee-simple patents were issued. They stretched across the eastern part of the Penokees in Townships 45 North Range 1 West and 44 North Range 2 West. Every single one of those patents was issued to individuals who had appeared earlier on Lucius Lyon's 1839 roll of mixed bloods eligible for payment under the 1837 treaty. Within a fortnight, on the June 23, Francis Belanger and his wife, Lizette, sold their patent to L. F. Leopold, the brother-in-law of Julius Austrian, for $100, that is, $1.25 per acre, the going rate, and $3,100 in 2020 dollars. In the days following, Joseph Vasseur and John Guignon did the same. Then John Baptiste Roy, Joseph Dejadon, and Charlotte Dupony sold their parcels to Leopold in July.[94]

Eighteen more patents were issued on August 18, and Louis "Newagou," a.k.a. "Nah-waw-goo." sold his eighty-acre for $100 to L. F. Leopold. Every one of those newly issued patents were in the western part of the range and all of them in Township 44 North Range 3 West, which was thought to be the heart of the iron range.

On August 13, in Washington DC, the commissioner of the GLO asked the commissioner of Indian affairs "whether the location of the scrip issued to the mixed bloods were made *under the direction of the President* and if not, whether they should not be submitted through the Indian office for his approval before issuing patents thereon."[95]

Commissioner Mix responded to Commissioner Hendricks and again, after consulting with the secretary of the interior: since "the certificates, or scrip, were issued with the approbation of the Department, he regards this as the act of the executive, and therefore it is not deemed necessary to approve the locations prior to the issuance of patents provided that there are no controversies in the premises."[96] This action ratified the movement of patents issued in fee into the marketplace and they were consolidated in short order.

The La Pointe Iron Company was incorporated into Wisconsin law as chapter 67 on March 5, 1859, less than a year after these patents were purchased. The five directors were Senator Henry B. Payne, Louis F. Leopold, Henry Goodman, Robert F. Paine, and the ubiquitous entrepreneurial business man, Julius Austrian. Julius Austrian was living in La Pointe at this time and appears on the enumeration sheet in the 1860 federal census. He is identified as a farmer with real estate valued at $10,000 and personal estate valued at $10,000 as well,[97] a total of $627,000 in 2020 dollars.

The company now had "full power and authority to open and work any mines of iron or any other ores and minerals that may exist on any lands which the said company may acquire within the state of Wisconsin."[98] I annotated the list of corporate properties[99] in figure 5.1 to reveal that the company's entire holdings had been patented to mixed bloods shortly before incorporation.

Less than a month later, on April 1, 1859, another mining company, the Wisconsin and Lake Superior Mining and Smelting Company, was incorporated under Wisconsin law.[100] Of the 1,960 acres, 960 were listed as "The List of Lands Belonging to the Company" in their papers of incorporation

LA POINTE IRON COMPANY,

OF ASHLAND COUNTY, LAKE SUPERIOR, WISCONSIN.

The following are the Lands of the Lapointe Iron Company.

TOWNSHIP No. 45, NORTH OF RANGE No. 1, WEST.

	Section	Town	Range	Acres	Patent holder
The South half of the N. E. quarter	25	45	1	80	John Guignon
" South " " N. W. "	25	45	1	80	John Baptiste Roy
" North " " S. E. "	25	45	1	80	Benjamin Morin
" North " " S. W. "	25	45	1	80	Louis Nah-waw-goo
" North " " S. E. "	26	45	1	80	Michael Duperez
" South " " S. E. "	26	45	1	80	Francis Belanger
" South " " S. W. "	26	45	1	80	Joseph Deiedord
" North " " N. W. "	35	45	1	80	Joseph Yapeur
" South " " S. E. "	27	45	1	80	Joseph Deiedon
" North " " N. E. "	34	45	1	80	Joseph Bazinet
" North " " N. W. "	34	45	1	80	Angeline Guadine
" North " " N. E. "	33	45	1	80	Angeline Brebau

TOWNSHIP No. 44, NORTH OF RANGE No. 2, WEST.

	Section	Town	Range	Acres	Patent holder
The South half of the N. W. quarter	1	44	2	80	Louis Defoe
" North " " S. W. "	1	44	2	80	Francis Cadotte
" South " " S. E. "	1	44	2	80	Michael Bazinet
" South " " S. W. "	1	44	2	80	Alexis Carpenter
" North " " N. E. "	12	44	2	80	Charlotte Godfroy
" East " " S. W. "	2	44	2	80	Joseph Roy
" South " " N. E. "	11	44	2	80	Stephen Butterfield
" North " " S. W. "	11	44	2	80	Antoine Roy
" South " " S. W. "	11	44	2	80	Joseph Dennis
" North " " N. E. "	10	44	2	80	Michael Balanger
" North " " N. W. "	10	44	2	80	John Morrison
" South " " N. E. "	10	44	2	80	John Baptiste Gaudin
" East " " S. E. "	10	44	2	80	
Lots No 1 and 2	15	44	2	88..90	Mary Soliere
The East half of the N. E. quarter	9	44	2	80	Antoine Gaudin
" N. W quarter of the N. E. quarter and the N. E. quarter of the N. W. quarter	9	44	2	80	George LeGros
The N. W. quarter of the S. E. quarter and the S. W. quarter of the N. E. quarter	9	44	2	80	John Baptiste Balanger
The South half of the N. W. quarter	9	44	2	80	Joseph Couture
" East half of the N. E. quarter	17	44	2	80	John Baptiste Huihle
" S. W. quarter of the N. E. quarter and the S. E. quarter of the N. W. quarter	17	44	2	80	Joseph Gaudin
The South half of the S. W. quarter	7	44	2	80	
" North half of the S. E. quarter	18	44	2	80	Paul Soliere
" North half of the S. W. quarter	18	44	2	77..70	Francis Huehle
					Thomas Conner
					John Baptiste Huehle

TOWNSHIP No. 44, OF RANGE No. 3, WEST.

	Section	Town	Range	Acres	Patent holder
The North half of the S. E. quarter	13	44	3	80	Charles Chaloux
" North " " S. W. "	13	44	3	80	Ambrose Deragean
" South " " N. W. "	13	44	3	80	Francis Decoteau
" North " " N. W. "	13	44	3	80	Michael Basquet
" East " " S. E. "	14	44	3	80	Alexie Bazinet
" East " " N. E. "	14	44	3	80	Joseph Heuhle
" whole of	15	44	3	640	
" South half of the S. W. quarter	10	44	3	80	J. Baptist Cadotte
" South " " S. E. "	9	44	3	80	Antoine Lamaroux
" South " " S. W. "	9	44	3	80	Augustus Bazinet
" North " " N. E. "	17	44	3	80	J. Baptist Defoe
" South " " N. E. "	17	44	3	80	Michael Bosquit
" South " " N. W. "	17	44	3	80	Antoine Cadotte
" North " " S. W. "	17	44	3	80	Joseph Defoe
" South " " S. E. "	18	44	3	80	Joseph Lemaroux
" North " " N. E. "	19	44	3	80	J. Baptist Bazinet
" North " " N. W. "	19	44	3	80	Andrew Moran [i]

Being together 4726.60 acres.

[i] The whole of Section 15 includes the eighty-acre parcels patented to Dennis Benjamin (N1/2 of NE quarter), Catherine Decoleau (S ½ of NE quarter), Charles Corbin (N1/2 of SE quarter) and John Baptist Gauthier (S1/2 of SE quarter)

Figure 5.1. Annotated list of LaPointe Iron Company's corporate land holdings with the names of the Lake Superior mixed-bloods to whom the parcels of land were originally patented in the column to the right.

that had been patented to two Dakota mixed bloods, Hercules La Chapelle and David Goutier[101] in March and April of 1859. Those patents were similarly unrestricted. As indicated earlier, a treaty with the Dakota in 1830 had established a mixed-blood reservation that would be held collectively "in the same manner that Indian titles are held."[102] However, Congress modified the treaty in July of 1854.[103] The Dakota mixed bloods' right to a 640-acre parcel *within* the reservation designated in that treaty was now converted to scrip certificates for the same amount of land elsewhere.[104]

This was the origin of nearly half of this company's land. Apparently, agents acting on behalf of the soon-to-be created corporation had made their way to Prairie du Chien for purposes of purchasing the right to these allotments from Dakota mixed bloods, who also, no doubt, affixed their "X" to legal documents transferring their interests.

This process reveals the ways in which the phrase "patent in the usual form" was improvisationally implemented in such a way as to plausibly deny responsibility for the outcome of dispossession. Highly restricted scrip was redeemed for entirely unrestricted patents. Because of the liminal, or threshold, quality of the mixed-blood category, designated by the attorney general of the United States as "not citizens, but subjects . . . yet still Indians," there was both a certain power as well as a certain danger in that liminal status. As a "different kind of Indian," to quote from later testimony from the White Earth Reservation, they were eligible for different kind of land. However, they were also not eligible by virtue of their difference for the same kind of protection that the government afforded the rest of the tribal population. Unlike their relatives, these "subjects" had the power to grant power of attorney over their property to whomever they wished for whatever reason.

The distinction of "mixed blood" and "full-blood" was by this time also an indigenous category by virtue of the force of law and interest that stood behind it. Although now in possession of some cash, yet still brown-skinned, most mixed bloods would become tribal members over the course of the rest of the nineteenth and into the early twentieth centuries. The distinction between themselves and their Indian relatives would grow more important when the allotment policy was implemented on the collectively held reservations as the difference came to index an entire cultural orientation.[105] But over time, largely due to the strength of settler society's racialized conception of belonging and difference, mixed bloods would be fully assimilated into the reservations societies.

At the same time, mining industries were capitalized by this dispossession. Railroad corporations—"the spinal cord of colonialism"—[106] developed lines connecting the source of the ore with Lakes Michigan and Superior, the

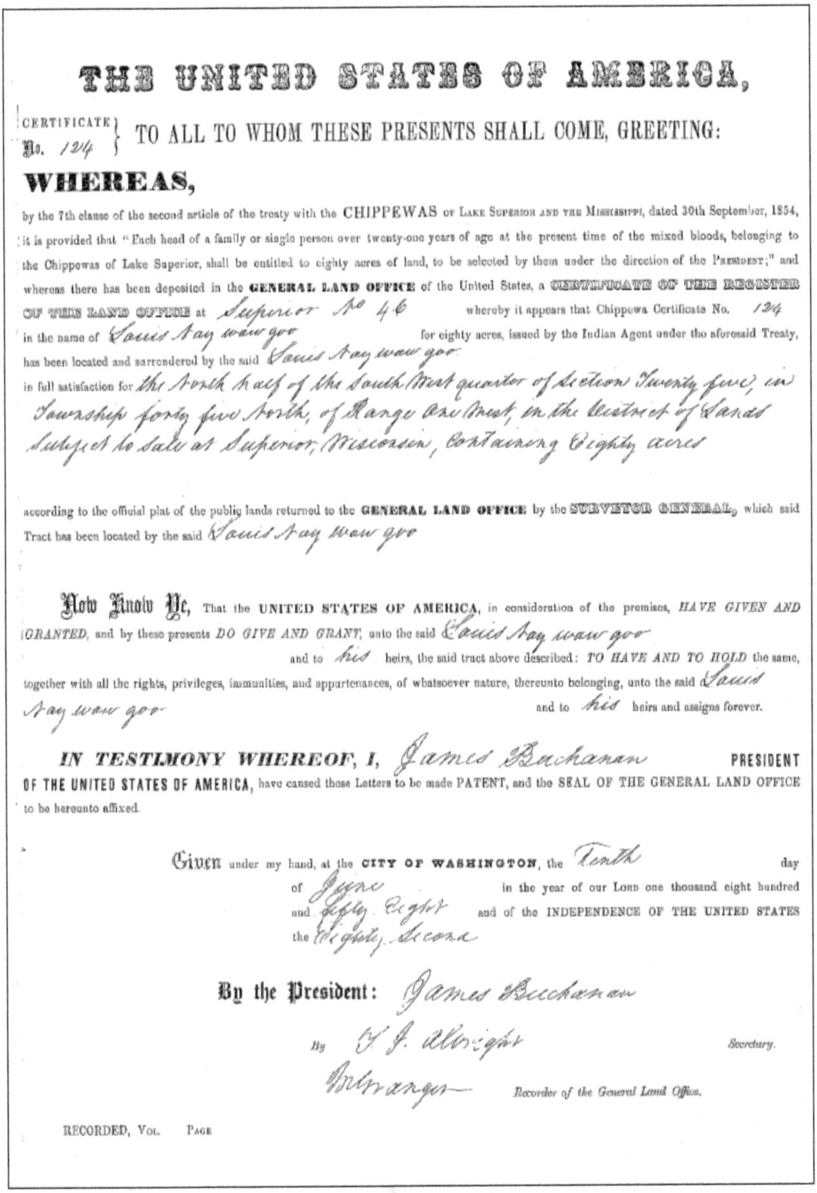

THE UNITED STATES OF AMERICA,

CERTIFICATE No. 124 } TO ALL TO WHOM THESE PRESENTS SHALL COME, GREETING:

WHEREAS,

by the 7th clause of the second article of the treaty with the CHIPPEWAS OF LAKE SUPERIOR AND THE MISSISSIPPI, dated 30th September, 1854, it is provided that "Each head of a family or single person over twenty-one years of age at the present time of the mixed bloods, belonging to the Chippewas of Lake Superior, shall be entitled to eighty acres of land, to be selected by them under the direction of the PRESIDENT;" and whereas there has been deposited in the **GENERAL LAND OFFICE** of the United States, a CERTIFICATE OF THE REGISTER OF THE LAND OFFICE at Superior No 46 whereby it appears that Chippewa Certificate No. 124 in the name of Louis Nay waw goo for eighty acres, issued by the Indian Agent under the aforesaid Treaty, has been located and surrendered by the said Louis Nay waw goo in full satisfaction for the North half of the South West quarter of Section Twenty five, in Township forty five North, of Range One West, in the District of Lands Subject to sale at Superior, Wisconsin, Containing Eighty acres

according to the official plat of the public lands returned to the **GENERAL LAND OFFICE** by the SURVEYOR GENERAL, which said Tract has been located by the said Louis Nay waw goo

Now Know Ye, That the UNITED STATES OF AMERICA, in consideration of the premises, *HAVE GIVEN AND GRANTED*, and by these presents *DO GIVE AND GRANT*, unto the said Louis Nay waw goo and to his heirs, the said tract above described: *TO HAVE AND TO HOLD* the same, together with all the rights, privileges, immunities, and appurtenances, of whatsoever nature, thereunto belonging, unto the said Louis Nay waw goo and to his heirs and assigns forever.

IN TESTIMONY WHEREOF, I, James Buchanan PRESIDENT OF THE UNITED STATES OF AMERICA, have caused these Letters to be made PATENT, and the SEAL OF THE GENERAL LAND OFFICE to be hereunto affixed.

Given under my hand, at the **CITY OF WASHINGTON**, the Tenth day of June in the year of our LORD one thousand eight hundred and fifty Eight and of the INDEPENDENCE OF THE UNITED STATES the Eighty Second

By the President: James Buchanan

By J. J. Albright *Secretary.*

Granger *Recorder of the General Land Office.*

RECORDED, VOL. PAGE

Figure 5.2. Image of the patent issued to mixed-blood Louis Nay waw goo under the authority of the seventh clause of the second article of the treaty made with the Chippewa in September 1854.

American towns of Ashland and Bayfield emerged, and tribal populations were concentrated at Red Cliff and Bad River, Lac Courte Oreilles and Lac du Flambeau in Wisconsin. This moment in the lives of the "mixed bloods, belonging to the Chippewa of Lake Superior" shaped the entire landscape of the Lake Superior basin. We turn now to an exploration of that postdispossession landscape.

6

Constituting Reservation Society on the Emerging Postdispossession Landscape

They were Indians but they were different . . . a different class of people.[1]

The consolidation and stabilization of the reservation communities took place in the context of mining and lumbering that transformed the ceded territories and circumscribed opportunities and possibilities for indigenous people. These modes of extraction not only changed the landscape, but they also produced great disparities between owners and workers, Indian and non-Indian alike. In this chapter, I first address the status of mixed bloods in the first decade after the 1854 treaty was signed and during the time they were dispossessed of their special property. I then sketch the particular history of the lands consolidated by the La Pointe and Lake Superior mining companies and then describe the impact of lumbering—the successor extractive industry—on the land and on the process of constituting the tribal populations on the reservations themselves. This was in the era of land allotment. I will give special attention to the integration of indigenous people designated as "mixed bloods, belonging to the Lake Superior Chippewa" and their descendants into the reservation communities. Finally, as exemplars, I examine the lives of Vincent Roy, Eliza Morrison, and John Morrison, all mixed-blood Ojibwes, to show how the larger economic and political forces were working to simplify the social and ethnic constitution of the landscape.

Several years before Julius Austrian, his fellow businessmen and competitors had begun to gather up powers of attorney over mixed bloods, locate lands in the iron-bearing Penokees ostensibly on behalf of those mixed bloods, and then purchase the patents and incorporate themselves as mining companies, the *Superior Chronicle* on October 9, 1855, published the reflections of a Toledo, Ohio, newspaper editor in a front-page description of the annuity payment under the treaty that made the land transfers possible. The author was pleased that the Indians were now being paid in goods rather than specie, which had all too quickly found its way into the coffers of the whiskey sellers so much to the detriment of "the former lords of these fairy isles scattered about us." After describing some spontaneous dancing and the face of the oldest woman he had ever seen, he made the following comment regarding tribal makeup: "Nothing more surprised our party more than the great proportion of their children, of all sizes, and I may add, shades of color, for the infusion of French blood from a long series of successive intermarriages, is found in every tribe."

Being from Ohio, the journalist was apparently unschooled in the mixed blood/full-blood or "half-breed"/"Indian" distinctions, now on the ascendancy in the sociological imaginations of the Euro-American settlers and soon to become the names of political factions on the reservations. He apparently saw only "Indians," or to be more precise, "their children," and despite the different "shades of color" indexing a rather homogenous Other from his perspective. Of course, Ojibwe people were all in attendance because all of their families, mixed and full-bloods alike were all recipients of the payments made in exchange for the land cessions, a stipulation that had been explicitly written into the Treaty of 1847 and practiced from the beginning of treaty making.

Yet, Hole-in-the Day the younger, a thirty-year-old outspoken aspiring leader who also attended the 1855 disbursement, not only had some things to say about "the folly of our chiefs" who characteristically "look to their own interests . . . when they make bargains." As he criticized the concentration of power that the treaty economy brought with it, he also explicitly addressed a named class of native persons. "You half-breeds, if you have any wise plans in your head that your chiefs ought to know, why not make them known to them before it is too late, that you may have no occasion to find fault with them for not acting wisely?"[2] Being, "your chiefs" these "half-breeds" were apparently well understood to be well within the native society and polity, and apparently being looked to once again for political advice in managing the changing political and economic landscape.

This advisory function of the mixed bloods, as a "different class of Indian people,"[3] is extensively documented in both the work of Theda Perdue on mixed bloods in the Southeast among the so-called "Civilized Tribes"[4] and Thomas Ingersoll in his study of mixed bloods throughout North America. Theda Perdue calls upon scholars to historicize the very use of terms like "mixed blood" or "half-breed" and characterized the use of terms as uncritically and anachronistically reproducing racial ideology. She argues that the matrilineal societies of the Southeast assimilated the children of Native mothers and non-Indian fathers to Native society and culture, seeing them as valuable resources in relations with Whites. They were not the agents of colonization they have been made out to be. Similarly, Ingersoll shows how some mixed bloods became "leading men," such as Joseph Brant, William Johnson Jr., and Alexander McGillvray[5] acting in the capacity that Hole-in-the-Day seems to be gesturing among the Ojibwe. Mixed bloods are not best understood as cultural brokers working between two worlds, because their actions indicate that they were committed to living lives in the tribal world.

In 1864, now ten years after the Treaty of 1854 was signed, and half a dozen years since at least three score of the mixed bloods had lost their eighty-acre parcels to mining interests in the region, nine Ojibwe chiefs composed a bilingual petition addressed to the commissioner of Indian affairs. The document was a report from their perspective on how the treaties were being implemented at the local level. The group had met "repeatedly and in council and at their homes" at Bad River over the course of the winter. As far as we can tell, Joseph Gurnoe of Bad River did the actual writing. Gurnoe was one of the "mixed-bloods, belonging to the Chippewa people." At the time, the entrepreneurial Gurnoe had been going around with fellow mixed blood James Chapman gathering the consent of other mixed bloods "to use their names in application for scrip."[6] They were responding to an opportunity recently created by the commissioner of Indian affairs when he liberalized the criteria for claiming the right to scrip thus establishing the conditions for lumber interests to gain access to lands in Minnesota. This did not disqualify Gurnoe from working with the chiefs.

On the topic of the chiefs' memories and understanding of the provisions for mixed bloods in the 1854 treaty that created the reservations and ceded their lands on the north shore of Lake Superior, the chiefs wrote: "Your Mixed Bloods are expelled from your Villages and Reservations. You will give them Six Thousand Dollars in Coin. [They] will then have eighty Acres of land outside of your Reservations."[7] Although the $6,000 was to be paid in agricultural implements, household furniture and cooking utensils, the idea that granting the eighty-acre parcels would have the effect of separating the mixed bloods clearly seems to indicate that the chiefs endorsed the intent of the treaty provision. It also reveals that before the treaty, the mixed bloods were living *within* their "Villages." The chiefs wrote, "Commissioner Manypenny also told us at La Pointe, those Mixed Bloods who are living on your Reservations and whom you like and wish them to stay, can remain with you always."[8] Indeed, some significant portion of this class never left their so-called full-blood relatives.

The people who were qualified to take the half-breed scrip that entitled them to an eighty-acre allotment in the ceded territory outside the borders of the collectively held reservations did not leave the communities in which they were living. By taking the scrip, they were marking themselves as members of a social category *within* tribal society, the federal government's intention of physically separating them from the same notwithstanding. And although the process of constituting stable reservation communities involved a good deal of conflict, these mixed bloods' altered status does not seem to be the reason for the conflict, even when this provision of the treaty was recalled and deployed to exclude individuals from full membership in reservation-based tribal communities.

It appears that the category "half-breed" or "mixed blood" was appropriated as a social category within the reservation communities in the second half of the nineteenth century and was deployed strategically by many different Indian people for political purposes into the first third of the twentieth century. The missionary Frederic Baraga had recorded a term for half-breed—"abitâwis" in his dictionary published in 1853.[9] With increasing interference and domination in the reservation period, Indian people needed to take cognizance of the ways in which they were understood by state and federal officials, missionaries, and other whites in positions of power. This practice represents a much weakened and partial continuation of the "middle ground" phenomenon Richard White first articulated wherein opposing groups try to prosecute their ends by "appealing to what they perceive to be the values and practices of those others" and generating novel cultural forms as a result.[10]

Resource Extraction History

The dispossession of the mixed bloods was a *de facto* government subsidy that played an important role in capitalizing and catalyzing the development of the region. From the native perspective, it was experienced as an enclosure movement that made their traditional subsistence practices, guaranteed by the treaties, into offenses against the state. The enclosure marginalized and proletarianized them and caused a vicious internal debate that would last for decades about how the Indian communities would articulate with the dominant society and who in those communities was a proper member and who was not.

While Agent Gilbert, the superintendent, and the commissioner of Indian affairs were working on implementing the mixed-blood provision of the treaty in 1855, the locks at Sault Ste. Marie opened, a critical step for the development of the extraction economy the treaties were intended to facilitate and the attendant transformation of lands and people in the Lake Superior Basin. "It would be hard to exaggerate the economic importance of the St. Mary's Falls canal, through which the vast mineral resources of the Lake Superior country moved to mills and furnaces on the lower lakes,"[11] John D. Dickenson wrote as the first line in his monograph on the canal and locks. From the perspective of the 1850s, both copper and iron ore from the newly discovered ranges could now be transported to mills in the East now that railroads connected the mineral ranges to Lake Superior.

Locally, in 1860, the county of La Pointe was subdivided to create Ashland County with the city of the same name as the county seat. The state legislature created roads between Ashland and Superior, and Ashland and Chippewa Falls,[12] on the Chippewa River accessing the Mississippi River and the entrepôt of St. Louis. In the 1870s, the Wisconsin Central Railroad connected the town of Ashland on Lake Superior to ports on Lake Michigan coming upon "an occasional Indian camp," as the railroad made its way north from Stevens Point through the ceded territories from which it received a grant of "a million acres of the finest standing timber on good soil."[13] The railroad also linked Ashland to the Penokees at the same time.[14] James Feldman writes that it was proximity to the rich iron deposits in the Penokee Range that caused the railroad to terminate at Ashland instead of Bayfield.[15] The railroad would soon carry minerals and then logs to metropoles for processing throughout the region.

According to Bruce K. Cox, author of the encyclopedic history of mining in the Gogebic Range, although the La Pointe Iron Company had already begun exploration in 1861, the "first shaft sunk on the Gogebic Range is attributed to this company" in 1874, "just west of the Penokee Gap on Section 15 [Township 44 North, 3 West]." The mine was on land that had originally been patented to Dennis Benjamin, Catherine Decoleau, Charles Corbin, and John Baptist Gauthier—all Lake Superior Chippewa mixed bloods. Today it is the site of Copper Falls State Park.

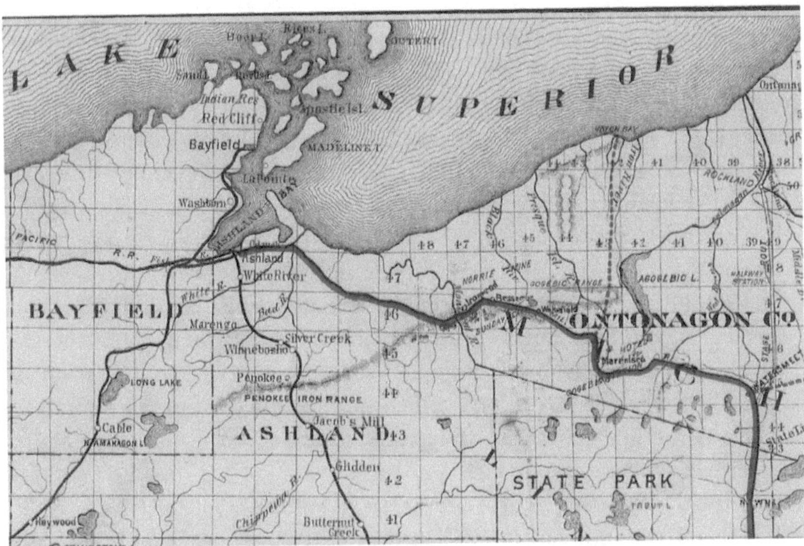

Map 6.1. Detail of map of the Milwaukee, Lake Shore, and Western Railroad, 1885. John Otis Thayer, cartographer. Image #91425. Courtesy of the Wisconsin Historical Society.

Earlier, in 1859, the *Ashland Press* reported that Captain Ray, Louis Leopold, and others "loaded with drills, wheelbarrows, &c," were in the area prospecting. They were anticipating the arrival of a railroad due the following year as their supplies had to be packed in by men and horses. The following year, Section 15 would yield six tons of ore that were packed in barrels and sent to Cleveland for assay and testing. In 1874, La Pointe leased the land to Bessemer Steel Works of Newport, Ohio. Two hundred tons of magnetic ore were mined and left on the hillside below a shaft that reached a depth of forty-five feet for wont of a means of transporting it profitably. Cox observed, "None of their holdings produced even a single shipping iron mine."[16]

The iron formation stretches about eighty miles, more than half of which are in Iron, Ashland, and Bayfield Counties. In all that distance in Wisconsin, only two mines made much money, the Cary and the Montreal, and they are well east of the La Pointe Company lands.[17] The mixed-blood provision of the treaty of 1854 did not capitalize successful mines in the region even if it did catalyze mineral development in the region generally.

Of the many mines on the lands originally patented to mixed bloods, only the Tyler's Fork Mine "made small shipments." The land which this mine worked was originally acquired by the Lake Superior Mining and Smelting Company and represents "the first serious attempt to exploit the iron ore deposits of the western Penokee," according to the geographer Arne Alanen.[18] Cox writes, "The Tyler's Fork Option company carried out explorations on an eighty in Section 34 and four eighties in Section 33 at the beginning of 1887." The land had been patented to Dakota mixed blood David Goutier. In an undated affidavit Goutier described himself as "an 'Eighth blood' of the Medawahkanton band of the Dacotah or Sioux Indians, and, as such am entitled to the portion of an eighth blood under the treaty of July 15th 1830 concluded at Prairie du Chien."[19] The Tyler Fork's Option Company would ultimately ship a total of about 60,000 tons by the time it was closed in 1890.[20] On a list of forty-seven Gogebic mines in order of importance, reflecting the relative richness of the range in the upper peninsula of Michigan, only twelve were in Wisconsin and Tyler Fork ranked next to last.[21]

Recall that the illustrious Increase Lapham had made a trip to the area on behalf of the Lake Superior Mining and Smelting Company in the late 1850s. As it would turn out, he "emphasized the importance of the magnetic formation at the [Penokee] gap," which had the effect of orienting interest to the western and ultimately rather unproductive end of the range as "no extensive operations were carried on in the west."[22] This was the land that was located by La Pointe and Lake Superior Mining companies.

This is certainly not to say that the effort wasn't made on those lands that had been patented to mixed bloods for a short time. In 1929, when mining was extracting 6 million tons of ore per year in the eastern part of the range, that is mostly in Michigan, the geologist H. R. Aldrich described the landscape of the entire Penokee Range as "a maze of pits, some shallow to be sure but some of considerable depth, shafts with carefully timbered walls, and the mounds of dirt and broken rock thrown out by those prospectors who literally combed the surface of the formation in search of iron ore. There are hundreds of these pits, shafts and trenches. There is not a "40" from end to end of the range across which the Ironwood formation occurs which has not been well pitted in this surficial and superficial manner."[23]

Additionally, self-published author Lawrence Roe wrote that in the period between 1884 and 1887, "the Gogebic area experienced a land rush unparalleled in the history of northern Wisconsin. In 1884 there were 184 mining companies and two years later only 15 remained."[24] Arnold Alanen writes that locations—named residential enclaves that were proximate to mines—such as "Annie, Germania, Hennepin, Kakagon, Minnewawa, Section 33, Shores, Trimble, Tyler Fork, and Windsor—existed on the place-name map of Wisconsin for a few years only."[25] The map published by Gage E. Tarbell and Company in 1887 reflected this early optimism showing the names of scores of companies holding sections and parts of sections of lands formerly patented to "the mixed bloods, belonging to the Chippewas of Lake Superior" on this newly imagined pitted landscape.

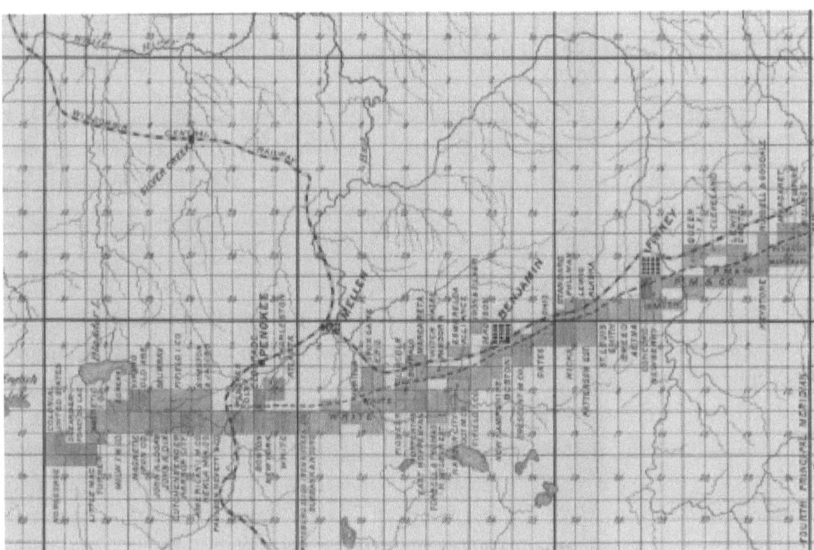

Map 6.2. Detail of Gage E. Tarbell's Gogebic Iron Range showing the mining properties in the western part of the Penokees from the Fourth Principal Meridian to English Lake. Image #96955. Courtesy of the Wisconsin Historical Society.

This optimism endured despite professional opinion about the viability of the ore in the Penokees. Already in the *Geology of Wisconsin, Survey of 1873–79*, the author of the chapters on the Penokees quoted from Increase Lapham:

> The Penokee Iron Range has now been examined in greater detail than any other area of corresponding extent in the state. The larger part of it has been traversed two or three times. . . . besides that which Mr. Wright has made . . . and the chief geologist himself has examined the eastern-most end. Every ore outcrop has been visited, sampled, and the samples analyzed. As far as purely geological work, without the aid of digging, is concerned, it may be safely said that the region is practically exhausted. . . . the geologist how hands over (further work) to the mineral explorer, who will find in the maps which we furnish, a reliable guide as to where to explore.

Charles Wright in the same volume writes even more candidly. Reporting that Wisconsin railroad people found nothing of value in the lower iron belts—meaning the western end of the range—but were confident of finding some in the north at some point in the future. He commented, "How soon will depend somewhat on the amount of attention those attractive and deceptive lower iron ore belt receive from future explorers." Wright described the land that contained the Penokee Range as "these worse than worthless lean ore belts."[26]

There was a lot of dissembling going on. In his study of law and mining in Wisconsin, James Lake off-handedly refers to the distance between predictions and outcomes as "the Penokee orgy."[27] David Mladenoff quotes from Mussey's early twentieth-century study of the corporate history of mining: "Many of the mines were managed with a view to the sale of stocks rather than ore. To sell securities, 'records' were necessary, and hence the mining captains strained every nerve to attain the maximum output possible the first year. The produce of 1885 was less than 125,000 tons; that of 1886 almost 750,000; of 1887 over 1,700,000. The mines were 'skinned' of their cheaply worked [surface] ores with a rapidity almost inconceivable, and the product was thrown on the market with a reckless disregard for the future."[28] Indeed, this earlier period is the beginning of what Iron County resident, chemist, engineer, and local mining critic Richard Thiede describes as the perpetual future bonanza that is always just out of reach in the Penokees. His caustic conclusion was, "It is and has always been a speculative charade."[29]

The charade is still available. In consulting University of Wisconsin-Madison scholar David Mladenoff's source, Mussey's early-twentieth century publication, it is telling to point out that fee holders in the Gogebic were to receive an average of fifty cents per ton of ore mined on their property. Presumably, this provision is still available, hence the value of the La Pointe Iron Company's holdings to this day. After 1927, the land could also benefit from Wisconsin's innovative forest crop law and taxed at a much reduced rate.[30] Despite the failure of the lands in the western part of the Penokee Range to live up to the hopes of those who were so eager to gain title to them in the 1850s, the lands were still in the possession of the La Pointe and Penokee Iron companies in the early twentieth century.

The combination of exploration, speculation, and actual employment in the mines of the entire Gogebic Range, the western part of which are the Penokees, reconstituted the demographic structure of the population by the turn of the century. By then, about half of the 22,000 residents were foreign-born: Finns, Swedes, Cornish, Canadians, Italians, Slovenes, Croats, Germans, Poles, Norwegians, and Irish,[31] many of whom were trying their hand at farming the cut over lands. They had been encouraged by the state to settle in the region as farmers.[32] Few had much experience living in multiethnic societies. Catalyzed by the ascendant Anglo-American racial ideology, the line was sharpening between immigrants who were becoming white and indigenous people.[33]

David Mladenoff calls attention to what he describes as "an ironic pattern" of land ownership in this region despite the boom and bust character of the landscape's productivity. Land owned by mining companies has shown the least change between the turn of the century and 1975. He points out that "although the range is not considered a viable mining area at present, it is being held as reserve properties for future use." Moreover, because owners of severed mineral rights pre-empt those of surface rights, "the future of the area is still in the hands of absentee corporations." In 1975, the biggest categories of land ownership in the sector of Iron County Wisconsin traversed by the Penokees were county forest (45 percent), small parcels (29 percent), and mining (14.5 percent).[34]

One gets the impression that the Penokees have always been about an elusive imagined future just beyond the reach of those who gaze upon the range, usually from a considerable distance. All the better to delude oneself, perhaps. Many of these lands would remain in the possession of La Pointe Iron into the twenty-first century when interest in the iron ore would again be revived as the mining industry was emboldened by the erosion of Wisconsin's progressive and environmental commitments that came with the Walker administration in 2011.

Allotting and Logging the Reservations

The relative failure of mining was followed by a successful lumbering industry. The town of Ballou was plotted on the eighty-acre parcel patented to mixed blood Joseph Roy in June of 1858. In the middle of the nineteenth century this land was part of La Pointe Iron's portfolio, and became a site of a sawmill in the 1920s. The mill can stand as an icon of an extractive industrial transition as it was lumbering and not mining that transformed this landscape most profoundly and created the context within which the reservation populations coalesced, consolidated, and stabilized.

As a measure of environmental transformation that took place on the lands ceded in the treaties of 1837 and 1842—lands upon which Indian people attempted to continue to live—by 1898, 87 percent of the pine trees in the twenty-seven northern counties were gone.[35] This was in addition to all of the hardwoods that were used in shoring up the mines, especially on the eastern end of the Gogebic-Penokee Range. Because the relatively soft hematite was prone to caving, the mines had to be extensively shored up, and David Mladenoff estimates that 200 square miles of hardwood trees were cleared for this reason alone.[36]

On the newly created reservations themselves, the Indian Office managed lumbering operations ostensibly for the benefit of Indian people wherein "logging revenue would fund the transition from an Indian economy dependent on annuities to one based on an exchange of goods and labor and thus integrated into the national economy."[37] *United States v. Cook*, a Supreme Court decision in 1873 that originated with the Oneida in Wisconsin, held that Indians did not own the timber on their individual land allotments for purposes of selling it other than as a means of developing the land for agriculture.[38] The result of this decision for the Ojibwe people in northern Wisconsin was that a billion board feet were taken off the four Wisconsin reservations in the 1880s within the La Pointe Indian agency under the authority of its agent. It was done in such an irresponsible fashion that the Senate conducted an investigation and found corruption at the highest levels.

The third article of the Treaty of 1854 permitted allotting individuals over the age of twenty-one an eighty-acre allotment of land on the collectively held reservations. Although ostensibly motivated by a desire to change hunters into farmers, this process began in 1875 at Bad River (1876 at Red Cliff, 1881 at Lac Courte Oreilles, and 1886 at Lac du Flambeau), and prospective Indian farmers began selling a portion of the trees on their land per the stipulations of *U.S. v Cook*. Because the last of the annuities payments were made in 1875, Indian agents and tribal people were concerned about how the members of the community would make their living.

Many Indian people asked to be allotted in order to create a source of income in the face of the end of treaty annuities.[39] As it would turn out, Indian allottees were underpaid for their lumber and underemployed in the work it took to remove it.[40] Nonetheless, they did benefit from the logging that took place. After reforms were initiated, another 1.25–1.50 billion board feet were harvested by the Stearns Lumber Company from the Bad River Reservation alone between 1894 and 1922—and the abuses continued.[41]

Logging of this magnitude characterized the transformation of the entire ceded territory. Of the 320 billion board feet of mostly white pine that were harvested from the Great Lakes forests,[42] 170 billion board feet came from the lands ceded in the treaties of 1837 and 1842.[43] William Gough, writing about the Wisconsin cutover region, describes the landscape by the end of the nineteenth century: "Brush, limbs, tops, and unwanted logs littered the ground, which still contained millions of stumps. With less vegetation, runoff increased, lowering stream levels, drying up marshes, and creating flood problems. In streams with lower levels and increased silting, increased penetration of sunlight changed the habitat for fish. There was also less game. Consequently, caribou and moose for example, were extinct in northern Wisconsin by 1900."[44]

Wisconsin's lumber harvest built Chicago, which in turn, further transformed landscapes from the Great Lakes to the Rocky Mountains, creating a "second nature," a story well told by William Cronon in *Nature's Metropolis: Chicago and the Great West*. The traditional subsistence base for native people was so compromised that they had to supplement what hunting, fishing, and gathering they could still do with wage labor in commercial fishing, lumber camps, and sawmills.[45] It was a *de facto* enclosure movement that drove this proletarianized population to the reservations in conjunction with allotting the lands in severalty to those who achieved tribal membership.

In 1910, Judge L. H. Mead, from the area between the Lac Courte Oreilles and St. Croix Ojibwe communities, observed the effects of the extraction economy on the Ojibwe population:

> You understand, there is nothing here for the Indians, as there was when I came here twenty-seven years ago. Practically all the blueberry fields are fenced in, the cranberry marshes are owned by other people, and a great many of the cranberry marshes are turned to use for hay meadows. The fishing that they had then has been taken over by the sporting element from the cities; and deer, duck, and game has been driven father west and north . . . These Indian boys could not go to one of our farmers, generally speaking, and get work as quickly as a whiteman could.[46]

The ascendant authority and power of the state contributed to this dispossession and to the passage of laws criminalizing indigenous subsistence practices by redefining the animal bodies that sustained indigenous human life as "game" to be marketed to sportsmen with the state and thereby creating hunting and fishing seasons, bag limits, and restrictions on methods of harvest.[47] Resources that had made up a tribal commons were now commoditized, which had the social effect of increasing the distance between settlers and native people. Many of the mixed bloods would be driven in the direction of the reservations yet assimilating them to the newly formed and unstable reservation communities was fraught with difficulties.

Constituting the Reservations

The 1854 treaty continued to shape these communities. These newly conceived reservations, and especially Bad River, had an immigration and boundary problem in the late nineteenth century. It was caused by the allotment policy and a proviso of the treaty that had created the Bad River Reservation "for the Lapointe Band, and *any other such Indians as may see fit to settle with them.*" Although allotment began in the 1860s, by 1882, the Department of the Interior granted the Chippewa the right to cut and sell timber from their allotments.[48] Having an allotment on a forested reservation represented a substantial income from the merchantable timber that could be harvested from it. This was a specific version of Edmund Danziger's observation that "Indians understood that bloated membership rolls meant less sustenance to share."[49]

The ascendancy of the racial system was becoming hegemonic throughout the United States. The reservation policy itself sought to concentrate Indian people for purposes of changing their cultures and societies. A binary system that divided all of society into whites and nonwhites made assimilation and integration, which had been envisioned earlier, unlikely. So-called mixed bloods living throughout the ceded territories who could not or would not pass for white—and of course, even those who could—had the choice of either migrating west to join the newly emerged Métis in the Red River Valley, or they could try to play up their local kin ties, seek an on-reservation allotment, and settle into life on one of the recently created Chippewa Indian reservations.

When lumbering interests sought to make the trees within the borders of the reservations into commodities, the federal government mobilized the allotment provision of the Treaty of 1854, and Indian people of all blood degrees and tribal commitment began to seeks allotments for their monetary value. The demographic change destabilized the leadership that was already challenged by the intrusion of federal power that came with the physical presence of federal agents decades earlier. I will explore the full implications of this reality in the next chapter.

By the time that the iron ore companies in the eastern part of the Penokee Range began to make money in the 1880s, the people whose property had capitalized the failing pioneers in the western part of the range were being integrated into the reservation-centered communities, and those communities retained the decentralized structure and geographic extension that they had in well before the treaty period. Ojibwe people in Wisconsin ceded lands in 1837, 1842, and 1854, stipulating each time that they would continue to hunt, fish, and gather on those lands. Indians had effectively only ceded the right to refuse non-Indians the freedom to live amongst them for purposes of harvesting pines and mining for copper, and little more. With the increasing numbers of non-Indians in the area and the threat of removal, the 1854 treaty effectively amended the previous treaties by designating townships within the earlier treaty cessions that whites could not locate upon and so created the reservations as sanctuaries.

Yet Indian people did not flock to these sanctuaries. "The natives" actively avoided settling on these reservations "relying on the plentiful supply of fish, as well as terrestrial game, wild rice and maple sugar,"[50] throughout the ceded territories, according to Edmund Danziger. They would only move to the reservations with allotment when they could sell the timber, and even then, they would live in settlements at some distance from their now-cleared individual tracts. These "natives" included the so-called mixed bloods who were living similar lives.

Patricia Shifferd described the way in which people at Bad River sought to rationally adapt to the "expansion of Euro-American commercial industrial society" and bemoaned the dearth of "secondary works adopting a holistic macro-sociological approach"[51] for the second half of the nineteenth century. This would finally come with Edmund Danziger's study, *Great Lakes Indian Accommodation and Resistance,* and I will rely upon it to sketch the general conditions in our own effort to describe what happened to the mixed bloods who had been dispossessed of their land, even if they were relatively flush with cash, if only for a short period of time.

Though Danziger does not explicitly address the mixed-blood trajectory into full tribal membership apart from noting the factionalism that characterized reservation polities when the reservations were being allotted, his work is helpful for contextualizing this process of tribal consolidation. Danziger describes several political scenes throughout the Great Lakes Indian communities as "complex and disputatious" with progressives favoring "formal education, Christianity and social status attended by achievement and wealth" competing with the traditional leadership,[52] a social distinction that was also cast in the idiom of blood in many of these communities.

This constitution of the tribal population into reservation-centered communities was fraught, but probably not because some of them took half-breed scrip in the late 1850s and early 1860s. Insofar as the very idea of reservations was new in the 1850s, the problems were more a matter of concentrating Indian people generally than integrating a particular class of Indian into communities already socially and geographically concentrated.

The "Letters Received" file from the Bad River Agency during this period reveals evidence of conflict and hostility between people over the issue of property in several of the reservations. It is not clear, however, that these conflicts are between people whom the whites call "Indians," "half-breeds," and "mixed bloods," although that language will be used by people in all of these categories to press their different agendas. In the late nineteenth century, the conflicts seem to be between a faction on the reservation that is seeking to restrict membership to long-standing community members and one that is open to admitting persons from distant Ojibwe communities. It may have been a matter of the desires of competing constellations of families for political power. There are also many letters from people using both their mixed-blood-French and their Anishinaabeg names identifying eighty-acre parcels on the reservation. They appear to be appealing to the chiefs making the decisions in multiple domains. In the twentieth century, as we will see in the next chapter, it was a debate about the inclusions of the Ojibwe living along the St. Croix river that divided the community.

For example, on September 2, 1881, the government farmer William Walker wrote to the agent that John Baptiste Mayotte's two-year-old steer had been cut with an axe by a person he knows.[53] I would speculate that this was done by someone less affluent, perhaps jealous of what he perceived to be Mayotte's success at assimilating to the new agricultural order. On April 10, 1882, Mr. Walker wrote to the agent reporting that Peter Marksman had his home broken into in October "by Indians belonging to this place," losing 1500 feet of lumber, four windows, two stove pots, one lamp, 9 bake pans, 12 plates"[54] etc. Marksman was a mixed-blood Christian minister living at L'Anse in Michigan. Significantly, he had signed the Treaty of 1854. Another example, in July of 1883, the Fond du Lac chief Nawgawnab wrote the agent complaining of "persons who don't belong here"[55] taking up eighty-acre parcels of land on the reservation. Several Cadottes and LaGards had written the agent the month before, referring to themselves as "the undersigned mixed blood Indians of the Fond du Lac Minnesota reservation,"[56] notably not "half-breeds" but also a distinct class of Indians. In April of the same year, twenty-five people with French or French-derived, last names made applications for allotments in two townships and eight contiguous sections of the Bad River Reservation, all of which would have been very likely to have been covered with pine trees[57] at the time and therefore quite valuable.

A letter from Gish ke tawug and Edawegeshik written in February of 1883 to the agent at Odanah states the matter plainly:

> Dear Sir. We want to ask you about some Half Breeds who have come here from Bayfield to take up land here.
>
> Have they any right to take eighty acres here? We think not. We think you should be told as you have the authority to permit or to prevent it. We trust you will forbid them before they take the land.
>
> The law was passed some time ago by our Great Father that Half Breeds were not to take land in the Reservation. Will you tell us how it is that they are now trying to do so. Please examine.
>
> We send this letter by the Bearers to who that we are united with them [sic] in the matter and await your answer to them.
>
> Yours respectfully,[58]

I suggest that it was these people's political affiliation as members of Buffalo's band, and not their mixed bloodedness, that was the real reason the chiefs sought to exclude them. The reference to "law passed some time ago by our Great Father" forbidding half-breeds from residing on the reservation appears to be an example of Richard White's middle ground wherein one group appeals to another in terms that the former imagines the latter will respond to. There is no such law. Placing the issue in the context of law permits the proponents to represent themselves more innocently and thus potentially allying federal power in a local political project.

Despite political conflict on these new reservations, Congress expanded the reservation at Red Cliff in 1883 to accommodate the many mixed bloods "scattered throughout the country equally entitled to allotments" and whom the Bad River "Indians of that reservation are unanimous in refusing to consent to their receiving patents."[59] However, not because they were mixed bloods. They were members of Ojibwe communities at some distance from the community at Bad River. And not because they were nominally Red Cliff Indian Catholics attempting to locate on Bad River's still mostly nominally Protestant and pagan Indian lands either. These beneficiaries of the expansion of Red Cliff were members of different bands, constellations of intermarrying families, each made up of people with different proportions of Indian and non-Indian forebears.

There is also conflict between leaders whom the federal agents unambiguously designated as "Indians." In April of 1885, the government farmer would write that "Edawageshik, the oldest chief on the reservation, wishes to tell you that Blackbird does not represent the Indians of this place . . . [He is] . . . always making trouble . . . [T]he old man wants the railroad money for the right-of-way to buy some equipment for making sugar."[60] The complaint may have something to it. A petition signed by forty-four residents—with both Anishinaabeg and Franconyms—to Agent Gregory at Ashland asked that James Blackbird's patent be denied for the land upon which they had established a village, and made valuable improvements upon, including a graveyard.[61] Several years later, Blackbird would be demanding rent from those people. Antoine Denomie would write to the agent: "Mr Blackbird is not recognized as chief but by his relatives, the Condecons who belong in Michigan."[62] Blackbird was a young man at the time of the signing of the Treaty of 1854 and regarded by some as the head of the band at Bad River, to the extent to which such a community can be regarded as a single political entity at all. He will play an important role in the community in the decades to come.

Again, the Bad River Reservation was a rather new idea at the time. At stake were the constellations of families (from Michigan or not) that would reside there. And more importantly, which families would legitimately govern the community in the eyes of the federal government. The idea that there was a Bad River Band, that is, a single social group geographically constituted, is erroneous. If anything, this was a political project. Social groups were constituted around charismatic leaders and the groups were characteristically fluid—as they had always been. The current political conflicts were motivated in a very traditional order of value, albeit in an unprecedented demographic context that included individually allotted landed trust property escalating the stakes.

If the conflict was described as mixed-blood/full-blood factionalism, a phenomenon that was common in many native societies in this region at the time, the difference represents social and cultural orientations and not genealogical differences as has been described and analyzed by several scholars already, especially Melissa Meyer in *The White Earth Tragedy* and Jill Doerfler in *Those Who Belong: Identity, Family, Blood, among the White Earth Ojibwe*. The powerful language of blood was deployed to represent the difference between conservatives, who were attempting to improvise survivance by reviving traditional practices, and progressives, who were attempting to preserve indigenous society and trading off those traditional practices. The result was that coalitions of families opposed each other.

Several petitions in the letters received are signed by people using both their Franconyms and their Anishinaabeg names. Nonetheless, we can read letters such as the one below, uncharacteristically written on a typewriter, which perhaps signals the writer's intention to enhance the letter's authority:

Jan 15, 1890

We, the chiefs, are satisfied to abide by the treaties that have been made with the government and our forefathers. The half breeds have been creating disturbances in the way of misleading us and caused division among ourselves.

Now we ask you to notify John Denomie and all other half breeds that any attempt to come into our councils and interfere with us in trying to get matters in a proper shape.

James Blackbird
George Messenger
Moses White
Joe Buffalo[63]

The same group wrote a petition to the commissioner of Indian affairs, dated February 26, 1896, that was sent through their agent calling for the expulsion of Antoine Denomie and John Morrison from the reservation for disturbing the peace and governance of the community. Antoine's brother, John Baptiste, was running two lumber camps and appears to be the only Indian lumber entrepreneur at this time. He represented a new form of capital accumulation and the political power that came with it, and he was in conflict with the leadership of one of the factions as a result. The Denomie brothers were soon to be elected secretary and treasurer of a business committee, suggesting a conflict between emerging democratic and waning gerontocratic political norms.

Denomie is identified as "a half-breed" in the petition.[64] Here, the chiefs are ringing a bell that the government officials would respond to. It is a kind of ethno-oriental practice, named by the anthropologist James Carrier, and referring to "essentialist renderings of alien societies by members of those societies themselves."[65] Here, the indigenous leadership knows that "half-breed" is also an important non-Indian category to whites for describing a sector of Indian society. The chiefs deploy it understanding its power. When so-called "half-breeds" write to the government, they refer to themselves as "mixed-blood Indians," apparently evoking the language of belonging in the treaty of 1854 and foregrounding their Indianness in their appeal.

Mixed bloods were taking a lot of blame at the time. Roger Patterson, the government farmer at Bad River, had previously written to the agent in January of 1896 describing "certain half-breeds" as having "swarmed in to this reservation," and they were having a "demoralizing effect on the plain Indians by introducing whiskey, inducing them to attend dances, teaching them to play cards and gamble and almost every other degrading practice." They tell the Indians that they are being cheated by the lumber company, causing "bitter factional fights between the Indians themselves." He concluded that "of course there are some very good and respectable half-breeds that came in and merely want to work for their living and these I think should be protected and allowed a chance."[66]

The "swarming" was not restricted to so-called "half-breeds." It included Ojibwe people associated with either no reservation—such as the St. Croix and Mole Lake bands—or smaller reservations that had less land to allot, fewer trees that made the allotments valuable, and no white-owned lumbering operations or a sawmill to provide employment.

Concerns about "swarming" motived research about mixed bloods and scrip. On March 1, 1897, thirty-nine years to the day that Julius Austrian located sixty-one mixed-blood parcels in the Penokees, the government farmer at Bad River wrote to the agent on behalf of tribal member Joe Martin asking for "some kind of book which he claims to have seen in your office which showed who in years passed have secured scrip.' "[67] The book may have been an ordinary leather-bound ledger, or it may have been the 1874 GPO publication of *Half-Breed Scrip. Chippewas of Lake Superior. Correspondence and Action Under the 7th Clause of the Second Article of the Treaty With the Chippewa Indians of Lake Superior . . .*", the 331-page report filed by the commission investigating the abuses to which such scrip had been put, which includes numerous lists of "half-breed" applications for scrip for eighty-acre parcels. The same request was made in September and the specific reasons stated plainly. The lists "are needed badly by a committee of Indians appointed by the agent to pass on the rights of certain of the halfbreeds who claim allotments on this reservation."[68] A political faction at Bad River was looking for a rationale to reduce the numbers of eligible allottees, from one perspective, or distantly related kinsmen from another, who were trying to make claims at Bad River. It wasn't that they had mixed parentage per se: it was that they were from other communities. And in some cases, they were descended from someone allotted once already with mixed-blood scrip, and that would permit the leadership at Bad River to credibly turn those applicants down.

Generally, Ojibwe people accommodated and resisted the forces of urbanization and industrialization. They developed a mixed economy that involved adding wage labor to traditional hunting, fishing, and gathering with all of its implications. Two legal cases on the Bad River Reservation speak to the importance of that on-going traditional economy and also to the relative cultural and political homogeneity of the community despite the factionalism being described in the language of blood.

In the first case, John Blackbird was arrested for setting fishing nets in Bear Trap Creek. In the second, Michael Morrin was arrested for setting nets in Red Cliff Bay on Lake Superior. Note their names. John was the nephew of Chief James Blackbird and grandson of the Chief Blackbird who signed the 1854 treaty and is designated as a full-blood on the 1910 census.[69] In contrast, Morrin descended from Benjamin François Morin of St. Suplice, who entered the fur trade in 1807 and married Margaret Bazinet. They were residents of La Pointe at the time of the 1837 treaty.[70] Morrin appears on the 1910 census with the occupation "fisherman" and is designated as one-quarter Chippewa Indian.[71] Despite the difference in their origins, both were contesting state domination and violation of usufruct rights their forebears had stipulated for in the treaty cessions. Both supplemented their incomes with fish, spoke, read, and wrote English, and wore whiteman's clothes.[72]

As the conflicts about membership and leadership at Bad River and many other Indian reservations played out, the metropole sought to extract Great Lakes copper, iron ore, petroleum, and lumber. This created opportunities for agricultural work, domestic work, road construction, lake shipping, employment at the Indian agency, and staffing the boarding schools. It also created the opportunity for Indian people to sell the trees on their lands. The effect, however, was that they were proletarianized, "burned at the bottom of the melting pot," as Danziger observed,[73] losing control of the means of reproducing themselves socially after the manner of their grandfathers and grandmothers.

Wage labor changed the nature of cooperation and dependence on kin. In her study of this time period at the White Earth Reservation in Minnesota, Melissa Meyer writes that the mixed-blood members who were taking advantage of new economic opportunities were less altruistic and more orientated toward wealth and social status than their full-blood relatives, perhaps like the aforementioned Mr. Mayotte and Rev. Marksman. This was a widespread phenomenon throughout Indian country at the time.[74] These forces, and different people's responses to them, led to disputes about who was an Indian—that is, who was really a trustable community member, committed to commonly held values, and thus entitled to annuities as well as allotments. Danziger would write that the rights of so-called mixed bloods were controversial.[75]

The ascendant racial ideology that had become hegemonic among the increasing numbers of Euro-Americans moving into the area made it difficult for aspiring Indian mixed bloods to become integrated into the dominant society. This created a centripetal force drawing such individuals toward the reservation communities. Two incidental references to Indian people from the *Ashland Press*, the newspaper published closest to the Bad River community, and five years apart, are indices of the consensus among Americans about anyone identified as Indian at the time. From the July 29, 1876, issue we read "Blueberries are ripe and the 'nitchies' [pejorative for Indians] are making themselves useful by serving the white folks with plenty of them at ten cents a quart." And from the March 26, 1881, issue: "Mr. Lo and his family can be seen any day preambling our streets with sacks of fresh pickerel for sale cheap for cash popy."[76] By this time, the phrase "Lo! The poor Indian" from Alexander Pope's eighteenth-century poem "An Essay on Man" had apparently been condensed, abbreviated, and morphed into the proper, if also generic name, Lo.

HON. VINCENT ROY.

Photograph 6.1. Drawing of Vincent Roy, "Uncrowned King of the Chippewas." Late nineteenth century. Verwyst, C., *Life and Labors of Rt. Rev. Frederic Baraga.*

At the level of the individual biography, Bad River community member Vincent Roy Jr.'s efforts to make a life for himself in the changing economy is also illustrative of the forces that kept him out of settler society and would attract him to Indian society despite his affluence. As discussed earlier, Roy was a prominent Anishinaabeg mixed blood born in 1825 into a mixed-blood fur-trading family. He was employed by the business men Louis Leopold and Julius Austrian as a translator, managing their posts at Fond du Lac and Vermillion Lake in the late 1840s and early 1850s. Chief Buffalo invited Vincent Roy to accompany the 1852 delegation to Washington to complain about the government's inaction in the face of white onslaught. Vincent apparently imagined himself a citizen of the United States and attempted to mobilize the preemption law that would permit a person to claim and purchase land upon making improvements upon it. The effort led to a court case. The August 3, 1858, issue of the *Superior Chronicle* reported the decision from the Government Land Office:

> Being thus entitled by reason of the Indian character to certain rights and privileges conferred by treaty, and having to some extent derived the benefits and advantages secured to them thereby, I am not disposed to regard the claim which they now assert to the right of pre-emption as citizens of the United States with any special favor and consideration. But these parties have entirely failed to show that they have settled upon and improved the land claimed by them in good faith for their own use and benefit. The facts disclosed by the evidence on file indicate beyond reasonable doubt that they were the employees of others under whose direction and for whose benefit they were acting.
>
> In view of the facts hereinbefore stated, the pre-emption entries of the said parties, Charles Brisette, Antoine Warren, Basil Dennis and Vincent Roy, Jr. are invalid, and I hereby direct that the same be cancelled.

It appears that these men—"of the Indian character"—were originally hired by two speculators to preempt land on their behalf for purposes of making a big profit on lands that would become part of the city of Superior. Recall that this was one of the methods used to secure mining lands in the Penokees and widely understood as "townsite fever."[77] In the news article itself, a contrast is drawn between the "three or four half-breeds claiming to pre-empt as 'American citizens,' and some six or eight real American citizens claiming some three hundred acres as a town site." The writer points out that "the Indians are not merely bogus citizens, they are bogus pre-emptors in the bargain, for they were hired men of Thompson and Stinson." The article interprets the aforementioned Attorney General Cushing opinion to preclude "a half-breed Indian, receiving annuities as such, recognized as a dependent of a tribe, and beneficiary of treaty stipulations" from becoming a citizen by anything other than "some positive act of Federal legislation,"[78] and certainly not by taking an eighty-acre parcel under the treaty aspiring to whiteness in the lifestyle register. Failing to secure the land as a US citizen, Vincent Roy would claim it under the mixed-blood provision of the Treaty of 1854 and hold the land for thirty-six years, whereupon he sold it for $25,000,[79] more than three-quarters of a million in 2020 dollars.

Vincent Roy Jr. also makes an appearance in Arthur Tenney Holbrook's trout-fishing memoir as an associate of Antoine Dennis and identified as "Vincent Roy (a full blooded Indian, who is said to have been the wealthiest Chippewa in the whole tribe)."[80] In a short biography of Vincent Roy in his hagiography of Father Baraga, Chrysostomus Verwyst, O.F.M. lauded Roy for his magnanimity and generosity to his fellow Indian people, calling him the "the best Indian of the Northwest." Fellow friar Father Oderic tiled an article for the Fr*anciscan Herald*, "An Uncrowned King of the Chippewas," singing Roy's praises as well.[81] With the simplification of the ethnic landscape and the reimagining of the ceded territory as a wilderness capable of restoring civilized persons to health, indigenous persons are now an instrument for realizing such a goal, and therefore all Indians belonged to a homogenous category. The racial binary has become hegemonic and Vincent Roy's mixed bloodedness completely eclipsed.

In contrast, the case of the mixed blood John Morrison is also revealing for the way in which he and his wife, Eliza, appear to have attempted to live on the ceded lands only to fail. He and his wife were reassimilated into reservation-based tribal society in the 1880s when the community was actively implementing the provision of the treaty that provided for allotment on the reservation itself. Morrison's eighty-acre tract in the Penokees was patented to him in March of 1858 and alienated soon thereafter. He appears on the 1860 federal census as a forty-year-old laborer.[82] Morrison has a personal worth of $100, exactly the amount he would have received for signing power-of-attorney documents that transferred his patent to an aspiring mining-company owner. Morrison's fourteen-year-old son, John Jr., was born in 1846. Now in his mid-sixties, he appears on the 1910 census, and he speaks, reads, and writes English and has his own income. Both John Jr. and his wife received allotments on the Bad River Reservation, and both are one-quarter Chippewa, designated as Indians living in a community with many other Indian people of various degrees of Indian bloodedness.[83]

Eliza wrote a series of letters that would become *A Little History of My Forest Life*. The book is introduced, edited, and insightfully interpreted by Victoria Brehm. Eliza (nee Morrin) Morrison, aunt of the aforementioned fisherman Michael Morrin, as it turns out, worked at the Chicagoan William Cunningham Gray family's camp on Island Lake where the Morrisons lived in the 1890s. These Morrisons are also mentioned in Arthur Tenney Holbrook's memoir, described as being part of "a group of Chippewas" including the Antoine Dennis and Joe La Pointe families.[84] In exchange for the Grays sending them barrels of food and clothing, Eliza wrote a series of letters to Catherine Gray describing her life and the lives of those with whom Eliza was familiar.

Eliza's book is a rare and intimate glimpse into the lives of mixed blood Indian people in the second half of the nineteenth century. Eliza's maternal grandmother was an Ojibwe Indian woman, and John Jr. had been brought up among the Ojibwe of the St. Croix River. She says that her husband is closer to and more familiar with Indian ways. Eliza never explicitly refers to herself as a mixed blood or a "half-breed" anywhere in her narrative. Insofar as she refers to Indians and whites in the third person, she does not appear to explicitly identify as either. At the same time, Eliza makes several references to "our native language,"[85] meaning Anishinaabemowin, though she can speak, read, and write English, having been schooled on Madeline Island in the 1840s. There are many references to sugar camp, fishing, and hunting. Eliza and John seem to spend their social time with Indian people as "Indian friends always stopped by to see us."[86] In 1881, twenty Indian people passed through their homestead intending to introduce a new dance at the village in Odanah. This was the Big Drum or Dream Dance, a late nineteenth-century religious revitalization that is still practiced in the region to this day.

Several of these pilgrims were cousins of John Morrison.[87] Even after they left their life in the woods and were living in the town of Ashland for a period of time, Eliza would write, "I had a good many of my Indian friends come by to see me."[88] When she bore one of her sons, she was visited by "many Chippewa women."[89] She describes her closest friend, a Mrs. Bousky (from Bousquets) as a full-blood. Michael Bouskie, referred to only as Eliza's friend's husband in the book, had "some of the Indian superstitious ways."[90]

Significantly, Michael Bouskie is the son of Michel, resident of La Pointe, and was sixteen years old in 1839 when Lucius Lyon compiled the list of eligible mixed bloods.[91] Michel's eighty-acre allotment under the 1854 treaty was by this time part of the landed capital of the La Pointe Iron Company. On the 1860 census, Michel identifies his occupation as fisherman, he has $300 in real estate, and his personal estate is worth $150.[92] The Bouskies also make an appearance in Holbrook's memoir; he working as a guide at the Knight-Vilas camp and she as a sexually abused mascot, described by Holbrook as "a repulsive looking squaw, who had but one or two teeth; and the traditional initiation into the Ashland lodge was for the neophyte to embrace Mary, and give her a warm kiss full on the lips!"[93] Clearly, these formerly liminal mixed bloods had been fully racialized and exoticized.

In describing accompanying her husband in the woods, Eliza writes "Of course we made ourselfs [sic] Indian and wife as much as we could," she walking behind him and carrying her "little squaw ax," and he in a red sash, a sign of "red and white blood."[94] Though he would mark trees using his personal totemic sign, being a Catholic, Eliza assures the reader, he made such marks for practical reasons, and "not because he believes any part of the Indian superstitions."[95] When carrying her little son, she did it "Indian style,"[96] using a cradleboard. She would use the same phrase in describing their use of a drying rack for the last two hauls of fish for the season.[97]

John and Eliza Morrison were Indian enough to have chiefs vouch for them and so receive an annuity payment at Red Cliff in 1865. Yet, although "we went on the old Indian way of tapping maple trees, . . . [o]ur sugar was much whiter and cleaner than what the Indians made."[98] They appear on the 1877 tribal roll. In 1894, she would write that her husband was going to get an eighty-acre allotment on the Bad River Reservation. As we saw from some of the correspondence above, the very possibility of him receiving an allotment on the reservation was a measure of how connected and committed he was to tribal members in authority, that is, embracing "tribal relations," as such a disposition was pejoratively described. Morrison fished, trapped, contract hunted, and worked as a laborer and mailman before he decided to take up the plow. Receipt of scrip, subsequent granting of power of attorney, and sale of the patent in 1858 were apparently nonevents in the couple's lives as they go entirely unmentioned. And insofar as it was likely known to residents of the reservation community that they had once taken scrip, it apparently was not held against them.

Eliza's story reveals how fluid community membership was at the time. On the one hand, referring to Indians effectively as "them" throughout Eliza's narrative and, on the other, describing a lifestyle and social life that are indistinguishable from those of many Indian people at the time leave the reader uncertain as to how she and her husband think about to whom they belong in ethnic or racial terms. If, in fact, they have such concerns at all. Eliza will write upon their move "from Spider Lake to Odanah, that is to the Indian village where I am living now . . . A person would naturley [sic] think it would be very pleasant to live with *my* people" (italic emphasis added). And although she missed the homestead and wild game, she would write, "I am quite satisfied to be where I am with some of my old acquaintances."[99]

Her immediate neighbors were Souliers, Goslins, and Beauregards, as well as many other Indian people whose lives probably had similar trajectories.[100]

On this issue of her identity, Victoria Brehm, the editor of what she calls a "métis autoethnography,"[101] concludes: "It was the legacy of this old, accommodating métis world of the Great Lakes that allowed people to be Indian or white or métis at the same time in the same place, depending on which was necessary to qualify for treaty payments, or homestead land, or take up an allotment on a reservation."[102] So it was as it had always been: social relationships were determinative.

The Morrisons, the Bouskys, the Roys, the Blackbirds, the Morrins were all still living in Anishinaabewaki, organized by committed kinship and social relationships with race having little standing as a means of determining belonging or difference. Yet the landscape was changing. Extractive industries attracted more and more non-Indians whose practices worked to enclose the resources upon which Indian people depended upon to reproduce their society. With this influx came the collapse of the continuum of social relationships that linked the centers of Indian and non-Indian society and caused a polarization determined by the ideology of race. The policy of allotment transformed the trees on the reservations into commodities and sources of employment for Indian people. In the early twentieth century, with allottable reservation land growing scarcer, the internal social distinction of mixed blood and full blood was mobilized to name an internal and polarizing political distinction. A crisis in reservation governance ensued, and it is this history to which we now turn.

7

Allotment and the Problems of Belonging

> People from all over are coming in here and saying, "I am a member of this band." That is the reason we are having so much trouble in getting our land allotted.
>
> —Chief James Doolittle, 1913

> The question of allotments in that country depended primarily upon the necessity of the lumbering companies for timber.
>
> —Dr. Wooster, 1921[1]

In the late nineteenth and early twentieth centuries, the distinction between full bloods and mixed bloods gave rise to groups within the various Indian communities engaged in bitter struggles for control of their communities. I want to document the structure and the change in these indigenous polities over time in order to validate the claim made by contemporary descendants of members of both factions that their mixed-blood ancestors were dispossessed in the middle of the nineteenth century, and some form of compensation is due the tribe as the entity that suffered a collective loss.

This chapter begins by exploring the conflict between mixed bloods and full bloods for political control of the Bad River Reservation that came to a head over the issue of which Ojibwe people would be permitted to live at Bad River and therefore receive allotments of land on that reservation. I draw upon records of visits to Washington DC, federal agents' and inspectors' reports, a manuscript describing meetings of the Bad River chiefs and headmen, archival records of marriage patterns, the town's short-lived newspaper, the writings of tribal members employed in a Works Progress Administration

(WPA) project, and a lone published account of Ojibwe mixed-blood life, all of which explicitly discuss the status of mixed bloods, making it possible to create a composite portrait of the polity in the early twentieth century.

If the annuity system that came with the treaties disrupted the indigenous authority to determine community membership, wherein the US government empowered certain cooperative leaders to decide who was a member of the treating polity and who was not with payments in specie at stake, then the legitimacy of authority was made even more precarious with the implementation of the allotment policy. At stake was the right to reside within the recently surveyed boundaries of the Ojibwe reservations in Wisconsin. More importantly, however, was the right to monetarily benefit from the sale of the trees on individual parcels of land within those boundaries. Yet, because the proceeds from the sale of timber on those individual allotments was controlled by the federal agents, and not the chiefs, the chiefs' role as loci of redistribution was diminished in the community. Since allotment was designed with very particular geographical entities in mind, it dealt a severe blow to the fluidity and flexibility that had been characteristic of belonging in Anishinaabewaki, the indigenous sociopolitical formation organized by kinship.

Within the Ojibwe communities in the Great Lakes region, Melissa Meyer's analysis of the impact of the allotment policy on the White Earth Reservation in Minnesota is the gold standard.[2] Dealing mostly with the years between 1889 and 1920, she shows the effects of the historical constitution of the White Earth Reservation in 1867. Bands living throughout Minnesota were settled on a formerly uninhabited landscape. The result was a polity that was polarized between conservative "full-bloods" and progressive or assimilating "mixed bloods." Formerly cultural or ethnic differences were now symbols of political positions. The actual assigning of allotments at White Earth was less fraught than at Bad River in that White Earth is several times the size of Bad River, ecologically more diverse, and its population was not built up around a band already in place. By contrast, White Earth's biggest problems came with reservation-specific congressional legislation in the early twentieth century that designated most of the population "mixed bloods" and made them eligible to sell their lands, which resulted in a massive dispossession. Mixed-bloodedness became a very salient status at White Earth in the first decades of the twentieth century and may have played a role in the focus placed upon mixed bloodedness at Bad River at the same time.

Katherine Ellinghaus complements Meyer's study and has shown how the allotment process refigured Indianness at the White Earth Reservation in Minnesota because both the authority to determine belonging and the criteria for making that determination were now nearly entirely controlled by the federal government.[3] Similarly, Thomas Biolsi has shown how allotment on the Lakota reservations fundamentally transformed the subjectivity of the Lakota people. They were individually "empropertied" and made into "red Lockeans" vis à vis their relationship to the land and to each other.[4] Also on the Plains among the Arapaho and the Cheyenne, at the same time, Loretta Fowler shows how authority was eroded and interfamilial cooperation declined with allotment.[5]

The allotment process had similar effects in the Great Lakes region and would also challenge the traditional leadership at Bad River. The chiefs had direct or immediate family memory of the treaty period, and this authorized their leadership. The value of the memory, however, was hotly contested in the community given the new realities of allotted reservation life, and the so-called mixed bloods' political power waxed.

Complementing this shift, federal officials would soon be inclined to default to genealogical descent abbreviated as blood quantum as a means of determining the competency of tribal members regarding property during this period. Yet agents continued to defer to tribal leadership to make the decisions regarding who belonged to the polity and who did not on the basis of kinship and descent. For example, in 1890, the commissioner of Indian affairs, Thomas Morgan, opined that though blood was important for purposes of allotment, it was not definitive. Two years later, he warned of the ramifications of denying allotments to mixed bloods in the face of their being recognized by their communities as tribal members. In 1894, the attorney general held that mixed bloods living on reservations were to be regarded as Indians for all governmental purposes. And though the general principle was contested in several legal cases, by 1918 the Department of the Interior held to this position on membership.

Blood quantum of mixed bloods was not regarded as dispositive for purposes of assigning allotments. Blood quantum only became important when the government sought to establish criteria for the *alienation* of allotments.[6] This was especially evident at the White Earth Chippewa Reservation in Minnesota where fraud led to the loss of 143,000 acres of land and a subsequent Supreme Court decision holding that among the tribal population "everyone was mixed blood who wasn't 100 percent full-blood."[7] The special status of mixed bloods under the treaties and the blood ideology that informed the creation of that status in the first place did, however, play a role in the process by which reservation leaders made their decisions regarding who belonged to the community and who did not.

The multiple means of including persons as members of social groups in earlier periods had been the prerogative of extended families, and this was a dimension of greater mobility on the landscape. Persons could be made members of indigenous social groups through marriage, as well as capture and adoption. As these communities were reservationized and engaged more regularly with the federal government, they were not so much forced to acquiesce in the government's conception of membership as they were to accept the federal government's conception of polity and governance. The role of federal law in this tribalization process has been well described by Carole Goldberg, who concludes that factionalism and instability were common outcomes.[8] This is certainly true at Bad River in the early part of the twentieth century.

Power had historically been concentrated in the hands of the headmen and chiefs, a centralizing process that had been going on since at least the treaty period if not before. By the early twentieth century, the power of chiefs and headmen was waning because reservation agents created advisory business committees and then disbanded those in favor of general councils. It was in these forums that the community debated membership criteria and drew upon the imposed and increasingly hegemonic discourse of blood in making their determinations. The terminology of this relatively new way of figuring belonging and difference was selectively appropriated by indigenous people as a rhetorical device in conflicts over access to reservation resources. Nonetheless, as among the White Earth Chippewa, it was not genealogy that determined one's status as a "half-breed," "mixed-blood," "full-blood," or "Indian," but one's "habits and mode of life."[9] In other words, "culture" was determinative, specifically in regard to how one ordered the relationship between one's commitment to kin and one's accommodation of the external forces bearing down upon reservation society.

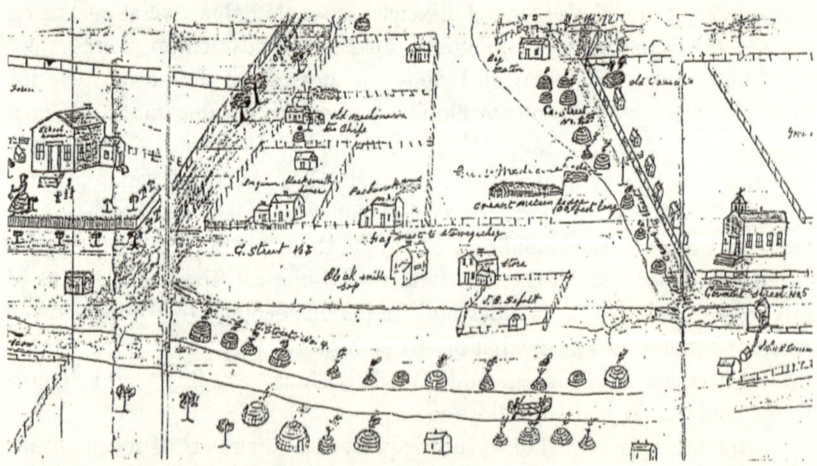

Figure 7.1. Detail of a hand-drawn image of the town of Odanah on the Bad River reservation, reputed to date to the late nineteenth century done in the birds-eye view style of the times. Joseph Green, the creator, signed the map and added "a full-blood Indian."

The La Pointe bands, now in the late 1800s and early 1900s, were reorganized as the Red Cliff and Bad River Bands. Red Cliff was populated by the descendants of the followers of Chief Buffalo, nominally Catholic, oriented toward fishing, and included thirty-some families of St. Croix River valley Chippewa who had migrated to Red Cliff in the 1860s. The agent described the community as populated by "almost wholly part blood citizens [and] are a progressive, quite industrious band."[10] Bad River, however, was a larger and more complex constellation of related families as we have seen, and somewhat more oriented toward farming, having concentrated at Odanah on the fertile Bad River flood plain, several miles south of Lake Superior in the 1840s at the encouragement of the missionary Leonard Wheeler.

In the half century since the signing of the Treaty of 1854, the town of Odanah at the heart of Bad River had grown from a small settlement with several houses, all associated with the school established by the missionary Leonard Wheeler, to a bustling little town of about two thousand. Residents were evenly divided between Indians and whites, and "the two races of citizens seem to be getting along without any friction whatever," according to the agent.[11] Figure 7.1 is an ethnocartographic representation of the central part of the town of Odanah.[12]

This hand-drawn bird's-eye view depicts a single community showing both wooden frame buildings and wigwams resonant of the political factions of "progressives" and full-bloods (or "vagabonds" as the Lapointe agent dubbed them)[13] and both groups contesting for power in the community. The cultural institutional plurality of the community is shown by the Grand Medicine Lodge, the school, and the church. A second church, St. Mary's, sponsor of the school, is just out of frame.

The growth and population makeup was largely attributable to the presence of the Stearns Lumber Company from 1894 until 1922. The company cut hundreds of millions of board feet of lumber and paid nearly $7 million to Indian people at Bad River in possession of allotments and over $1 million dollars in wages to Indian lumberjacks, and to the 150 to 200 Bad River tribal members who were sawmill workers.[14]

By the second decade of the twentieth century, the town also had two churches and three schools (public, Catholic, and Methodist), blacksmith shop, billiard hall, bowling alley, tailoring shop, two theaters (one of which had Vaudville on Sunday nights), carpenter shop, and confectionary shop. By 1913, 75 percent of the Bad River Band lived in the town.[15] According to the agent, 90 percent of that population used alcohol. The town of Ashland lay ten miles away by the train, which ran three times a day and boasted fifty-three saloons—a problem widely and extensively discussed within the community. Odanah hosted both a yearly Indian fair celebrating the anniversary of the

1854 treaty and several Indian Farm Institutes, the latter the outcome of a relationship developed with the University of Wisconsin-Madison that hosted the fourth annual meeting of the Society of American Indians in 1914 attended by several Bad River members.[16]

Rather significantly, the community had its own newspaper. *The Odanah Star* was the only reservation-based weekly newspaper in the state of Wisconsin. Writing her dissertation on newspapers of this era, Patty Loew described the paper as "a passionate, informative, and entertaining chronicle of life on the Bad River Reservation, a reflection on the lives of its mixed-blood readers who were undergoing a period of intense cultural reconstruction." Loew concluded, "Sometimes unpredictable, often contradictory, *The Odanah Star* was a confusing admixture of assimilationist themes, consumerism, and chest-thumping protests about the 'Octopus' (Stearns Lumber Company) and graft within the Indian Service."[17] All true, and yet it was more.

This progressive newspaper was published from June 12, 1912, to June 30, 1916, and at the time when the community was actively debating who belonged there and who didn't, how individual landed property should be allocated, and what kinds of values and commitments were desirable among its members. Frequent critical articles revealed the editors seeking to hold accountable the Indian agent and Stearns lumber mill, as well as officials in nearby Ashland. It published critiques of federal Indian policy and the workings of the Indian Office in DC, as well as texts of proposed bills and court decisions and letters from a few tribal members and US congressmen. The *Star* reported developments at the White Earth Reservation in Minnesota, the Lac du Flambeau and Lac Courte Oreilles Chippewa, and the Menominee reservations in Wisconsin.

The *Star* joyously reported local improvements, complained about the lack of good roads, cheered businesses opening and lamented their closing, and enthusiastically told of the triumphs and travails of the local baseball team. It argued in favor of agricultural and other forms of development, acknowledged and decried the factionalism, and sought to tamp it down with appeals to "the welfare of our village." The paper was certainly supportive of allotment as means of development and reported on the community meetings that dealt with the topic.

At the same time, the editors repeatedly evoked and fiercely supported the Treaty of 1854, especially for its value for prohibiting the sale and use of alcohol in all of the ceded territories, but also for the treaty's recognition of the right to hunt, fish, and gather on those lands free of state regulation. The actions of many of the leaders of the local community appeared in its pages, often without editorial commentary. The paper was a concrete means of imagining the Bad River community and its relationship to the region, other tribes, and its place in the nation at a critical moment in the community's history. The newspaper rarely used the words "mixed blood" and "half-breed," but when it did, it was usually in relation to other tribes but never associated with political factionalism at Bad River.

The St. Croix Chippewa Problem

Bad River and Red Cliff both had begun to allot individuals in the mid-1870s under the Treaty of 1854 although most of the allotments would come in the 1890s and the first decade of the twentieth century.[18] Allotment was the means to extract millions of board feet of timber from the reservations.

The federal government implemented the La Pointe Plan in 1893 to manage the harvesting of Indian timber. A single contractor—the Stearns Lumber Company—won the right to negotiate with tribal members for the timber on their allotments. Prices were fixed by species. The contractor would locate a mill and preferentially hire Indian people.[19] The policy change incentivized allotment claims on the four Wisconsin Ojibwe reservations, although people continued to actually reside in villages both on the reservations and throughout the ceded territories. Furthermore, allotment was formally similar to receiving annuities, although the agent now displaced the chiefs and headmen as the locus of distribution, a change that had considerable political implications.

Bad River became a magnet for Ojibwe people due to the second paragraph in Article II of the 1854 treaty describing the land that became the Bad River Reservation, initially for the LaPointe band, "and such other Indians that may see fit to settle with them." Chairman Moses Claff of the US Senate Committee characterized the community in 1909. From earlier hearings, he decided that "this reservation . . . was the only reservation to which all could come who could not go anywhere else for land . . . [and this] has made this reservation the worst reservation in the State on that account . . . the worst characters among the mixed bloods and the Indians would naturally come here if they could not get lands in other reservations. It made this sort of unloading place for them all."[20] Of course, "the worst characters" were among *both* "the mixed bloods and Indians."

This had been a long-term problem as Congress attempted to liquidate the nearby Lac du Flambeau and Lac Courte Oreilles Reservations in 1872 and remove their populations to Bad River. In the early twentieth century, those "other such Indians," especially those from the St. Croix River area, but also Ojibwes from L'Anse and Ontonagon in Michigan, were making so many claims on Bad River that Congress decided to intervene in the enrollment process by calling for the creation of a new roll in 1905. The process would have to be repeated again in 1908 after it was alleged that the "half-breeds . . . [had been assigned] . . . the best lands on the reservation."[21]

By 1901, more than a thousand residents had been allotted an eighty-acre parcel on the reservation under the authority of the Treaty of 1854. Some allotments were worth as much as sixty thousand dollars for the merchantable timber, making some tribal members the equivalent of millionaires in 2020 dollars. However, others had almost no timber on their land at all. According to the commissioner of Indian affairs at the time, there were contested allegations that half-breeds were getting the most valuable land.[22] Another chief complained that St. Croix people were getting allotments in favor of the children of Bad River community people. According to agent Samuel Campbell, those who had been allotted wanted their children to receive allotments "so as to keep them in idleness in the future because when the money of the older ones who have allotments gives out, they fall back on the allotments of their children."[23]

As a measure of the instability brought by lumbering and allotment, in 1907, the LaPointe Band reconstituted its government, dispensing with "an old form of government which has existed from the earliest ages, in which the ruling power has been under the control of hereditary chiefs, and handed down from generation to generation" and created an elected Advisory and Business Committee of twelve men. Twenty-three men had been nominated, and the top twelve were selected. In the pamphlet published memorializing this transition, photos and short biographies of the new committee were appended to the narrative and documentary account of the process. Each began with the phrase "Is a full-blood," or "Is a mixed-blood," and there were six of each although not by explicit design, thus pointing to the political makeup of the total community at Bad River.[24]

The allotment process created vocal divisions. In the fall of 1909, the US Senate Committee on Indian Affairs came to the hinterland and interviewed Indian people about its implementation. It was apparently motivated by the frequency of complaints from the reservation concerning who was getting allotted and who was getting what lands, their quality varying considerably. James Blackbird, son of a treaty signatory and now a member of the new governing committee, testified as to the political makeup of the Bad River Reservation by identifying which chiefs and their followers belonged there, and he registered his doubts about St. Croix people.

At that time, several hundred St. Croix band members were living landless and roaming in poverty a hundred miles to the southwest. They no longer had access to their usual and accustomed locations for purposes of hunting, fishing, and gathering because of white settlements. Worse, they did not receive a reservation in the 1854 treaty. The agent at LaPointe appears to have been genuinely moved by these people's circumstance having spent four years in St. Croix county as undersheriff and then sheriff.[25]

Chief Blackbird articulated his reasons for excluding these Indians from Bad River and voiced what he considered to be an ancient principle of inclusion. "We were given to understand that we were all separate bands, and we were given to understand that if any Indians should come and settle with us outside of our band that we could give them lands, if they so desired, but we did not agree to give them any lands for the reason that they have not settled with us and that they are living separate and apart from us . . . It was the custom of our forefathers and it is the custom today."[26]

To understand the significance of Blackbird's opinion and the conflict, we turn to a document generated twenty years later. In the late 1930s, an anonymous entry titled "Chief Ya Banse" in the WPA Chippewa Historical Project that employed Bad River tribal members, sheds light on the significance of this conflict. According to the account, Ya Banse, the leader of this group, had signed six treaties and was "a very able warrior, courageous, shrewd, cunning, aggressive and a natural leader with oratorical abilities." As he was said to be responsible for "the massacre of the Sioux in the vicinity of our Solon Springs"[27] (about forty miles west of Bad River), the sense that Bad River's historic security was owed to him and his people must have been a widely held memory among the Bad River leadership in the early twentieth century and the source, therefore, of considerable ambivalence about including his band at Bad River.

Over four hundred people at Bad River signed a petition to the commissioner of Indian affairs opposing enrolling St. Croix Indians and endorsing earlier legislation taking the age limits off the allotments in order to enfranchise their children. Special Agent Downs had produced the objectionable roll. He, too, was sympathetic to the plight of the landless, marginalized Ojibwe Indians living on the east side of the St Croix River, referred to as "Rice Indians" by Bad River chief Blackbird, cleverly othering these people. Bad River leaders testified that though they valued building up the population of the reservation, that didn't mean granting allotment to people who didn't reside amongst them.[28] Subsequently, a committee appointed by the tribal leaders ratified the addition of several hundred local people for purposes of allotment. Notably, the committee was made up of both full- and mixed-blood men.

Chiefs and Headmen versus the Progressives

By 1913, the conflict between mixed bloods and chiefs was more rancorous, and the issue of what to do about the yet-to-be-allotted qualified members led to a proposed piece of legislation. It would authorize the sale of the merchantable timber on the unallotted lands of the reservation. The proceeds derived were to be credited to the accounts of the unallotted members of the band, who would then be allotted land. In the debate over whether or not to endorse this legislation, putative memory of the mixed-blood provision of the treaty signed, now six decades earlier, emerged in speeches given by two of the chiefs. George Messenger spoke against the legislation, concluding his remarks, "What the chiefs say is true, the half breeds have been given their portion, the scrip." James Doolittle added that that while the mixed bloods received "lands outside the reservation," some "came in and settled with the Indians" and we "looked at the half breed and took pity on him and divided some of his land that he was going to give to his children," thus fully enfranchising him, "when the half breed showed his intention of settling here."[29] Indeed, the community would agree to send a delegation to Washington made up of members from each faction and reflective of the political constitution of the recently created Advisory and Business Committee.

The mixed-blood editors of *The Odanah Star* took a strong position on the St. Croix Ojibwe, a group they referred to as "renegade Chippewas" and a "Lost Tribe." In their first article about the issue, the newspaper reported the St. Croix to number five thousand. How anyone could have found that number of Indian people living only one hundred or so miles away remotely credible is hard to imagine. Nonetheless, even if the estimate was taken to be one of the frequent typographical mistakes by the newspaper, and assumed to be five hundred, this would have alarmed their largely mixed-blood readership. The newspaper also suggested that they were mostly mixed bloods and had "left their tribe" before the 1854 treaty. This would have weakened their claim on Bad River. The editors placed the responsibility for the St. Croix's unfortunate circumstances on the St. Croix themselves, assuring readers that there was "no deep seated ill feeling" between Bad River and St. Croix, but that they "looked with envy upon the fortunate members of the regular tribes who have drawn rich allotments."[30]

Nonetheless, a month later, the new roll was completed, and it included the St. Croix. The editors let it fly, saying that "some who appear on the list are illegal . . . others ignored . . . a bungling job. . . . a grave justice has been done . . . the present roll is ROTTEN TO THE CORE" (caps in original). [31] A month after this diatribe, the paper claimed that these Indians were members of the Chief Buck or Ai-Yaw-Banse band (a Lac Court Oreilles chief who signed the 1854 treaty), thus implying that if they were eligible for allotments anywhere it was at Lac Courte Oreilles and not Bad River since they "live as well as the white neighbors with whom they have intermarried."[32]

The issue of legitimate membership in the community was again dealt with several years later, in 1919, when the community held another rather contentious meeting. The main issue was whether or not to replace the advisory and business committee that the chiefs and headmen now came to see as usurping their treaty-grounded authority. By now, a faction of mixed bloods calling themselves "Progressives" dominated the committee.

The meeting was so contentious that procedural issues took up the first part of it as the group rejected the first three nominees to act as interpreters. When the meeting finally got started, Chief James Blackbird—in the habit of shaping agendas for decades—evoked the Treaty of 1854, noting it did not authorize a business committee. A mixed-blood woman responded: "We do not want to live like an Indian, we want to live like white people, we want to follow the ways of the white people, we do not want to follow the Indian."[33] Another said that nothing in the treaty authorizes the chiefs and headmen to "control the affairs of our tribe now or in the future."[34] There was an accusation that the chiefs were hoarding allotments: "We do not want Chiefs, every chief had two or three eighties, I can prove that, my husband saw the books," one woman charged. The very constitution of the band was at stake. William Obern, self-described mixed blood and elected interpreter for the meeting, called for a change of the guard motivated by the necessity of recognizing that old political forms were no longer efficacious:

> We looked upon the full breed Indians as our friend, they took us in when the white man did not. We inherited the white and Indian traits of our parents, but as a rule the Indian side of our relation took better care of us than the white side of our parents, that is our white parents. As a rule the white parent abandoned his children and the Indian women has taken care of them, what we get here, we get through our Indian blood, and it is quite natural we would be in sympathy with them, we do not want them to be put out, but we have come to a point where we must organize ourselves as the white man has. We must meet the white man, and battle with him, shoulder to shoulder with his own tools and his own methods. We have come to a time when we cannot do business as we did 40 or 50 years ago. Conditions have changed.[35]

A particularly hot set of exchanges over this issue of proper governance took place over two days. Tribal member Reverend Philip Gordon, the first American Indian ordained by the Catholic Church in the United States and the last president of the Progressive Era's Society of American Indians, challenged the octogenarian Chief Blackbird to show him where the treaty gives the chiefs the right to "direct the affairs of the reservation," a copy of which the priest had in front of him. Blackbird responded by recounting his memory of the treaty conference nearly seventy years earlier and concluding that "the Chief was to make his home on that reservation and rule and look after the affairs belonging to the reservation and that whoever wants to make a petition for [sic] the behalf of the Band residing on what lands has already been laid aside is to make petition to the Agent."[36] Here he was allying traditional power with the federal government.

Gordon denied that such matters were dealt with at the time of the treaty and held the written text of the treaty as proof. The symbolism is hard to miss: competing conceptions of authority and history, with actual eye (or ear) witness manifested in memory and narrated publicly on the one hand, and an official government text written in English on the other. The following day, Gordon escalated his rhetoric analogizing the rule of the chiefs and headmen on the reservation to the rule of the recently defeated Kaiser in Germany, with whom the United States had recently fought a war. Bad River had sent forty or fifty young men as part of the effort. Gordon suggested that the Congressional Committee on Indian Affairs should judge the competency of the current tribal leadership on the reservation, here, perhaps, evoking the language of the 1906 Burke Act that enabled trust and patent holders to be declared competent and capable for purposes of selling their land.[37]

Progressives and conservatives were polarizing. Immediately, millions of dollars in payments and policy regarding who was eligible for allotments was at stake. In the longer run, it was a debate about whether gerontocracy or democracy was a more desirable form of government. The conflict was stated quite explicitly by the chairmen of the Business Committee, mixed-blood James Denomie: "The committee has usurped some of the authority of the Chiefs and Headman, but I want to say that what they usurped, they usurped legally. It was by motion of the Council held on the 25th of June [1907], and concluded on the 15th of July that gave them the right and authority to usurp that authority."[38]

Denomie also addressed the long-festering issue of what to do about the fact that more than five hundred people at Bad River were still waiting for allotments. It was well known that there wasn't enough unallotted land to grant each an eighty-acre tract. Denomie went so far as to accuse the chiefs and headmen of claiming that the reservation's very borders were incorrect. He charged that they "have given out the impression *for the purpose of obtaining a following* that this reservation is much larger than what it is now marked out to be"[39] (my emphasis). He accused the chiefs of trying to get the issue to the Court of Claims which would have the effect of increasing the numbers of people claiming land and holding up payments to tribal members, just like it had for the Cherokees recently.

Chief James Scott responded to Denomie by accusing him of fraud, and he mocked the mixed bloods' characterization of the chiefs and headmen: "They have always called the Chiefs and Headmen the ignorant class. They do not know anything. They are not capable of doing anything for the behalf of the people. That is the way that that intelligent class of people are calling the chiefs and headmen."

Mixed-blood interpreter, and full-blood sympathizer William Obern responded: "Well, all you people, you want lands, I do not blame you. I would give it to you, if I had it, but you cannot get blood out of a stone, you have got it. . . . We have these people coming in here from other reservations, to take money, coming in here for years, and expecting to get allotments here." This was an old theme.

Despite the attack on traditional authority, James Blackbird later articulated the place of mixed bloods or "these half breeds," as he referred to them, reiterating the criteria for community membership, actual blood notwithstanding and pointing out their dependence upon each other:

> And I never make up any arguments against the mixed bloods, the half breeds, but it seems that the government has set records about mixed bloods in that ruling, which I refer to in 1854, and it is always hurting our mixed bloods whenever that question is raised from that Treaty. They do not like to listen to it, to be talked about, and we are not talking about it, because it is in the record, it is the action of our, of my father and the President. Now, ever since I have been taken by my fellow Indians as Chief and always looking back, *I see and like these half breeds and always welcome them and take them in and come here and reside with us, and I never tried to drive them away, but I always am glad to receive them and associate with them* . . . [if?] you take the mixed bloods on one side and the old full bloods standing on one side we would not be anywhere at all, if we done this. We always welcome them to come and sit with us and take rights on this reservation, and yet as you see, they call us foolish people, ignorant, not able to transact any affairs, we are not able to do anything for the behalf of the band.[40]

Despite the conflict, and as Blackbird's comments suggest, there was a public recognition that the full bloods and mixed bloods were bound to each other by their shared history, committed co residence, moral obligation, and the relatively recently appropriated category of race, as they all seemed to see each other as Indian. The traditional chiefs and headmen prevailed at this meeting as the outcome was to abolish the business committee, happily reported by Agent Everest in his report for the year as due to "a spirit of jealousy and rivalry."[41]

According to the bilingual mixed-blood William Obern, testifying at a hearing of the US House Committee on Indian Affairs in 1921, and who described himself as "in the real estate and brokerage business, and do[ing] considerable interpreting for the Indians before the courts and before other such places as they ask me to go, . . . the allotting question was almost solely in the hands of the Indian chiefs."[42] He is designated as Indian of 1/8 blood on the 1910 census, although he would represent himself as "about one-quarter" when he testified at the Senate Committee on Indian Affairs hearing the year before.[43]

The conflicts that motivated the House Committee hearing appeared to be between mixed bloods and full bloods, but it could not simply have been a matter of allotting full-bloods and denying mixed bloods. As of this date, there were 1063 Indians enrolled at Bad River, and only forty-six individuals were genealogical full-bloods, 358 were more than half, and 679 were half or less, according to Edgar B. Meritt, the assistant commissioner of Indian affairs.[44] That is, 96 percent of the people in this community had mixed family heritage.

Heritage itself was not the difference that made a difference per se, but rather cultural orientation similar to and perhaps even influenced by the contemporaneous situation at White Earth, an issue that drew national attention. This is suggested by the relationship between Antoine Denomie and Henry Ashmun, Bad River tribal members who published *The Odanah Star,* and Gus Beaulieu, who at the same time was publishing the *Tomahawk* at White Earth. The *Star* occasionally ran reprints of articles that appeared in the *Tomahawk.* Ashmun and Beaulieu both attended the 1914 Society of American Indians annual meeting in Madison—only open to Indians—all three identifying themselves as Chippewa.[45]

This genealogical heterogeneity was also reflected in the surnames in the reservation communities at the time. The 1910 US Census for the Bad River Reservation[46] reveals that of the 223 households in which it was possible to designate last names as French, Indian, or Anglo-American, about 35 percent were French or originally French, 38 percent were Anglo-American, and 25 percent were Anishinaabeg. At the nearby Red Cliff Reservation, 60 percent of the fifty-four households were French or originally French, 21 percent Anglo-American, and 16 percent Anishinaabe. The Franconymic Lac du Flambeau community with 131 households had 16 percent French, 21 percent Anglo-American, and 61 percent Aninshinaabeg. In all three cases, some of those Anglo-American names were translations of Indian names or had been adopted by Indian people for tactical reasons and obscure their parentage as a result.

At the 1921 US House of Representatives hearing, Assistant Commissioner Merritt also testified that there were two factions on the Bad River Reservation and they had been fighting for fifteen to twenty years over who should be on the rolls.[47] As Melissa Meyer found at White Earth,[48] the factions were not really organized by blood quantum. Instead, these factions represented their difference from political foes by using the idiom of blood given its rhetorical power in the ears of community members and the federal agents, the latter quite sympathetic, if not fully committed, to the racialist idea that the more white blood that ran in one's veins the more one was capable of assimilating civilized ways, managing one's own affairs, especially for purposes of imagining land's exchange value.

At the same time, the Bad River band had sent a delegation to Washington and had their secretary testify to the House Committee. The letter signed by "members of the La Pointe Band of Chippewa Indians and ex-soldiers of the World War"—signaling their patriotism—and authorizing the Washington delegation. It was signed by twenty-two service veterans, ten of whom bore Franconyms, such as Soulier, Gordon (an Anglicization of Gaudin), Cadotte, La Fernier, Pero (from Perrault), and Rabideax. According to William Obern, the group raised the funds for the trip by making promises to contributors that their investment would be repaid many fold taking advantage of naïve people's hopes. He alleged that the faction sought to open a recently closed roll for purposes of gaining more allotments for individuals, often from other Ojibwe communities, allegedly denied the same in their own communities.[49]

Blackbird's Memories and the Political Aspirations of the Full-Bloods

Those very chiefs to whom William Obern referred apparently met regularly as there is a partial record of several meetings that took place in January and February in 1920 that addressed allotment and membership as well as a number of other issues.[50] This was the leadership of the full-blood faction, and it included the following individuals: Chief James Blackbird, Chief Joseph Current, Chief James M. Scott, Headman Joe Stoddard, Chief Antoine Jocko, Headman Geo. Starr, Headman Antoine Kebec, Headman John Frost, Headman Frank Whitebird, Headman John Shebiosh, John Carpenter, Headman John Diver, Horace Greeley, and Ed Haskins.

JAMES BLACKBIRD

Is one of the hereditary chiefs of the La Pointe Band. Is a full-blood and was born near the falls of the Bad River on the reservation in 1837 and has always lived there; he is a son of MAW-CAW-DAY-PE-NAY-SE, who was spokesman for his people at the negotiation of the treaty at La Pointe, Wis., September 30, 1854; he is a man of integrity and large influence among his people; the owner of several dwellings in the village on the reservation; and has and lives on an eighty acre farm all improved; cuts and markets from his farm upwards of 75 tons of tame hay each year; he is and has been a faithful follower of Christianity of the Catholic faith since early manhood.

Photograph 7.1. Chief James Blackbird. Rev Thomas, "full-blood" pastor of the Methodist Church at Odanah since 1897 appears to be responsible for compiling the *Proceedings of La Pointe Band* in 1907 documenting the transition from a tribal council to an elected council. The publication included photos and biographies of the twelve men elected.

Many of the patronyms are still present at Bad River to this day. In fact, the tribal administrative center is named after Chief Blackbird. Indeed, much of the thirty-three-page document records Chief James Blackbird's recollection of the Chippewa negotiators' understanding of the Treaty of 1854. He had been present at the deliberations when he was in his teens and likely was being groomed for political leadership by his father and others.[51] Ten years before, he had testified that although he didn't fully understand what was going on at the 1854 treaty council, "What I heard in our own wigwam where my father used to come and talk the matters over, that I understood thoroughly well."[52] The issues that appear in the records of the meetings at Blackbird's home also include the dispute about the establishment and survey of the borders of the Bad River Reservation, the political organization of the Lake Superior Bands of Chippewa, the cooperation between the chiefs and the federal government regarding criminal jurisdiction, the liquor problem and the establishment of Indian police, visits to Washington DC during the Lincoln and Garfield administrations, and the legal status of the "Half breeds."

At a February 3, 1920, meeting at the home Chief James Blackbird, attended by three other chiefs and six headmen, their anonymous non-Indian amanuensis recorded the following regarding what Blackbird remembered of what was said about those of mixed blood at the time of the 1854 treaty. Note how he uses a specific attribution style that gives his memory credibility as to the source:

> The opening statement was made between the Acting Commissioners for the United States Government to Chief Buffalo, acting chairman in behalf of the LaPointe Bad River Band of Lake Superior Chippewa Indians, and the ruling agreed upon in regard to the status of those of mixed blood (half-breeds, quarter-breeds, one-eighth and all of only part Chippewa blood) that they were not to have any rights whatever within the reservation, as to allotment of tribal land, but that the United States government would pay those of mixed blood $90,000 and furnish them with agricultural implements, household furniture, carpenter tools, etc., and permit them to select 80 acres of land anywhere in the ceded Chippewa Territory, outside the reservation, to each who was then a head of a family in 1854 and each young man then 21 years of age, and patents issued to them for the same in the usual form.

The figure of $90,000 comes up repeatedly over the course of the second half of the nineteenth and into the first couple of decades of the twentieth centuries. The exact figure does appear in the Treaty of 1854 but in reference to a payment made to the chiefs. It reads: "The United States will also pay the further sum of ninety thousand dollars, as the chiefs in open council may direct, to enable them to meet their present just engagements." James Blackbird's father, who spoke publicly at the 1855 payment, clearly indicated at the time that he understood that it was money intended for the chiefs to pay their debts to the traders.[53] Since a number of the traders were, in fact, mixed-blood people, and the $90k was to pay debts to those traders, I will speculate that this provision for the mixed bloods was condensed in memory over the decades. The conflation also works to make the claim that the forebears of the people who this faction sought to exclude have already been compensated.[54]

Perhaps more strikingly, he claims to remember the mixed bloods rather negatively: "not to have any rights whatever within the reservation," and allotted outside of it. His memory contrasts strongly with the agent's letter written immediately after the treaty negotiations, wherein the chiefs insisted on consideration for "our relations," which I discussed extensively in chapter 5. Can this difference be reconciled by recognizing that mixed bloods weren't what they used to be six-and-half decades earlier?

James Blackbird continued: "Moreover, the agreement was entered into, and the ruling made that any Indian woman of the band, intermarrying with those of mixed blood who has a script [sic] or married to a white man, their children would forfeit their right within the band to tribal property forever."

The problem of white men marrying into the band was not the same problem in 1854 that it was three and four decades later during the allotment period with so much valuable property at stake. There were far more whites living in close proximity when the allotment policy was being implemented, often taking Indian wives to get access to their property. Claiming that the issue of Indian women marrying mixed bloods or whites was a problem in the mid-nineteenth century, when the treaty was negotiated and that it was discussed as part of the negotiations is not credible to me. It is one of the reasons why I believe the memories recounted at this and other meetings at Blackbird's home are best thought of as aspirationally legislative.

I also find it hard to believe that the implementation of the allotment provision was extensively discussed during the treaty negotiations. There was no mention of it in treaty commissioner Gilbert's letter of transmittal to the commissioner of Indian affairs.[55] The reservation policy, after all, was a new idea at the time and allotting parcels within them to individuals, although provided for in the treaty in Article 3, likely seemed abstract and remote. Bad River wasn't even surveyed for almost ten years after the treaty was signed.[56]

What we are seeing here is authority being constituted and consolidated. The power of the chiefs and headmen was waning and being contested, although they could still draw upon the authority of their witness and fluency in what everyone understood to be traditional cultural matters. The power of the progressives was on the ascent. The dislocations created by the implementation of the allotment policy provided a motivation for this consolidation of legal opinion.

Mixed bloods who had attempted to mobilize the eighty-acre provision were retrospectively marked as a class, now seen as morally equivalent to white men, and therefore presumptively suspect. Is it too crude to suggest that if the traditional faction at Bad River was seeking to exclude people making allotment claims, then one tactic might be to disqualify them as opportunists and scrip-taking, patent-selling mixed bloods whether or not, in fact they were? Was this a way to smear the so-called mixed-blood progressive political opposition? The last scrip was issued in 1870, fifty years before this meeting at Blackbird's home. The youngest scrip-taking reservation-allotment seeker in 1920 would be over seventy years old. I find it unlikely that these few septuagenarians were either seeking allotments or were the targets of this allegation.

By this point, quite a few of the descendants of those individual mixed bloods "belonging to the Lake Superior Chippewa" who received scrip and patents in 1858 were already part of the community, and they had been allotted on the Bad River Reservation. And at least John Carpenter—one of the headmen listening to Blackbird's recitation—is included in that group as his forebear Alexis's patent was part of La Pointe Iron Company's landed capital. There were many others.

Marie, Carl, and Paul Soulier took eighty-acre parcels under the mixed-blood provision of the treaty. The lands were located for them in the Penokees and then alienated. Paul and Marie were husband and wife, in possession of $600 worth of real estate and $100 in his personal estate. Presumably, some of that money came from the sale of the eighty-acre parcel in 1858. He was a laborer from Canada and appears on the 1877 tribal roll. His wife is designated as Indian on the census of 1860, although she had been an eligible mixed blood. They had nine living children; Michael, Antoine, Francois, Suzette, Angelique, William, Paul, Marie, and Rosalie. William appears on the 1910 census as a man in his early fifties, very likely the son of Paul. He is working as a rafter and is widowed living at Bad River. He has a son, also William, born in the mid-1880s. Both father and son had allotments on the Bad River Reservation. Eight other Souliers had allotments at Bad River as well.[57]

John Baptiste Denome was one of the mixed bloods who had an eighty-acre allotment located for him in the Penokees, and today the land is within the borders of Copper Falls State Park. Denome was born in 1835 and had seven siblings,[58] giving rise to the extended Denomie family, many of whom would settle upon the Bad River Reservation. At least thirty-nine different Denomies held patents in fifty-six different sections within six different townships on the Bad River Reservation under either the authority of the 1854 treaty or the Allotment Act.[59] In her book about Lake Superior Ojibwe labor history, Chantal Norrgard writes of the cultural and social significance of berry-picking in the early twentieth century by drawing extensively upon an essay written by Florina Denomie, working for the Bad River WPA project in the 1930s,[60] a small measure of the extent to which Denomies had become central to tribal life by this time. Denomie Creek is a well-known geographical feature on the reservation, having been named after John Baptiste Denomie, well-respected tribal diplomat who had an allotment through which the creek ran.[61]

Four Cadottes of the regionally famous and prominent Cadotte family took mixed-blood eighty-acre allotments that would be located in the Penokees in 1858. Antoine claims $100 as his total personal worth on the 1860 census. It may very well be the payment he got from La Pointe for his patent. Fourteen different Cadottes took a total of twenty-eight allotments on the Bad River Reservation typically taking a portion in 1919 and then another in 1924.[62] These appear to be the former group's children and grandchildren, or certainly collateral descendants. Likewise, Joseph Vasseur took a mixed-blood allotment that was patented on June 10, 1858, like so many others in the Penokee Iron Range. Later, he would receive two noncontiguous forty-acre patents on the Bad River Reservation itself. In 1910, a descendant was living unmarried in his fifties on the Bad River Reservation.[63]

Having ancestors who took mixed-blood scrip and received unrestricted allotments in the Penokees or elsewhere for that matter, only to lose them in short order, did not categorically exclude these people nor their descendants from being considered as members of reservation communities. As such, they qualified to be allotted thereon because the qualification for membership was a social commitment, rather than blood, just like it had always been.

Indeed, the attorney general of the United States had weighed in on this matter, addressing himself to the question as to whether or not Sioux mixed bloods who had received scrip, an individual property under the 1830 treaty, were precluded from the full benefits of tribal membership. He wrote, "Half-breeds residing with their tribes have, as a general rule, always been regarded as Indians, and even whites adopted by the tribes have been regarded as Indians so far as property rights are concerned . . . It is well settled that an Indian may hold individual property under treaty allotment and at the same time rejoin her [sic!] tribe without objection, so far as the United States is concerned."[64] So, despite the ascendency of a racialized conception of group membership generally held among the settlers, the federal government acquiesced in the indigenous conceptions of belonging and difference.

The assistant commissioner's data on blood quantum, the rough surname survey presented above, and these genealogies indicate that Bad River, as well as all of the other reservations in the region, already included many descendants of that class of mixed bloods as fully enfranchised members of their tribal communities. Nonetheless, the push of white settlement and the pull of allotment was generating enough social insecurity to motivate some members to base their criteria of inclusion and exclusion in the treaty and rehearsing the distinction between community members and so-called "half-breeds." The language reflected the diffusion of the dominant society's racialist thinking, but the substance was political. This conflict was taking place even as community members with French surnames and Ojibwe surnames married each other at rates that indicate that the distinction was insignificant. I will return to this point after contextualizing the concern over marital property.

James Blackbird continued his account, including specific attribution, of all that transpired regarding these particular matters at the proceedings of the Treaty of 1854:

> *Moreover, the open statement was made by Acting Commissioner in the United States Government, and the chiefs of the Lake Superior Chippewa and to Chief Buffalo, acting as chairman in behalf of the Lake Superior Chippewa Indians and the agreement entered into:*
>
> If an Indian man belonging to the Lake Superior Chippewa of the LaPointe-Bad River Band marries a Chippewa Indian woman or half breed Chippewa woman, from another reservation who is without land, the woman by marriage is adopted with the band wherein her husband belongs, and the children of said marriage are also adopted within said father's band inasmuch as they are of his blood; but if the Indian woman has already been allotted in her home reservation or by script has received land, she herself is not entitled to allotment with her husband's reservation, but is adopted within the band,—but her children are entitled to allotment, inasmuch as they are of their father's blood. Moreover if a Chippewa Indian of the Lake Superior LaPointe-Bad River band marries a white woman, she by her marriage is adopted within the band of her husband, is not entitled to allotment, but her children are entitled to allotment, as they are of their father's blood.

This provision would codify the ascendency of the patriarchy that came with holding property in severalty. Again, from the perspective of 1854, as almost no land would be allotted for nearly three decades, this provision is more proposed legislation for the 1920s than recollection of the 1850s. There could not have been talk of scrip as the mechanism by which land would be located and patented at the treaty negotiations in September of 1854 because the method of administering this provision was not settled upon until two years later.

Blackbird continued, repeating his formulaic introductory statement:

> *Moreover, the open statement was made by the Acting Commissioner for the United States Government and the Chiefs of the Lake Superior Chippewa Indians and to Chief Buffalo, acting as Chairman*

> *on behalf of the Lake Superior Chippewa of the LaPointe-Bad River band, and the ruling made,*
>
> If a Chippewa woman of the LaPointe band marries a Chippewa Indian or Half breed Chippewa outside the Reservation, who have not been allotted within their reservation or by script [sic] received land from the Gov't, when he enters the Lapointe-Bad River Reservation if he be of good moral character, not a disturber of the peace and wellfare [sic] of the Band, when the question of allotment comes up, he may become adopted by the will of the Chiefs and Headmen and the members of the Band, and so voting and consenting in open council of the Band, he may be allotted; but if he be not of good character, a disturber of the peace and well fare [sic] of the band, he shall not be adopted or enrolled for allotment.

Here the chiefs appropriate for themselves the power to create kinship relations and citizens, that is, to adopt members. A power that had always belonged to families would now be a tribal governmental prerogative. Something similar to this took place in Cherokee Country nearly two centuries before with the emergence of a central government that usurped clan authority to adjudicate disputes and punish wrongdoers.[65]

Allotment not only drew St. Croix Chippewa and mixed bloods from various locations to Bad River, but it also changed the status of Indian women, making them desirable marriage partners of white men. Blackbird articulated the concern:

> If a Chippewa Indian woman marries a white man, he has no rights within the band nor his children inasmuch as they are of his blood. However, if a Chippewa Indian woman marries a Half breed Chippewa from without the Band, who becomes adopted and is allotted, he is not entitled to a voice in council, or to participate in the affairs of the Band. He must remain a good character, protecting the rights and well being of the Band who has received him. But if [he] becomes an immoral character, or a disturber of the peace and well being of the band, in any tribal affair, the Chiefs and Headmen will sit in Council with a representative of the Federal Government or Indian Agent so called, and the Federal Representative or Indian Agent will be so instructed by the Chiefs and Headmen to remove such person in question from the reservation after the charges are heard and proved against him. Any member of the Band, who is of bad character,

> or a disturber of the peace and well-being of the Band, or tribal affairs, upon the [unreadable] of the Chiefs and Headmen to the Federal Representatives or Indian Agent, shall be removed from the Reservation. Also any white man who shall disturb the peace or well being of the Band, being of bad character, shall be removed by Federal authority from the Reservation by the [unreadable] of the Chiefs and Headmen."

At this point, the right that Chippewa Indian women and their families had been exercising for two centuries in marrying non-Indians, first working-class French voyageurs, then mixed-blood men, and incorporating them as kin was now subject to the approval of a ruling council, further consolidating their power. Ethnic confrères from other Anishinaabeg communities could be assimilated as second-class tribal citizens only by the direct action of the chiefs and headmen. They were also claiming the right to command the enforcement capacity of the federal government, which was indicative of the cooperative governance being envisioned. This alliance was just the sort of consolidation of power that figures such as Antoine Denomie, Henry Ashmun, and John Morrison—prominent early twentieth-century Bad River Reservation mixed-blood, progressive citizens—were so critical of in the pages of *The Odanah Star*. It was a political stance they paid for dearly as they would be banished from the reservation for several years.[66]

Blackbird continues beginning with his authorizing introduction:

> *Moreover the open statement was made by the Acting Commissioner on behalf of the United States Government, to the Chiefs and Headmen of the Lake Superior Chippewa Indians, and to Chief Buffalo of the LaPointe-Bad River Band, and Acting Chairman of the Lake Superior Chippewa Indians,* again and again, the agreement made, that the Chippewa Indians of the LaPointe-Bad River Band are the sole heirs of the LaPointe Bad River Reservation, which is theirs and to be theirs and their heirs forever.

Recall that two efforts in the early 1850s had been made to remove the Chippewa from Wisconsin into Minnesota. In exchange for ceding their lands on the north shore of Lake Superior—where the Mesabi Iron Range would soon be discovered—they were guaranteed that they would not have to remove west of the Mississippi. The passage focuses on the term "sole heirs" and the highlighted "again and again" (underlined in the original), and emphasizes that the resident dominant band's leadership was asserting its authority to interpret the meaning of the phrase in the treaty regarding the creation of the reservation, to wit: "For the La Pointe band, and such other Indians as may see fit to settle with them."[67] The leadership group was asserting its right to be legislating matters of belonging and difference, inclusion and exclusion, validated by the federal government speaking "to the Chiefs and Headmen."

At his home, on February 12, at the last meeting for which there are minutes, Blackbird opined on the meaning of that phrase in the treaty:

> This clause "such other Indians" does not mean white men, half breeds or persons of part Indian blood, but does mean only full-blooded Indians of the Lake Superior Chippewa, not Mississippi Chippewas whose reservations are determined under some other treaty. Any full blooded Chippewa Head of Family, widow or young man, twenty-one years of age of the Lake Superior Chippewas, who is of good moral character, not a disturber of the peace and well fare of the Bad River-La Pointe Band, who has not been previously allotted on his own reservation or in the ceded Chippewa Territory, may be recognized by the Chiefs and Headmen of the La Pointe-Bad River Band in open Council of the band, only, and then may be allotted by the Chiefs and Headmen.

Note the collation of criteria excludes full-blooded Chippewas allotted in the ceded Chippewa Territory. However, only mixed bloods, or in Blackbird's terms, "half-breeds" were allotted in the ceded Chippewa Territory. The provision indicates that "full-blooded" could only have meant someone with no non-Indian forebear in anyone's living memory. And "half-breed," a person whom the group remembered as having a non-Indian forbear, likely an American in the first ascending generation. I read this as another dimension of the full-blood faction drawing upon putative history and tradition to delegitimize the mixed-blood progressives.

Finally, Blackbird paints a detailed portrait of the proper relationship between the mixed bloods and full bloods that was allegedly envisioned six decades earlier:

> *Moreover, the open statement was made by the Acting Commissioner for the U.S Government* to the half breeds and those of part Chippewa blood dwelling among the LaPointe-Bad River Band, granting them the privilege of choosing their 80 acre script [sic] land west of the LaPointe-Bad River Reservation and laying out their holdings in adjoining eighties, there farming a rectangular block of land—this land west of the Bad River-LaPointe reservation

> was as well timbered as the Bad River reservation. Those of the half-breeds who designated their acceptance were given a slip of paper by the Acting Commissioner with their name thereon and the statement that they were entitled to 80 acres therein stated, and all they had to do was file on their eighty acres and receive their patents at once. Some of them took these slips and peddled them out among the white people, for sale for $10 or $15 or $25 ~~or for a few quarts of liquor~~. [crossed out in the original] They also received $100 per head.

Blackbird's memory acknowledges the presence of "half-breeds" at the 1854 treaty proceedings, and though none signed that treaty unlike previous treaties, several mixed bloods did act as interpreters and a number were traders who received compensation for debts. Furthermore, the chiefs and headmen in 1920 interpreted the intent of the mixed-blood treaty provision and imagined a separate mixed-blood agricultural community with "adjoining eighties, there farming a rectangular block of land" and of equal value to the land on the reservation being "as well timbered." The chiefs at Blackbird's home were imagining a kind of mixed-blood annex to the reservation community. It is also notable that only a subset of these mixed bloods took the scrip option indicating the current leadership's awareness of the gradations of commitment individuals had to the tribal collective, as well as mixed-blood interest and capacity to live in this new fashion. They were not "given a slip of paper by the Acting Commissioner" at the time of the signing of the treaty, and it was certainly not the case that "all they had to do was file on their eighty acres and receive their patents at once."

As I have shown, the process of implementing the mixed-blood provision of the treaty took nearly four years. Blackbird's recollection condenses an administrative process for the moral force of the claim and was a means of setting apart a class within the tribal population. And no doubt, these gathered chiefs and headmen had certain families in mind. An even smaller subset of mixed bloods allegedly squandered their right. Those who "received $100 per head" were the ones who got the market value from people like Julius Austrian and others who had gained power of attorney and then located the lands in the Penokee Hills along the Iron Range. But even many of these people and their descendants had been fully enfranchised at Bad River by this time.

Blackbird specifies the status of mixed bloods, honoring past practice of sharing annuities with them, but excluding them from eating from the "tribal dish," a metaphor for the tribal capital of land. He starts with his attributional authorizing formula again:

> *The agreement was further made between the Acting Commissioner in behalf of the United States Gov't and the Chiefs and Headmen of the Lake Superior Chippewa Indians*, and Chief Buffalo acting as Chairman in behalf of the Lake Superior Chippewa Indians, that the half breeds dwelling with the La Pointe-Bad River Band, should receive annuities for a period of twenty years, after which there should be no further payment made to them, as they had no right within the Reservation or to any further share of tribal property . . . [they have] the right to eat out of the "annuity dish"—but were not entitled to a share of the tribal property—or reservation property of the Band, nor entitled to eat out of their "tribal dish"—before or after the annuities were paid, and therefore are not entitled to allotment.

This was another attempt to demote certain families to the status of second-class tribal citizens since they would have "no right" nor "any further share." And although they were not being expelled, their applications for allotments were clearly unwelcome. The chiefs and headmen had exercised this power more than twenty years earlier when they evicted the aforementioned Antoine Denomie, who saw himself as a patriot contesting the power of the federal agents who were interfering in internal tribal governance.[68]

In her 1998 dissertation titled, *Newspapers and the Lake Superior Chippewa in the "Unprogressive Era,"* Patty Loew spends a full chapter on members of the Denomie family in the late-nineteenth and early twentieth centuries. By this time, they were a rather large, extended family. As educated mixed bloods, they were a threat to the autocratic government agents who were facilitating the transfer of different forms of Indian wealth into the hands of private business interests all in the alleged interest of civilizing tribal members. Antoine Denomie was particularly critical of what he saw as the agent's meddling in internal political affairs of the community. He may have also been critical of what he regarded as collusion between the home-grown gerontocracy and the federal agents. In 1897, he and thirty-seven other people referred to as mixed bloods were evicted from the reservation. After a stint in Alaska, Denomie returned to the reservation in 1905 and continued to agitate. He established *The Odanah Star* in 1912. Loew describes him as a "cultural broker" and a believer in Christianity, education, business, and commerce, although "at his core, he remained Indian."[69]

At the White Earth Reservation in Minnesota in 1915, just five years before this series of meetings at Bad River, *Ahbowegeshig*, a member of the so-called "full-blood" faction in that community, expressed the opinion that the half-breed scrip was given to the mixed bloods to "leave the tribe." As it would turn out, Edgar Merritt, assistant secretary of Indian affairs, did not share that interpretation, instead arguing in favor of recognizing that mixed bloods had always been recognized by both Indians and the federal government as part of the tribal community [70]

Blackbird, too, had an opinion about mixed bloods and their scrip which he expressed at that last meeting of chiefs and headmen: "After they had consumed up their script [sic] and annuities, these half breeds continued to come into the LaPointe-Bad River Reservation whenever they hear and there was to be an enrollment for allotment and by grant were allotted and continued to consume tribal property."

Blackbird's allegation is more rhetorical than substantive. It seems that the half-breeds who had taken the scrip, yet never left the La Pointe community, had by this time been reintegrated into the tribal community, or had never really been alienated from the community in the first place. Their taking scrip and selling the patent then, was a nonevent vis à vis fellow community members. As noted above, insofar as the very youngest of the scrip takers would already be in their midforties in the early years of allotment at Bad River in the early 1880s—and it should be noted that there were only about three hundred patents issued for allotments in all of the Wisconsin reservations combined by this time.[71] *All* blood degrees of Anishinaabeg persons from nearby communities making claims on Bad River were seen as the problem—especially people from St. Croix. Allotment of the reservations transformed the criteria of belonging.

With the exception of a few somewhat self-serving pages in Benjamin Armstrong's *Reminiscences of Life among the Chippewa*, there is no comparable, contemporary, published or archival record of the proceedings of the treaty of 1854 apart from Henry Gilbert's transmission letter.[72] It is difficult, therefore, to decide with confidence whether James Blackbird's memory from more than six decades before was as precise as this account suggests. The 1920 gatherings at his home appear to be efforts to legislate under the guise of recollecting these negotiations, especially with the current chief repeatedly evoking the authority of the revered Chief Buffalo. Rhetorically, the repetition of the opening phrase "*the Acting Commissioner on behalf of the United States Government, to the Chiefs and Headmen of the Lake Superior Chippewa Indians, and to Chief Buffalo of the LaPointe-Bad River Band, and Acting Chairman of the Lake Superior Chippewa Indians*," framing the recollections/provisions that followed, gives those putative memories authoritative status. In either case, the current, if also contested traditional leaders of the band in the early 1920s, appeared to be attempting to make law, coming to a consensus about the contours of the community that they desired and aspiring to constitute themselves as the legitimate government of the community in the face of mixed-blood political, progressive ascent.

In sum, the implementation of allotment caused the population of Anishinaabeg people living throughout the ceded territories to attend to what was taking place on the newly created reservations. As life on the ceded lands grew more precarious, as an increasingly binary model of society took hold with only "whites" and "Indians" on the landscape, the need for a source of income and the desirability of living within the borders of one of the reservations grew. This concentration of people and the transformation of a network organized by actionable kinship relationships that were not what they used to be was a very conflictual process. The new regime of private property exacerbated issues of both internal lines and external borders in the Bad River community. The result was that members fiercely debated how to govern the reservation and the ways in which it should articulate with the larger settler-colonial state.

Actual Marriage Patterns and the Decline of the Mixed-Blood/Full-Blood Distinction

Tracing the numerous descendants of the three-score mixed bloods whose lands were consolidated by aspiring iron ore companies, let alone the several hundred who had been patented by the time these companies filed their incorporation papers, is a task beyond my capabilities. Some of these persons decided to make the effort to pass for white and assimilate into the dominant society. Many others were assimilated to the reservation-centric communities receiving allotments of land in exchange for living amongst and committing themselves to kin. I don't think the effort to give a comprehensive account of all the cases would yield a pattern that can't be discerned using less energy and time-consuming methods. We first look to marriage patterns, therefore, as a measure of the actual decline of the significance of the social categories of "mixed blood" and "half-breed" and trace several exemplary genealogies.

In the first half of the nineteenth century, when the fur trade was still viable, it may be that mixed bloods married each other more often than they married people called "Indians." Cultural brokerage was marketable, and the conditions for a broader Métis ethnogenesis were still possible.[73] However, during the second half of the nineteenth century, when indigenous life was importantly shaped by the treaty economy, allotment, and lumbering, the fur-trade-based niche that had been dominated by the class of mixed bloods was no longer viable. With the increased presence of Anglo-Americans, and their racialist ideology shaping social dispositions, which included prescriptive endogamy, we should expect more marriages between what the Anglos called "mixed bloods" or "half-breeds" and full-blooded "Indian" people. In fact, this is just the pattern that emerges.

Between 1874 and 1907 in the Bad River community, this resulted in Blackbirds marrying Gauthiers, Mayottes, Neveaux, and Coutures. A Denomie would marry Gijigokwe, another Denomie, Naganab, and another, Anassigijig. A Bresette married a Cloud; a Frost, a Sharette; a Green married a Buffalo, another Green, a Whitefeather. John Kakagon married Margaret Decoteau. Frank LeClaire married Catherine Crow. Antoine Lemieux marred Katie Buffalo. Peter Marksman married Wa-sa-je-wa-no-kwa. And there are more in the 279 marriage registration records compiled by Fond du Lac Band of Lake Superior tribal member Michael Munnel in 1993, who created "this American Indian marriage directory."[74] Whether or not Munnell was explicitly interested in the issue of bloodedness is not clear, although he does call attention to the variety of terms referring to "Color of parties" used to describe these marriages listing "Red, Copper, Halfbreed, Mixed Blood, Indian Chippewa, etc."[75]

Bloodedness, as figured by non-Indians, is not predicting marriage choices. Because a great variety of community members adopted American names, we set these aside and only consider the marriages between people who bear names that are clearly French, Ojibwe, or direct translations in English such as Stone, Martin or Blackbird. This smaller sample yields a total of about ninety unambiguously French names and fifty Ojibwe names of people who married each other at Bad River during these years. There were forty marriages between people who bore Franconyms, twenty-four between people who had Ojibwe names, and twenty-five between people with Franconyms and Ojibwe names. If people married each other randomly, we would expect thirty-seven intra-French name marriages, forty mixed marriages, and eleven intra-Ojibwe name marriages.[76] Although there is a bias with more people with Ojibwe names marrying each other in this data set, these numbers fall within what we expect if people were marrying each other randomly.

"Color of parties," speaks to the increasing significance of race in the community. Over four-decades, the proportion of people who designate themselves—or are designated—as "Indian" on the marriage form who marry each other declines from half the recorded population in the first decade of 1874–84 to one-quarter in the decade between 1897 and 1907. Over the course of the total four decades, the most common description for these marriages is "mixed," or "Mixed White and Indian," for a total of ninety-seven (34 percent). This is followed by marriages between people who are both "Indian" or "Red," (eighty-two of 279, or 30 percent). A full 104 individuals of the 558 include "white" either in part or wholly how they are designated.

When the parties are racially designated individually, most of the "white" or "mixed white" are men. This reflects an interest on Indian women's part in accessing resources in the dominant society as well as white men's interest in the security of holding Indian land. There are thirty marriages described as "White and Indian," all but one contracted between 1891 and 1907, and twenty-three in the twentieth century, all pointing to the significance of allotment for the social makeup of the community. "Mixed" appears eighty-four times in the data. "Half-breed" appears only four times. I think "mixed" refers to people who have been mixed for generations and "half-breeds" to the offspring of recent Indian/non-Indian marriages, likely with Americans. It appears that with the increase of white Americans marrying into the community, the social distinction between mixed and full-blood Indians began to lose its significance, while at the same time, the distinction between progressives and traditionals was more sharply drawn.

Between 1936 and 1940, the WPA sponsored the Chippewa Indian Historical Project at the Bad River Reservation employing about a dozen tribal members who interviewed fellow tribal members and generated scores of documents on a great variety of historical, cultural, social, economic, and religious topics. Ben Morrison, a collateral descendent of Morrisons discussed earlier, addressed the topic of mixed bloods in "Scrip Act-Mixed Blood Chippewa Indians."[77] His short essay is presented in full:

> The full-blooded Indian always had a jealous disposition concerning those of mixed blood. This for one of several reasons, besides the lack of understanding each other, has caused a lack of harmony and even had feeling between the two classes.
>
> After the Declaration of Independence and even previous to the adoption of the Constitution by the United States, the Federal Government made treaties with the Indians.
>
> In the course of this treaty-making, the full-blooded Indians did not want the mixed bloods to have a voice in the matter concerning treaties. Their attitude led the Government to adopt a course of action to cope with the situation. Treaties that they made with the Indians about this time explicitly stated: the mixed bloods ~~are~~ were Indians and had a voice in matters of business the same as the full bloods. This proved to be a stumbling block to the full bloods.
>
> A percentage of mixed bloods had no desire of being bound by treaty stipulations which would herd them on any reservation, and because of this fact, the Scrip Act was passed which gave the mixed-blood Indians the privilege of taking their own choice of land on any public domain. Many of the latter availed themselves of this opportunity.
>
> By taking the Scrip claim they were barred from taking an allotment on any reservation. At any rate the Scrip Act, as it was

> understood, was equivalent to holding an allotment, but it did not in any way deprive the mixed-blood Indian or any Indian from taking a homestead. Therefore, many took advantage of this claim including my father and several others of the family. Father did not come within the meaning of the Scrip Act law, as he was one of the early allottees on the Bad River Reservation.

Writing from the perspective of a well-connected tribal member, although also a descendent of mixed bloods, Morrison notes the antagonism between mixed and full-bloods. And note his use of the term "class" to distinguish them. The provision of the treaty has now achieved the status of separate federal legislation in the form of "the Scrip Act," a measure of a change in legal historical consciousness. He represents the "act" as a kind of safety valve for disenchanted mixed-blood Indians whom the federal government wanted to be included within the indigenous polity. The claim that scrip-takers were barred from taking allotments on the reservation is contradicted in another account from the same WPA corpus.

In an account titled "Tom O'Connor," by John Condecon, we read of the failed attempt on an unnamed white man's part to get Tom O'Connor to quit claim his deed for an allotment in Duluth that he had gotten through "the half-breed scrip." He concludes the account with the following: "Mrs. Mary O'Connor, the wife of Tom O'Connor also possessed a scrip allotment in Duluth, which was situated on the top of the hill. She also had another allotment here on the reservation. It frequently happened in those days, that Indians were inadvertently given two allotments."[78]

In one sentence, implying bureaucratic inefficiency, the author has plausibly solved the riddle of how it could be that "Indians" who were beneficiaries of the 1854 mixed-blood treaty provision could also become or always had been full members of the reservation polity and yet receive allotments on the reservations. The tone of this document from the 1930s suggests that the mixed blood/full-blood distinction was now archaic and had lost traction in the community, especially as the region attracted more and more non-Indians, creating an enclave of indigenes surrounded by settlers. At the same time, the Indian Reorganization Act passed while this historical project was running. It defined Indians as members of tribes, their descendants living on reservations and others who are one-half or more Indian not living on reservations,[79] thus fully enfranchising resident reservation community members despite blood quantum. All three Bad River tribal members who certified the adoption of the constitution and bylaws under the IRA identified themselves as mixed bloods on the 1930 census,[80] an index of the progressive mixed-blood factions' consolidation of power in the community.

The Long-Term Legacy

In the long run, the descendants of the mixed bloods considered in the 1854 treaty became central figures on the reservations in the region. Twelve different people carrying the surname "Gauthier" took scrip under the Treaty of 1854,[81] and three of them held patents in the Penokees for a short period of time. More than a century and half later, their descendants going by Gokey, Gochee, and Guthrie are tribal members in one of the several Anishinaabeg communities in the western Great Lakes. At Lac du Flambeau, the Guthrie family played an important role in the early twentieth century in developing commerce in the community and in the late twentieth century, in taking the leadership in getting the band to build a tribal museum.[82]

In 1988, as the treaty rights conflict was coming to crescendo in northern Wisconsin, Lac du Flambeau community member, Professor Gail Guthrie Valaskakis of Concordia University in Montreal published an important essay in *Cultural Studies* that is an effort to historicize and decolonize conceptions of belonging and difference drawing upon then-recent new understandings of culture, narrative, and biography. Valaskakis implicitly addresses the capacity of indigenous culture and society to appropriate novelty in different registers.

> I knew that my great-grandmother moved past the Catholic altar in her house with her hair dish in her hand to place greying combings of her hair into the first fire of the day, securing them from evil spirits. And I knew that I was yoked to these people through the silence of ancient actions and the kinship of the secret. Later I realized that we were equally and irrevocably harnessed to each other and this Wisconsin reservation land through indigence, violence, and ulcerated exclusion, recoiling among outsiders and ourselves; and that I was both an Indian and an outsider.[83]

Valaskakis describes her great-grandparents as Christian half-breeds, he allotted at Lac Courte Oreilles, and she at Bad River, and she would testify at the 1910 hearings called by Senator LaFollette to address the problems created by allotment, timber contracts, and the monopoly held by the company store. Valaskakis's great-grandmother would also assist ethnographers Frances Densmore, Victor Barnouw, and A. I. Hallowell.[84] Valaskakis writes of the complexity of community identity "like the names, we were suspended between Christian ritual and Chippewa custom." Recognizing her forebears who married non-Indians in the last two generations, she writes, "Like many other since, my brother and I are living boundaries between the city and the reserve, the Chippewa and the outsider." Yet, "we are distinct, bound through common Chippewa grandfathers rooted to this place." And finally, "Colour, language, custom; schooling, dress, bloodlines; religion, craftsmanship, residence: all contribute to effervescent definitions of who is an Indian now."[85]

In assembling the list of mixed bloods eligible for payment under the 1837 treaty, Lucius Lyon took testimony from several hundred people at LaPointe. Three different related Gournons were found eligible, and one signed that treaty on behalf of the Red Lake Chippewa. Joseph Gournon accompanied a delegation to Washington in 1855. Fourteen people bearing versions of this surname took scrip under the 1854 treaty. Nearly a century later, nine Gurnoe families appear on the 1937 Indian census roll for the Red Cliff Reservation. The thirteen-year-old son of Edward Gurnoe would grow up to terminate the state of Wisconsin's authority to regulate Chippewa Indians fishing in Lake Superior by winning in the Supreme Court of Wisconsin that upheld the rights retained in the Treaty of 1854, thereby consolidating an Indian commercial fishing industry in the area.[86] The so-called Gurnoe decision in 1972 has become an icon of tribal sovereignty for Chippewa bands. Gurnoe's daughter, Rose, was tribal chair for a period of time in the 2000s. Gurnoe's kinsmen, Donald, was chief judge at Red Cliff from 2006 until his death in 2014.

Similarly, thirteen St. Germaines took scrip mobilizing the mixed-blood provision under the 1854 treaty,[87] yet none of them losing it through power of attorney to men seeking land in the Penokees, as far as we can tell. Spelling their name now with a "J" in favor of the "G," ten St. Jermains took allotments on the Lac du Flambeau Reservation in the first decade of the twentieth century under the authority of the General Allotment Act.[88] One of the two Josephs on the Chippewa Half Breed lists in the document produced by the 1874 congressional investigation is likely the grandfather of Thomas St. Germaine. Born in 1879, Thomas grew up in the Lac du Flambeau community during the period when it was being allotted and logged. He attended the Haskell Indian School and then studied law at Highland Park College in Des Moines, Iowa, and also at Yale. After a career playing football, St. Germaine would return to Lac du Flambeau in 1925 and would testify about the significance of the treaties at a Congressional Committee on Indian Affairs in 1929 that commenced a period of legal activism on behalf of tribal members.

Thomas St. Germaine was also a delegate to the Hayward Congress wherein regional Indian leaders met to discuss the proposed Indian Reorganization Act of 1934 that would recognize tribal sovereignty and transform community governance. He spoke of the importance of their rights to hunt, fish, and gather on the lands that were ceded in the treaties. He also litigated two cases in 1933 and 1940 involving treaty rights in the Wisconsin Supreme Court, and although he lost those cases, his advocacy maintained community consciousness of the importance of treaties with the federal government.[89] In 1939, he cofounded the Lac du Flambeau Commercial Club, which sought to chart development of the reservation in the areas of tourism, conservation, arts and crafts, and employment.[90] This initiative would facilitate the reproduction of a traditional way of life by commercial means.[91]

Thomas' grandnephew, Dr. Richard St. Germaine, who was born in a log cabin on the Lac Courte Oreilles Reservation, taught American History at the University of Wisconsin-Eau Claire and has authored a history of the reservation community. He also served as tribal chairmen several times in the 1970s and 80s and has been active on the Big Drum in his community. His brother, Ernie, was the chief judge of the Lac du Flambeau community for most of the 1990s. A founder of the American Birkebeiner—the largest cross-country ski race in North America in the early 1970s—an artist, and an educator, he, too is committed to the maintenance of traditional ways as well as *Anishinaabemowin*, the indigenous language. And yet traces of his distant mixed parentage linger in family stories.

As a boy, Ernie was visiting his grandparents' home. He told the story that as he and his grandfather walked out the door, his grandmother called out, "Shut the door!" and Grandpa said back, "I—love—you—too—honey." It would be years before Ernie understood that "Shut the door" sounds close enough to "J' ador" (I adore you) for Grandpa to respond the way he did. Of course, "I adore you," is "*Je vous adore*," in proper French. Was Grandpa speaking the local dialect? Was he teasing his wife? In any case, evoking this moment speaks to a creole heritage that has been fully indigenized.[92]

In the same vein, five people bearing the surname Dennis took half-breed scrip and were allotted eighty-acre parcels in several different townships. One of them was likely the parent of Antoine Dennis, who appears on the Bad River tribal roll in 1887. Milwaukee physician, outdoorsman and author Arthur Tenney Holbrook would memorialize Antoine Dennis in the pages of the *Wisconsin Magazine of History* subtitling his essay "Last of the Chippewa Mail Runners."[93] Holbrook would write of Antoine, " 'Me, I am born, you know in La Pointe,' began Antoine. 'My mother, she has French blood, yes sir; but my father she [sic] is full blood Chippewa,' " leaving us to conclude that despite that his father bearing the surname Dennis, indicative of mixed-blood origins, by the early twentieth century, he had been so fully assimilated into the reservation community, his son could credibly claim that it is only his mother's line that accounts for both his Franconyms.

At nearby Red Cliff, descending from one or more of the seven Defoes (Dufault) whose forebears took eighty-acre allotments under the mixed-blood provision of the treaty, Marvin Defoe, builds *jiimanag*—birchbark canoes—carrying on this ancient art and technology that was one of the critical conditions of the possibility of the fur trade.

Eight Corbines associated with La Pointe took scrip under the provision in the late 1850s and 60s.[94] Six Corbines received restricted patents for land on the reservations under the authority of either the 1854 treaty or the Allotment Act in the first two decades of the twentieth century.[95] Corbines have been in positions of leadership and responsibility at Bad River for decades. Dr. Joseph Corbine currently works in the health clinic as a counselor and serves as the chief judge for the community having been president of the tribal council in the 1980s.

The Newago name is prominent in the Red Cliff community. Louis Newago's X on a power-of-attorney document gave Julius Austrian the right to locate an eighty-acre parcel for him in 1858. Over a century later, in the mid-1980s, Thomas Newago, along with John Pero (Perrault) and John Lemieux, all three Bad River tribal members, sought to have their conviction for fishing in restricted waters overturned in the Appeals Court of Wisconsin. Their very effort indexes treaty rights activism that would ultimately succeed.

Another treaty rights activist at Red Cliff, Walter Bresette was a descendent of one or more of the nine Brisettes or Bresettes[96] who took scrip under the mixed-blood provision. A preeminent local intellectual during the treaty rights conflict of the 1980s, Bresette started the Lake Superior Greens and motivated the organization Witness for Non-Violence, a mostly non-Indian treaty rights support group that was a mediating presence at the protests on the boat landings from non-Indian anti-treaty-rights protesters. Bresette is the co-author of *Walleye Warriors: An Effective Alliance against Racism and for the Earth*, an account of the alliance formed in support of the exercise of off-reservation treaty rights in the 1980s and 90s.

Many examples of these Ojibwe leaders could be collated from Bad River, Red Cliff, Lac Courte Oreilles, St. Croix, Mole Lake, and Lac du Flambeau, as well as the tribal communities in Minnesota and Michigan. These Franconymic descendants of people who played mediating roles in the fur trade of the eighteenth and nineteenth centuries, and who were designated as "mixed bloods, belonging to the Lake Superior Chippewa," in the Treaty of 1854 were fully assimilated into the reservation-based tribal communities over the course of the late nineteenth and early twentieth centuries.

Nonetheless, the process of allotting the reservations exacerbated tensions between those mixed bloods and people whose Indianness was less contested. Some measure of the settler society's blood ideology referred to as "blood quantum" that underlays this distinction was also assimilated over the course of the late nineteenth and early twentieth centuries.

Yet, the legal force of the distinction and the power of that ideology was overcome by very long-standing conceptions and practices of belonging despite race becoming hegemonic in the settler society that surrounded this and other indigenous communities.

Conclusion

> Indian policy, as reflected in laws and treaties as well as in the hopes of men of good will of both cultures, was distorted cumulatively, a little at a time, by men in the field—businessmen, government officials, and Indians—who were willing to go beyond legal and traditional limits in order that they might pursue individual gain.[1]

Inawemaagen or "our relations," as they were called by Anishinaabe, "mixed bloods" and "half-breeds," as they were called by non-Indians, represented a class of indigenous person, typically integrated into the larger indigenous community by the obligations of kinship and marriage. In a version of Richard White's middle ground, wherein both Indians and non-Indians acquiesced in the other's categorization, these mixed bloods were considered and distinguished in several treaties in the region.

Explicitly included as part of the polity in earlier treaties with the Chippewa, in the Treaty of 1854 at La Pointe, they were made eligible for eighty-acre parcels of land that they would hold in fee simple, that is, in the same manner as United States citizens, though they were explicitly not citizens, but subjects. As such, they were liminal, sometimes a powerful status, almost always a dangerous one. People designated as mixed-blood Indians were simultaneously within and adjacent to the legal and political category of Indian. They were designated as mixed-blood Indians, yet they also were described as "belonging to" as if they were the possession of another entity from which they were separate and distinct. This ambiguous status left them vulnerable.

That status raises a question: How is it that someone defined as a subject, and not an autonomous citizen, has the right to alienate a federal patent by granting power of attorney to a private interest unmediated by the federal trust responsibility? By mobilizing this provision of the treaty, mixed bloods were acting on their "tribal relations" and thus not qualified for citizenship according to the state constitution.[2] At the same time, the mixed blood is not eligible for other benefits of citizenship. I answered that question in a close examination of the implementation of this treaty provision.

This is the locus of the failure of the federal officials to act on their trust responsibility and the site of the magic of the law in transforming a subject into a quasicitizen for the moment of transfer. As subject, s/he is eligible for a patent under the treaty. Acting on this right, s/he is now equivalent to, but not yet, a citizen, and so empowered to grant power of attorney as if s/he were a citizen. The provision of the treaty does not explicitly entail citizenship, and we are years away from the Civil War amendments to the Constitution that would even potentially address this issue.[3] The citizenship provision would be written into the General Allotment Act three decades later, so we can regard this 1854 treaty provision as a moment in the decades-long rehearsal for the allotment policy and program of dispossession.[4] Indeed, designating most of the reservation population at the White Earth Reservation in Minnesota "mixed bloods" resulted in the near total loss of their lands.

The intention of at least the official architects of the treaty provision was to separate this class of persons from their relatives, have them take up the plow, become integrated into the emerging, dominant economy and society, and act as teachers of their relatives on the newly created Indian reservations. Certain non-Indian private citizens saw in this provision the possibility of gaining access to land in a more efficient and less expensive way than using the preemption laws, which required assembling, sustaining, and paying squatters and then purchasing titles from those squatters once they had proven up their investments in the land. Those entrepreneurs were able to persuade members of this class of Indians to place their "Xs" on pieces of paper that gave those citizens power of attorney over those indigenous persons for purposes of siting those eighty-acre parcels of land for them. Some mixed bloods may have colluded in this transfer of a claim into the hands of private interests. Perhaps they even argued for the language in the provision that was decisive, that is, the phrase "patent in the usual form." But these mixed bloods were very likely an elite and in the minority.

An eighty-acre parcel of land, sold at the time for $100 and represented $3,136 in 2020 in the years immediately before the Civil War. The enumeration schedules of the 1860 federal census at La Pointe listed $100 in the section entitled "personal estate" for a number of mixed-blood people. When eligible mixed bloods put their "Xs" on powers-of-attorney documents and received that money, they were still living in the ceded territories, still members of families, still living within networks of kin obligations variously maintaining their "tribal relations," which was the diagnostic index of indigeneity at the time.

Within weeks of the lands being located, then patented, those non-Indian citizens purchased the patents. Shortly after that, they consolidated their purchases as capital and incorporated themselves as mining companies. This same process capitalized lumber interests in Minnesota and motivated a Congressional investigation.

It was the inattention, or failure of imagination, if not collusion, of federal officials that subverted the stated policy goal of the mixed-blood provision of the Treaty of 1854 with the Chippewa. Because of the in-between status of the mixed bloods and the jurisdictional ambiguity of the region, those officials were able to plausibly deny that they acted irresponsibly in honoring powers of attorney signed, or "X-ed," by noncitizen illiterate subjects of the United States, repeatedly referred to as "Indians" and therefore presumptively protected by the trust responsibility.

The failure of the treaty provision's intent subsidized the aspirations of the first mining industrial efforts in northern Wisconsin. And though those first efforts at mining the iron ore were not particularly successful, the subsidy capitalized and catalyzed the development of the region in causing the Penokee-Gogebic range to be perpetually imagined by businesses as a source of future wealth.

At the same time, the Indian communities that lost these tens of thousands of acres of land were further diminished. The *de facto* enclosure movement of which this dispossession was a part, resulted in the marginalization and proletarianization of nearly all of the members of the tribal communities, actual blood quantum notwithstanding. The mixed bloods did not establish a meaningful coherent tribal presence beyond the borders of the reservation communities in the lands they had ceded in the treaties of 1837 and 1842 as had been envisioned.

Moreover, the state of Wisconsin criminalized tribal members' treaty right to continue to hunt, fish, and gather on those lands in the nineteenth century, interdicting the use of those lands and resources for more than a century, further polarizing and simplifying the ethnic landscape of the region.[5] And rather like the dispossession that took place at White Earth, the effect of losing access to those resources resulted in poor nutrition and declining health.[6] In a set of hearings undertaken by the Senate Subcommittee on Indian Affairs in 1929, the year after the Meriam Report found so many shortcomings in US Indian policy, testimony from tribal members and government officials on the reservations in Wisconsin repeatedly reported poor health in the communities.[7]

Recall that the Bad River leaders who gathered at Chief James Blackbird's home in 1920 listened to their host putatively remember the intention of the mixed-blood provision of the treaty. The "half-breeds" would take up their parcels of land "west of the Bad River-La Pointe reservation" as the land "was as well timbered as the Bad River reservation" itself. They too could sell the stumpage and grow crops on the cleared land just like their relatives on the reservations themselves. The gathered chiefs were imagining a more complicated indigenous landscape and community than was envisioned by the architects of the reservation policy. It was a vision that was similar to Anishinaabewaki, the kinship network that organized space and people in the pretreaty economy.

The leaders were imagining the "adjoining 80s" as part of their community, west of Bad River, yes, but more than likely contiguous to the reservation as well and articulated with the new city of Ashland. This vision is concordant with the central concern of Eric Olmanson's *The Future City on the Inland Sea: History of Imaginative Geographies of Lake Superior*, a study that describes in detail the converging forces that shaped perceptions of the towns and their hinterlands on Lake Superior, Ashland amongst them. The articulation that the chiefs and headmen were imagining just might have entailed the reproduction of a traditional and evolving modern collective indigenous life accomplished by largely commercial means.

Both Gustav Brohaugh in his 1906 MA thesis on the Sioux and Chippewa scrip and William Folwell in his appendix treatment of the same topic fifty years later, noted the importance of the mixed bloods in securing tribal leadership's agreement to the terms of the Treaty of 1854. Recall that this treaty sought the remaining Chippewa lands east of the Mississippi in Minnesota on the north shore of Lake Superior and thought to hold iron ore at the time. The promise of iron was fulfilled with the discovery of the Mesabi Iron Range, in the 1860s, which yielded 150 billion tons of iron ore from the part of the range lying within the 1854 land cession.[8] By 1903, the Mesabi Range "exceeded the combined output of all the other Lake Superior iron ranges, and its domination increased steadily thereafter,"[9] according to geographer Arnold Alanen. "Between 1900 and 1980, the Mesabi range alone provided 60 percent of the ore mined in the U.S. At its peak, the range supplied 90 percent of all ore used by the nation's steel industry."[10]

Arguably, the mixed-blood provision of the treaty was compensation for their assistance in facilitating a land-and-resource transfer that was one of the essential conditions of the very possibility of the industrial development of the region and beyond. And although some of these savvy mixed bloods played a critical role in effecting the Treaty of 1854, it turned out that the compensation to the Lake Superior Chippewa would be determined to be inadequate. The Minnesota Chippewa Tribe brought a claim to the Indian Claims Commission (ICC) on behalf of the Lake Superior Chippewa in the 1960s alleging that the payment received for 1854 land cession was "grossly inadequate and unconscionable." The commission first found that the Lake Superior Chippewa were the sole owners of the territory ceded in the 1854 treaty. Hearings were held to determine whether or not the amount of money the US government paid for the land represented fair market value. Nearly 6 million acres were transferred. At the time, it was thought the lands would have some value for minerals but mostly for timber, though its accessibility, quality, quantity, and marketability were hotly contested.[11] Nonetheless, the ICC assessed the pine's value at $3,250,000 (55 cents per acre at the time). The government paid 8.2 cents per acre for the cession at the time of the treaty,[12] just less than one-seventh of its true value.

When the extractive industrial interests reached the borders of the reservations, the provision of the treaty that envisioned allotment *on the reservations* became the mechanism that availed corporate access. But allotment of land, making Indian people into the owners of property, exacerbated the problem of belonging and difference for the Anishinaabe people throughout the Lake Superior region.

The authority to constitute community was centralized in the political leadership. Individuals and families would be required to identify with kin located in particular reserved townships. The chiefs and the headmen competed with local insurgent progressives—now pejoratively called "mixed bloods"—over the criteria for membership and the qualifications for leadership. Along with the traditional requirement of residential commitment, community members appropriated non-Indian means of determining who belonged and who did not as they elaborated the category of mixed blood in the competition to govern the reservation. Both progressives and conservatives sought to delegitimize the other in the language of blood. The meetings held in Blackbird's home in 1920 reveal the extent to which the allotment policy moved the leadership to attempt to legislate tribal citizenship in terms of blood even as the actual marriage patterns and genealogies revealed a more complex tribal population.

As the indigenous community debated the significance of internal lines, the settler society's racial ideology refigured the total landscape in terms of Indians and whites. The postlumbering tourist economy in northern Wisconsin encouraged this binary form of figuring belonging and difference, creating opportunities to market cultural performances for indigenous people, all now members of spatially defined societies, marginalized and exoticized. This new reality and the long-standing indigenous conception of belonging informed the membership criteria in the six Wisconsin Ojibwe constitutions.

Additionally, the Indian Reorganization Act created tribal constitutions in the 1930s. All six of the Wisconsin Ojibwe tribes require descent from persons on rolls established at a specified date without specifying blood quantum of that person per the definition of an Indian in the IRA. Neither Bad River nor

Red Cliff uses blood quantum to figure membership. Lac du Flambeau and St. Croix require children of tribal members to be one-quarter and one-half Lac du Flambeau and Indian blood, respectively. And Lac Courte Oreilles requires that those born after 1966 must be either one-eighth LCO blood or one-sixteenth LCO and one-sixteenth other Ojibwe blood. This provision encourages reservation endogamy, implicitly discouraging relationships with other Ojibwe communities, further complicating aspirations to reconstitute Anishinaabewaki. All of these tribal constitutions also specify the territory over which the tribe asserts jurisdiction and stewardship in the first section of the first article (Bad River, Red Cliff, Lac du Flambeau, Lac Courte Oreilles) or second article (St. Croix and Sokaogon) thus spatializing and segmenting what had once been a more unified multicentric community articulated by webs of kinship presumptively dominating a landscape.[13]

The moment in the late 1850s had important consequences for an entire landscape in northern Wisconsin. The men who formed the La Pointe Iron Company and the Lake Superior Iron and Smelting Company, as well as other such companies for which we have yet to discover similar origins, were either the *de facto* codrafters of the treaty provision that made their aspiration possible, or they were the opportunistic beneficiaries of that provision. Ambiguities within the language of that single-sentence provision in

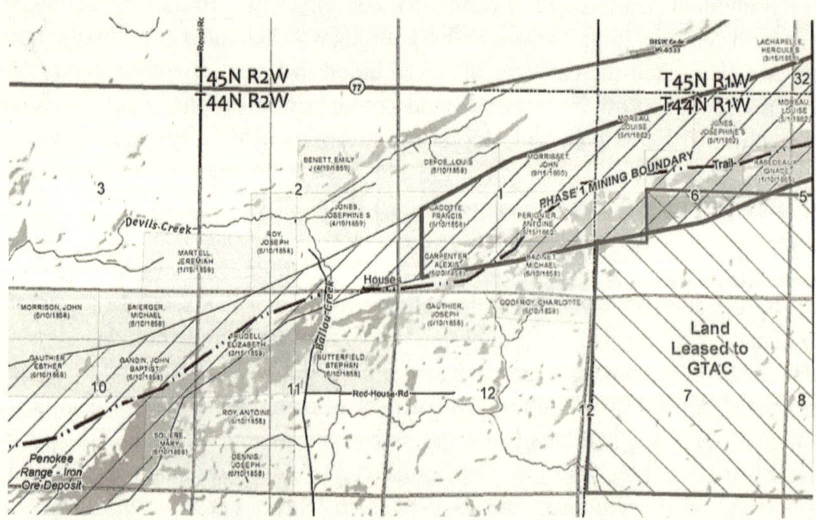

Map C.1. Detail of page 32 of 97, cultural/historic sites in the Bad River Watershed by Bad River Natural Resource Department (K. Sundeen) created 3/30/2015 showing the western part of the proposed Phase 1 Mining Boundary superimposed on the mixed-blood allotments from the mid-nineteenth century.

the 1854 treaty made its administration complicated enough to be exploited by astute business interests. These entrepreneurs laid the groundwork that gave the Penokee Hills their imaginative existence gazed upon as a perennially renewable future resource by those who consolidated half-breed scrip.

The La Pointe Iron Company has been marketing this image of the Penokees for the past century and a half. As of the early 2000s, the La Pointe Iron Company was headquartered in Hibbing, Minnesota, and owned surface and mineral rights on almost two thousand acres in Iron county and more than one thousand in Ashland County with mineral rights on four-thousand in Iron and eight-thousand in Ashland. The company tried to promote its holdings in 2003 by attending a meeting of the Iron County Comprehensive Plan Steering Committee, where it claimed that its land held 2.1 billion tons of magnetic taconite, "representing 10–12% of the iron ore resources in the U.S. An open-pit mining operation was considered feasible by the company, which could stand to collect royalties. It was said an open pit would go as deep as 800 feet and employ as many as 1000 people at an average wage of $25 per hour. . . . An open pit mine could operate for about 30 to 60 years, they said. All would be needed to get started is a mining company to lease their property, as the La Pointe Iron company itself is only the owner of real estate—not an actual mining company."[14]

Currently, Richard Thiede, an outspoken local citizen of the region, has carefully studied and monitored the history and complexity of corporate interest in the Penokees and has come to the conclusion that the most recent effort to mine the iron ore in the range was "a speculative charade."[15] In his blog, he argues that the pattern of the company's activity did not fit a serious effort to mine but rather the owner's "asset appreciation model." He writes that in 2006, the La Pointe Iron Company came to the conclusion that a mine was not feasible and that opinion is widely shared by industry experts. However, by investing a few million dollars, the appearance of feasibility can be created so that money can be made by buying and selling reserves, "like corn futures."[16]

In the early twenty-first century, the distinction between "full" and "mixed" is a distant memory as "mixed blood" is rarely heard, and "full-blood" has become a rare and prestigious designation connoting cultural competence and authenticity in this age of identity precarity anxiety, and for more than just indigenous people. And although blood remains salient as an index of belonging, tribal membership or citizenship at Bad River and Red Cliff is exclusively a matter of lineal descent, true to their long histories of assimilating others to their social and cultural orders. Of course, much that has been written about "blood politics," the different ways in which full "social citizenship" is accomplished and assessed applies to these communities.[17] But political divisions on Ojibwe reservations in the Lake Superior are no longer understood in terms of bloodedness.

In 1989, the Wisconsin Ojibwe's conflict with their non-Indian neighbors over the exercise of off-reservation treaty fishing reached a peak with hundreds of non-Indians arrested for interfering with this federally guaranteed right.[18] Many of the names of these Ojibwe Indian tribal members originated as French names. As such, they are the legacy of a process by which creoles were indigenized in the Western Great Lakes region. Robert Ritzenthaler had noted this decades earlier in his mid-twentieth-century article in the *American Anthropologist*, entitled "The Acquisition of Surnames by the Chippewa Indians." Therein he listed the following: St. Germaine, Soulier, St. Arnold, Corbine, Cadotte, Baptiste, Gokey from Gauthier, La Ronge, Bisonette, Surrette, Guibord, La Roche, Demarais, Bellisle.[19] These tribal members are the descendants of both "full-bloods" and "mixed bloods, belonging to the Lake Superior Chippewa," people whom the federal government sought to set apart from the "Indians" in the mid-nineteenth century.

Clearly, the policy of separating so-called mixed bloods from their "Indian" relatives failed. Yet it continued to disrupt and shape those communities while the category circulated and groups of families competed for political power. The policy had important consequences for the constitution of tribal communities as well as for the larger landscape of northern Wisconsin, revealing that there is often a long distance between the intentions of policies and their actual effects.

The failure reminds me of a provocative image in the work of the Mexican American writer, Richard Rodriquez. When the Franciscan priest offered the Indian woman the Eucharist in the sixteenth century, she swallowed the host, and she swallowed the priest as well.[20] I have always liked this story and told it in class as a way of disrupting the declension narrative of the vanishing or assimilating Indian that students typically bring to the study of Native North America. True enough that Franciscan priests in Mexico—as well as Protestant and Catholic missionaries and the US government's Indian agents in the Great Lakes region—had their *intentions* with respect to Indian people. And it is true enough that indigenous societies transformed a great deal as the result of those intentions and the forced interaction with non-Indians. However, for a long time, that interaction in the Great Lakes region was between parties of approximate equal power, and the intentions of each side—indigenous and settler—were mediated by the capacity of the other side to resist and appropriate the desires, designs, practices, and concepts of the other. After all, the French in North America were on the periphery of their system of the world, and the local indigenous people were at the center of theirs, giving the latter an advantage, at least for a while.

This is Richard White's now well-known "middle ground" thesis[21] that usefully revised how scholars have come to think about the relationship between colonial intentions and their consequences in the Great Lakes region from the seventeenth through the nineteenth centuries and one that has, in part, inspired this inquiry. Richard White's contribution is the springboard for Michael Witgen's insight that the engagement of Europeans and indigenous people in the Great Lakes region created an indigenous New World, Anishinaabewaki and Michael McDonnell's work revealing the centrality of Anishinaabe people in the imperial ambitions of Europeans and Euro-Americans. One important aspect of that indigenous New World was the emergence of a class of indigenized creoles within indigenous polities and then the transformation of those indigenous polities themselves.

This has been the story of the emergence and disappearance of a social category and the transformation of a human and physical landscape. The category "mixed blood," alternatively—and more disparagingly and therefore, tellingly—"half-breed," emerged in the Southeast of the United States when the so-called Civilized Tribes contested colonial domination by trading off elements of culture in an effort to preserve and enhance society and polity. At the same time, a racialist ideology of figuring belonging and difference was on the ascent. The effort to resist this domination on the part of those tribes was often led by people who had indigenous mothers and settler fathers; thus, they were in possession of cultural and social capital from both aspiring dominators and the eventually dominated. Mixed-bloods, therefore, were a settler invention born of that ascendant racial ideology. The term's use sought to inhibit and delegitimize the transformation of indigenous polities.

In the Western Great Lakes region, racial ideology diffused to the tribes by the middle of the nineteenth century even as band-level societies had diversified over the course of two centuries to include different classes of people with the tendrils of indigenous society penetrating the settler's. The category of mixed blood was largely imposed upon the indigenous polities in the treaty process even as those indigenous polities themselves were being constituted and transformed in the treaty relationship. Over time, this category would serve to disrupt those internal divisions making coherent unified resistance to domination difficult to achieve. As more and more Euro-Americans settled in the region, their totalizing, binary, and asymmetrical racial model of unmarked "whites" and marked "nonwhites" diffused to, and was appropriated by, the indigenous communities. This had the effect of diminishing the difference between nonwhite people with homogenous and heterogeneous genealogies, so that by the middle of the twentieth century there were only "Indians" or "tribal members," and they were physically or genealogically tied to lands specifically reserved for them.

Indigenous society before the treaty economy was multicentric and had no fixed geographical boundaries being organized by kinship. Once the region was ceded, private ownership and then mining and lumbering worked as an enclosure movement constituting identities and society in spatial terms. Indigenous society would now have geographical boundaries even if it preserved its multicentric character with the reservations.

Epilogue

The proposal to mine the Penokees in the second decade of the twenty-first century was a major crisis for the Bad River community and the catalyst for this study. The threat of "mountain-top removal," as Bad River tribal chairman Mike Wiggins put it, in the headwaters of the Bad River that flows across the reservation, the home of 1,800 tribal members, put the community on a defensive war footing. The prospect threatened the health, welfare, and the cultural identity of the band. Tribal officials redirected time and resources to first comprehending the magnitude of the proposed project and its implications for the reservation and then in taking action to oppose it. Tribal leaders and members attended six state-sponsored public hearings in different parts of the state responding to slipshod efforts on the state's part to consult with the tribes. They attended county meetings and rallies. Chairman Wiggins took the opportunity to speak to citizens' groups and university audiences. The Bad River Natural Resources Department redirected its efforts and tooled up to assess the environmental impacts of the proposed mine. Meetings were held with the Army Corps of Engineers. The tribe asked the United Nations Rapporteur on the Rights of Indigenous Peoples to intervene.

The depth and breadth of these responses are a measure of the on-going vulnerability of this community to the whims of land-owning corporations in their hinterland and at their doorstep. As long as the minerals remain in the ground, the new extraction industry-friendly laws remain on the state books, and the land available for lease, the band must remain vigilant, willing, and able to shift its governmental and political priorities from managing the ordinary needs of the community to defending the community from an outside threat.

The Penokees are the source of the Bad River communities' water and traditional subsistence. They are also within the territory ceded in the 1842 treaty. All of the Ojibwe bands—articulated with each other by generations of intermarriage despite some of their current membership rules—have usufructuary rights on this land. There are deer, bear, and other fur bearers in

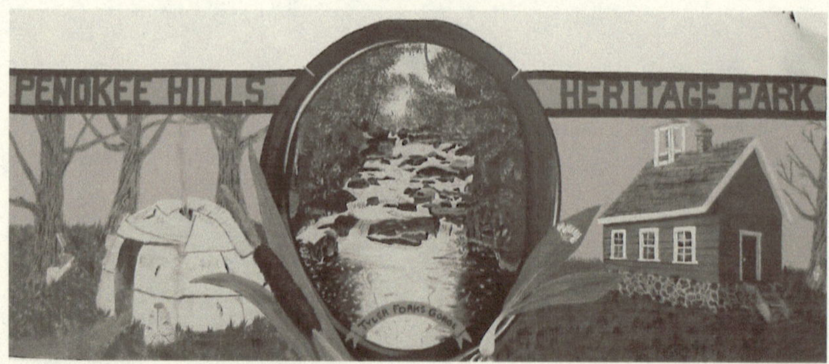

Photograph E.1. Cover photo of a painting by Gregg Jennings of the "Citizens Preserving the Penokee Hills Heritage" for the group's Facebook page showing an imagined bicultural sustainable landscape.

the Penokees, fish in the streams, and many maple and birch trees, good for making sugar and harvesting bark for baskets and canoes.

Efforts to reimage this hinterland as the Penokee Hills Heritage Park continue. Paul DeMain, long-time editor and publisher of *News from Indian Country*, has taken out a patent for *Penokee Gold*, maple syrup made from the trees that grow in the area. *Discovering the Penokees*, by Joel Austin, a book-length photo essay featuring the natural beauty of the region suggesting "a more sustainable future for this area" was published in 2014.[22] Old Baldy, also known as St. Peter's Dome in the western Penokees, has been revitalized as a prayer site in recent years. All of this activity is undertaken in the face of the reality that LaPointe Iron Company still seeks to lease the land for mining and that the government of the state of Wisconsin has been all too eager to facilitate such a use of the land. However, in reparation, the Penokees, or some significant part of them, could be repatriated to the Bad River Band or the Chippewa of Lake Superior in some form or another in recognition of LaPointe's originary moment when ambiguously defined indigenous persons inadvertently subsidized the capitalization of aspiring mining companies, and in doing so, set the regional landscape on a course of development that has left its original people in a precarious position.

Notes

Introduction

1. Nancy Langston, "Iron Mines, Toxicity, and Indigenous Communities in the Lake Superior Basin," in J. R. McNeill and George Vertis, eds., *Mining in North America: An Environmental History Since 1522* (Berkeley: University of California Press, 2017), 315.

2. Ramsar Convention on Wetlands, 2012. "USA Names Lake Superior Bog Complex," https://www.ramsar.org/news/usa-names-lake-superior-bog-complex. Accessed January 19, 2018.

3. See Albert Jenks (1901) *The Wild Life Gatherers of the Upper Lakes: A Study in American Primitive Economics* (Washington D.C.: GPO, 1901); Thomas Vennum, *Wild Rice and the Ojibwe People* (St. Paul: Minnesota Historical Society, 1988); and James M. McLurken, *Fish in the Lakes, Wild Rice, and Game in Abundance: Testimony on Behalf of Mille Lacs Ojibwe Hunting and Fishing Rights* (East Lansing: Michigan State University Press, 2000).

4. Rebecca Kemble, "Bad River Chippewa Take a Stand against Walker and Mining," *The Progressive*, May 28, 2013; Nancy Langston, "Iron Mines," 331.

5. Glenn C. Reynolds, "A Native American Water Ethic," *Transactions of the Wisconsin Academy of Sciences, Arts and Letters* 90 (2003): 143–61; Larry Nesper, "Law and Ojibwe Indian 'Traditional Cultural Property' in the Organized Resistance to the Crandon Mine in Wisconsin," *Law and Social Inquiry* 36, no. 1 (Winter 2011): 151–69.

6. Anonymous. 2013. LCO Harvest and Education Camp. http://www.savethewatersedge.com/camp-plummer-updates-lco.html. Visited September 14, 2017.

7. The EPA granted the Bad River Band treatment-as-state status in June of 2009. https://www.epa.gov/wqs-tech/water-quality-standards-regulations-bad-river-band-lake-superior-chippewa-tribe. Visited April 16, 2018.

8. Thomas F. King, *Places That Count: Traditional Cultural Properties in Cultural Resource Management* (Walnut Creek, Calif.: Altamira Press, 2003).

9. *Chequamegon History: Primary Research about the Chequamegon Region before 1860. https://chequamegonhistory.wordpress.com/.*

10. Edmund Jefferson Danziger, "They Would Not Be Moved: The Chippewa Treaty of 1854," *Minnesota History* 43, no. 5 (1973): 175–85.

11. Gustav O. Brohaugh, *Sioux and Chippewa Half-Breed Scrip and Its Application to the Minnesota Pine Lands.* Master's thesis, University of Wisconsin, 1906, 452.

12. Folwell, William Watts, *A History of Minnesota* (St. Paul: Minnesota Historical Society, 1956), 470–78.

13. Richard White, *The Middle Ground: Indians, Empires, and Republics in the Great Lakes Region, 1650–1815* (Cambridge: Cambridge University Press, 1991), 52.

14. Michael A. McDonnell, *Masters of Empire: Great Lakes Indians and the Making of America* (New York: Hill and Wang, 2015).

15. Michael, Witgen, *An Infinity of Nations: How the Native New World Shaped Early North America* (Philadelphia: University of Pennsylvania Press, 2012).

16. Witgen, *An Infinity of Nations*, 233.

17. Pierre Bourdieu, "The Force of Law: Toward a Sociology of the Juridical Field," *Hastings Journal of Law* 38 (1977): 814–53, 838.

18. 10 Stats. 1109, Treaty with the Chippewa, 1854.

19. Paul Wallace Gates, "Introduction to the John Tipton Papers," in Nellie Armstrong Robertson and Dorothy Riker, eds., *The John Tipton Papers, 1809–1839* (Indiana Historical Collections 24; Indianapolis, 1942), 18.

20. Henry Safford Neal, et al. *Half-Breed Scrip. Chippewas of Lake Superior. The Correspondence and Action under the 7th Clause of the 2nd Article of the Treaty with the Chippewa Indians, and the Mississippi, Concluded at La Pointe in the State of Wisconsin, September 30, 1954 . . .* (Washington: GPO, 1874).

21. Kathleen Neils Conzen, "The Winnebago Urban System: Indian Policy and Townsite Promotion on the Upper Mississippi," in Rondo Cameron, ed., *Cities and Markets: Studies in the Organization of Human Space* (Lanham, Md.: University Press of America, 1997): 269–310.

Chapter 1

1. William Whipple Warren, *History of the Ojibway People* (St. Paul: Minnesota Historical Society Press, 1984), [1885]: 119.

2. "Wausau" in Anishinaabemowin, Referring to Its Visibility from a Great Distance, Virgil J, Vogel, *Indian Names on Wisconsin's Map* (Madison: University of Wisconsin Press, 1991), 138.

3. Larry Nesper and Chantal Norrgard, *Mashkii Ziibii: Human Water and Landscape Rep*ort (2014). Report prepared for the Bad River Band of Lake Superior Chippewa Indians, 64–66.

4. Lawrence Martin, *The Physical Geography of Wisconsin,* Madison: Wisconsin Geological and Natural History Survey Bulletin, no. 36 (1932): 367–95.

5. John Pastor, *What Should a Clever Moose Eat? Natural History, Ecology and the North Woods* (Washington, D.C.: Island Press, 2016), 19.

6. David J. Mladenoff, et al., "Broad-Scale Change in the Northern Forests: From Past to Present," in *The Vanishing Present: Wisconsin's Changing Lands, Waters, and Wildlife* (Chicago: University of Chicago Press, 2008).

7. Pastor, *What Should a Clever Moose*, 2.

8. A. W. Schorger, "The Beaver in Early Wisconsin," *Transactions of the Wisconsin Academy of Science, Arts and Letters* 54, 149–79.

9. Pastor, *What Should a Clever Moose*, 49–51.

10. Douglas A. Birk, "When Rivers Were Roads: Deciphering the Role of Canoe Portages in the Western Lake Superior Fur Trade," in Jennifer S. H. Brown, W. J. Eccles, and Donald P. Heldman, eds., *Fur Trade Revisited: Selected Papers of the Sixth North American Fur Trade Conference, Mackinac Island, Michigan, 1991* (East Lansing: Michigan State University Press, 1991): 359–75, 365.

11. Frederic Baraga, *Chippewa Indians as Recorded by Reverend Frederick Baraga in 1847* (New York-Washington, Studia Slovenica, 1976), 9. Spellings, underlinings, and lowercase in the original.

12. Marshall Sahlins, *Islands of History* (Chicago: University of Chicago Press, 1985), 146.

13. Michael Witgen, "The Rituals of Possession: Native Identity and the Invention of Empire in Seventeenth-Century Western North America," *Ethnohistory* 54, no. 4 (2007): 639–68, 648.

14. Ibid., 658.

15. Charles Callendar, "Great Lakes-Riverine Sociopolitical Organization," in Bruce G. Trigger, ed., *Handbook of North American Indians, the Northeast* (Washington D.C.: Smithsonian, 1978): 610–21, 610.

16. Theresa M. Schenck, *The Voice of the Crane Echoes Afar: The Socio-political Organization of the Lake Superior Ojibwe, 1640–1855* (Routledge, 1997), 29.

17. Heidi Bohaker, "'Ninddodemag': The Significance of Algonquian Kinship Networks in the Eastern Great Lakes Region, 1600–1701," *The William and Mary Quarterly* 63, no. 1 (January 2006): 23–52, 32.

18. Harold Hickerson, "The Genesis of Bilaterality among Two Divisions of Chippewa," *American Anthropologist* 68, no. 1 (1966), 1–26.

19. Here I allude to the debate about whether tapping maple trees antedated the French entrada or was indigenized so creatively and thoroughly that the iconic practice has become a symbol of Northeast Indian indigeneity. See Carol I. Mason, "A Sweet Small Something: Maple Sugaring in the New World," in James Clifton, ed., *The Invented Indian: Cultural Fictions and Governmental Policies* (New Brunswick and London: Transaction Publishers, 1994) 91–106.

20. Robert E. Ritzenthaler, "Southwestern Chippewa," in Bruce G. Trigger, ed., *Handbook of North American Indians, The Northeast* (Washington D.C.: Smithsonian, 1978), 743.

21. Schenck, The *Voice of the Crane.*

22. Harold Hickerson, "The Sociohistorical Significance of Two Chippewa Ceremonials," *American Anthropologist* 68, no. 1 (1963): 67–85.

23. White, *The Middle Ground,* 14.

24. Schenck, *The Voice of the Crane*, 37–54.

25. Susan Sleeper-Smith, Indigenous Prosperity and American Conquest: Indian Women of the Ohio River Valley, 1690–1792 (Chapel Hill: University of North Carolina Press, 2018).

26. See for example, Harold Innis, *The Fur Trade in Canada: An Introduction to Canadian Economic History* (New Haven: Yale University Press, 1930); E. E. Rich, *The Fur Trade and the Northwest to 1957* (Toronto: McClelland and Steward Limited, 1967); Arthur J. Ray and Donald B. Freeman, *Give Us Good Measure: An Economic Analysis of Relations between the Indians and the Hudson's Bay Company Before 1763* (Toronto: University of Toronto Press, 1978); Sylvia Van Kirk, *Many Tender Ties: Women in Fur Trade Society, 1670–1870* (Norman and London: University of Oklahoma Press, 1980); Arthur J. Ray, *Indians in the Fur Trade: Their Role as Trappers, Hunters, and Middlemen in the Lands Southwest of Hudson Bay, 1660–1870* (Toronto: University of Toronto Press, 1998); Carol Podruchny, *Making the Voyageur World: Travelers and traders in the North American Fur Trade* (Lincoln and London: University of Nebraska Press, 2006).

27. Rhonda Gilman, "The Fur Trade in the Upper Mississippi Valley, 1630–1850," *Wisconsin Magazine of History* 58, no. 1 (1974): 2–28.

28. Marshall Sahlins, "The Economics of Develop-Man in the Pacific," *Anthropology and Aesthetics* 21 (1992): 12–25.

29. Gilman, "The Fur Trade," 4.

30. Arthur J. Ray, "Indians as Consumers in the Eighteenth Century," in Carol M. Judd and Arthur J. Ray, eds., *Old Trails and New Directions: Papers of the Third North American Fur Trade Conference* (Toronto: University of Toronto Press, 1980), 255–57.

31. McDonnell, *Masters of Empire*, 43.

32. Christopher L. Miller and George R. Hamell, "A New Perspective on Indian-White Contact: Cultural Symbols and Colonial Trade," *The Journal of American History* 73, no. 2 (September 1986): 311–28.

33. Frederick Jackson Turner, *The Character and Influence of the Indian Trade in Wisconsin: A Study of the Trading Post as an Institution* (New York: B. Franklin, 1970), 24, 29.

34. Ibid., 33.

35. Frank E. Ross, "The Fur Trade of the Western Great Lakes Region," *Minnesota History* 19, no. 3 (Sept., 1938): 271–307, 277.

36. Michael Witgen, *An Infinity of Nations: How the Native New World Shaped Early North America* (Philadelphia: University of Pennsylvania Press, 2012), 218, 260.

37. Ross, "The Fur Trade," 278.

38. Turner, *The Character and Influence*, 59.

39. Michael Witgen, *Infinity of Nations*, 126–32; Michael McDonnell, "Rethinking the Middle Ground: French Colonialism and Indigenous Identities in the Pays d'en Haut," in Gregory D. Smithers & Brooke N. Newman, eds., *Native Diasporas: Indigenous Identities and Settler Colonialism in the Americas* (Lincoln: University of Nebraska Press, 2014), 49–62.

40. White, *The Middle Ground*, 94–141.

41. Ibid., 97–98.

42. Marshall Sahlins, *Stone Age Economics* (New York: Aldine, 1972), 1–40.

43. Turner, *The Character and Influence*, 78.

44. Sylvia Van Kirk, *Many Tender Ties: Women in Fur-Trade Society, 1670–1870* (Norman: University of Oklahoma Press, 1983), 28, 46.

45. Jennifer Brown, "Fur Trade as Centrifuge: Family Dispersal and Offspring Identity in Two Company Contexts," in Raymond J. DeMallie and Alfonso Ortiz, eds., *North American Indian Anthropology: Essays on Society and Culture* (Norman: University of Oklahoma Press, 1994), 197–217, 206.

46. Richard White, *The Middle Ground*, 127.

47. James Clifton, "Michigan's Indians: Tribe, Nation, Estate, Racial, Ethnic, or Special Interest Group?," *Michigan Historical Review* 20, no. 2 (1994): 93–152, 113.

48. Bruce White, "Give Us a Little Milk": The Social and Cultural Significance of Gift Giving in the Lake Superior Fur Trade," in Thomas C. Buckley, ed., *Rendezvous: Selected papers of the Fourth North American Fur Trade Conference, 1981* (Norman: University of Oklahoma Press, 1984), 185–97.

49. David Scheider, *American Kinship: A Cultural Account* (Chicago: University of Chicago Press, 1980), 61.

50. White, "Give Us a Little Milk," 185.

51. Eric Wolf, *Europe and the People without History* (Berkeley: University of California Press, 1983), 193.

52. Witgen, *An Infinity of Nations*; McDonnell, *Masters of Empire.*

53. White, "Give Us a Little Milk," 187.

54. A conclusion I draw from a reading of Sahlins and Graeber's recently published *On Kings* (Chicago: Hau Books, 2017).

55. White, "Give Us a Little Milk," 189.

56. Sahlins, *Stone Age Economics*, 222.

57. Clifton, "Michigan Indians," 213.

58. Melissa Meyer, *The White Earth Tragedy: Ethnicity and Dispossession at a Minnesota Anishinaabe Reservation, 1889–1920* (Lincoln: University of Nebraska Press, 1994), 20.

59. Thomas Ingersoll, *"To Intermix with our White Brothers: Indian Mixed Bloods in the United States from Earliest Times to the Indian Removals* (Albuquerque: University of New Mexico Press, 2005), 52.

60. Ibid., 114.

61. Robert Hall, *An Archaeology of the Soul* (Urbana: University of Illinois Press, 1997), 1–8.

62. Bruce White, "The Meanings of Merchandise in the Ojibwa Fur Trade," in Sylvia Depatie et al., eds. *Vingt ans après, Habitants et marchands: Lectures de l'histoire des XVII et XVIII siècles canadiens* (Montreal [Que.]: McGill-Queen's University Press, 1998), 115–37, 130.

63. Maurice Block, *In and Out of Each Other's Bodies: Theory of Mind, Evolution, Truth, and the Nature of the Social* (Routlege, 2013); Marshall Sahlins, *Kinship, What Kinship Is . . . and Is Not* (Chicago: University of Chicago Press, 2014).

64. Matt Hooley, "The Autoethnography of William Whipple Warren," *Wicazo Sa Review* 20, no. 2 (Fall 2012): 75–98, 77.

65. Warren, *History of the Ojibway People*, 118–19.

66. White, "The Meaning of Merchandise," 117.

67. Warren, *History of the Ojibway People*, 78–82; Walter James Hoffman, "The Midewiwin or 'Grand Medicine Society' of the Ojibwe," Smithsonian Institution, U.

S. Bureau of Ethnology Report No. 7 (Washington D.C.: GPO, 1891): 149–299, 166; Selwyn H. Dewdney, *The Sacred Scrolls of the Southern Ojibway* (Toronto: University of Toronto Press, 1975): 57–80; Edward Benton-Banai, *The Mishomis Book—The Voice of the Ojibway* (St. Paul: Red School House Publishers, 1988): 95–103.

68. Barbara J. Heath, "Commoditization, Consumption, And Interpretive Complexity: The Contingent Role of Cowries In the Early Modern World," in Barbara J. Heath, Eleanor E. Breen and Lori A. Lee, eds., *Material Worlds: Archaeology, Consumption, and the Road to Modernity* (Routledge, 2019): 56–76.

69. Jan Hogendorn and Marion Johnson, *The Shell Money of the Slave Trade* (Cambridge: Cambridge University Press, 1986), 13.

70. Vecsey, *Traditional Ojibwe Religion*, 184–85.

71. Hickerson, *The Chippewa and Their Neighbors: A Study in Ethnohistory* (Prospects Heights, Ill.: Waveland Press, 1988), 44.

72. Hallowell, A. Irving, "Ojibwe Ontology, Behavior and World View," in Raymond Fogelson et al., eds., *Contributions to Anthropology: Selected Papers of A. Irving Hallowell* (Chicago: University of Chicago Press, 1976), 383.

73. Georg Kohl, in his 1860 *Kitchi-gami: Travels Round Lake Superior* (London: Chapman and Hall, 1860) writes that "bojo" is corruption of "bonjour," 193.

Chapter 2

1. Heidi Bohaker, "'Ninddodemag': The Significance of Algonquian Kinship Networks in the Eastern Great Lakes Region, 1600–1701," *The William and Mary Quarterly* 63, no. 1 (January 2006): 23–52, 38.

2. Bethel Saler, *The Settlers' Empire: Colonialism and State Formation in America's Old Northwest* (Philadelphia: University of Pennsylvania Press, 2015), 225.

3. Theresa Schenck, *All Our Relations: Chippewa Mixed Bloods and the Treaty of 1837* (Madison, Wis.: Amik Press, 2010), 236.

4. Patrick Wolfe, "Land, Labor, and Difference: Elementary Structures of Race," *American Historical Review* 106, no. 3 (June 2001): 866–905.

5. Jill Doerfler, *Those Who Belong: Identity, Family, Blood, and Citizenship among the White Earth Anishinaabeg* (East Lansing: Michigan State University Press, 2015), 1–30.

6. Thomas Ingersoll, *To Intermix with Our White Brothers: Indian Mixed Bloods in the United States from Earliest Times to the Indian Removals* (Albuquerque: University of New Mexico Press, 2005), 174.

7. Harriet Gorham, "Families of Mixed Descent in the Western Great Lakes Region," in Bruce Cox, ed., *Native People, Native Lands: Canadian Indians, Inuit, Métis* (Montreal: McGill-Queens University Press, 1987), 41–42.

8. Frederic Baraga, *A Dictionary of the Ojibway Language* (St. Paul: Minnesota Historical Society Press, 1992), 124, 421.

9. Reginald Horsman, *Race and Manifest Destiny: The Origins of American Racial Anglo-Saxonism* (Cambridge: Harvard University Press, 1981), 43–61; Robert

Bieder, "The Representation of Indian Bodies in Nineteenth Century Anthropology," *American Indian Quarterly* 20, no. 2: 165–79.

10. Robert Bieder, *Science Encounters the Indian, 1820–1880: The Early Years of American Ethnology* (Norman: University of Oklahoma Press, 1986), 73, 79.

11. Francis Paul Prucha, *Indian Policy in the United States: Historical Essays* (Lincoln: University of Nebraska Press, 1981), 192.

12. Robert Bieder, "Scientific Attitudes toward Indian Mixed-Bloods in Early Nineteenth Century America," *Journal of Ethnic Studies* 8, no. 2 (1980): 17–30.

13. Francis Paul Prucha, "Scientific Racism and Indian Policy," in *Indian Policy in the United States: Historical Essays* (Lincoln: University of Nebraska Press, 1981).

14. See especially Circe Sturm, *Blood Politics: Race, Culture, and Identity in the Cherokee Nation of Oklahoma* (Berkeley: University of California Press, 2002).

15. Jennifer S. H. Brown and Laura Peers, "'There Is No End to Relationship among the Indians' Ojibwa Families and Kinship in Historical Perspective," *History of the Family* 4, no. 4 (1999): 529–55.

16. Brian Hosmer, "Reflections on Indian Cultural "Brokers": Reginald Oshkosh, Mitchell Oshkenaniew, and the Politics of Menominee Lumbering," *Ethnohistory* 44, no. 3 (Summer, 1997: 493–509, 495.

17. Brown and Peers, "There Is No End . . . ," 539, and citing five sources supporting their claim.

18. Bohaker, "'Ninddodemag': The Significance of . . . ," 38.

19. Ingersoll, *To Mix with Our White Brothers*, 39.

20. Ibid., 109.

21. Ibid., 52.

22. Schenck, *All Our Relations*, 36.

23. John Comaroff, "Of Totemism and Ethnicity: Consciousness, Practice and the Signs of Inequality," *Journal of Anthropology* 52, nos. 3–4 (2010): 301–23, 302.

24. Ibid., 306.

25. Ibid., 307.

26. White, *The Middle Ground*, 105; Wolf, *Europe and the People without History*, 171.

27. Schenck, *The Voice of the Crane.*

28. Gorham, "Families of Mixed Descent," 38.

29. Jacqueline Peterson, *The People in Between: Indian-White Marriage and the Genesis of Metis Society and Culture in the Great Lakes Region, 1680–1830* (PhD dissertation, University of Illinois at Chicago, 1981).

30. Ibid., 5; emphasis added.

31. Jacqueline Peterson, "Many Roads to Red River," in Jennifer Brown and Jacqueline Peterson, *The New Peoples: Being and Becoming Métis in North America* (Lincoln: University of Nebraska Press, 1985), 41; "Rocking the Cradle of the Plains: The Emergence of a New Aboriginal People in Northern North American" (paper given at the 2017 Society for Ethnohistory Meeting in Winnipeg, Canada).

32. Lucy Eldersveld Murphy, *Great Lakes Creoles: A French-Indian Community on the Borderlands, Prairie du Chien, 1750–1860* (Cambridge University Press, 2014), 14.

33. Jacqueline Peterson, "Many Roads," 41, emphasis added.

34. Peterson, *People in Between*, 137.

35. Ibid., 66, 10–11, 29, 34, 43, 45.

36. A term used by Jerry Schultz in his 1994 review of Meyer's *The White Earth Tragedy*, *Great Plains Research* 4, no. 2 (August 1994): 332–34.

37. Rebecca Kugel, *To Be the Main Leaders of Our People: A History of Minnesota Ojibwe Politics, 1825–1898* (East Lansing: Michigan State University Press, 1998), 113.

38. Ibid., 77, 88; Register of Meeting of Association of American Indians at Madison, October 6–11. Papers of the Society of American Indians, State Historical Society of Wisconsin.

39. Schenck, *All Our Relations*, 1.

40. Witgen, *An Infinity of Nations*, 122.

41. This and other criticisms that follow from it were the substance of Jennifer Brown's review of the book appearing in *The American Historical Review* 105, no. 2 (Apr., 2000): 543–44, which I was pleased to find well after my own critique was written.

42. Brown and Peers, 539.

43. Keith R. Widder, *Battle for the Soul: Metis Children Encounter Evangelical Protestants at Mackinaw Mission, 1823–37* (East Lansing: Michigan State University Press, 1999), 9–10.

44. Ibid., xix.

45. Ibid., xx.

46. Johann Georg Kohl, *Kitchi-gami: Life among the Lake Superior Ojibway* (St. Paul: Minnesota Historical Society Press, 1985), 260.

47. Schenck, *Voice of the Crane*, 60.

48. Widder, *Battle for the Soul*, 11.

49. Ibid., 19.

50. Ibid., 15.

51. H. M. Robinson, *The great fur land; or, Sketches of life in the Hudson's Bay territory* (New York: Putnam, 1879): 53–59.

52. George Nelson, *My First Years in the Fur Trade: The Journals of 1802–1804*, eds. Laura Peers and Theresa Schenk (Minnesota Historical Society Press, 2002), 41.

53. Widder, *Battle for the Soul*, 18.

54. R. David Edmunds, " 'Unacquainted with the Laws of the Civilized World' ": American Attitudes toward Métis Communities in the Old Northwest," in Jacqueline Peterson and Jennifer S. H. Brown, eds., *The New Peoples: Being and Becoming Métis in North America* (Lincoln: University of Nebraska Press, 1985), 185–94.

55. Ingersoll, 82.

56. Ibid.

57. Ibid., 110.

58. Ibid., 130.

59. Ibid., 131.

60. John L. Hurd, "The Unprofitable Life of Sherman Hall," nd. Manuscript, State Historical Society of Wisconsin.

61. Widder, xv.

62. Ibid., 133.

63. Ibid.

64. Ibid., 134.

65. Keith Widder, *Battle for the Soul*, 62.

66. Richard Jenkins, "Different Societies? Different Cultures? What Are Human Collectivities?" in Sinisa Malesevic and Mark Haugaard, eds., *Making Sense of Collectivity: Ethnicity, Nationality and Globalization* (London: Pluto Press, 2002): 12–32, 18.

67. Ibid., 29–30.

68. Rebecca Kugel, "Reworking Ethnicity: Gender, Work Roles, and Contending Redefinitions of the Great Lakes Métis, 1820–42," in R. David Edmunds, ed., *Enduring Nations: Native Americans in the Midwest* (Urbana and Chicago: University of Illinois Press, 2008): 160–81, 168.

69. Ibid.

70. Mattie Harper, *French Africans in Ojibwe Country: Negotiating Marriage, Identity and Race, 1780–1890* (PhD dissertation, University of California, Berkeley, 2012), 30.

71. Ibid., 48, quoting James Doty.

72. Ibid., 46.

73. Ibid., 55–56.

74. Ibid., 68.

75. Tanis Thorne, *The Many Hands of My Relations: French and Indians on the Lower Missouri* (Columbia and London: University of Missouri Press), 175.

76. Jennifer Brown, *An Ethnohistorian in Rupert's Land: Unfinished Conversations* (Edmonton: Athabasca University Press, 2017), 154.

77. Consul Wilshire Butterfield, *History of Crawford and Richland Counties, Wisconsin* (Springfield, Ill.: Union Publishing Company, 1884), 379.

78. Schenck, *All My Relations*, 3.

79. Account of DuBay, M951 Roll 3: 409–10, July 2, 1839. Records of the Wisconsin Superintendency of Indian Affairs, 1836–1848 and the Green Bay Subagency. United States National Archives.

80. Ibid., 4.

81. "Chippewa Halfbreeds to Daniel P. Bushnell," July 24, 1839. 28 *Territorial Papers of the United States* 16, Wisconsin.

82. Merton E. Krug, *DuBay: Son-in-Law of Oshkosh* (Appleton, Wisc. C. C. Nelson Publishing Company, 1946), 13–18.

83. "Petition to the President by the Chippewa Half-Breeds, March 7, 1838," *Territorial Papers of the United States* 27, Wisconsin, 934–35.

84. Dodge to Harris, October 9, 1838, *Territorial Papers of the United* States 27, Wisconsin, 1074–75.

85. 7 U.S. Statutes 536; emphasis added.

86. Schenck, *All Our Relations*, 5.

87. Account of DuBay.

88. Ibid., 8.

89. Helen Hornbeck Tanner, "The Career of Joseph La France, Coureur De Bois in the Upper Great Lakes," in *The Fur Trade Revisited: Selected Papers of the Sixth North American Fur Trade Conference, Mackinac Island, Michigan, 1991* (East Lansing: Michigan State University Press, 1994), 171–188.

90. Gorham, "Families of Mixed Descent," 51.

91. Morton Fried, "On the Evolution of Social Stratification and the State," in Stanley Diamond, ed., *Essays in Honor of Paul Radin* (New York: Columbia University Press, 1960), 713–31.

92. David Graeber and Marshall Sahlins, *On Kings* (Chicago: HAU Books, 2018), 240.

93. Thomas W. Overholt and J. Baird Callicott, *Clothed-in-Fur and Other Tales* (New York: University Press of America, 1982), 74–75.

94. Bruce M. White, "The Power of Whiteness, or, The Life and Times of Joseph Rolette, Jr.," *Minnesota History* 56, no. 4 (1998–99): 178–97, 194.

95. William E. Culkin, "Early Protestant Missions in the Lake Superior Country, Volume II: Journals of the Rev. Sherman Hall together with his letters to the Rev. David Greene, 1831–1844," 1936. Manuscript, State Historical Society of Wisconsin, 26; emphasis added.

96. Reverend Alfred Brunson, *A Western Pioneer, or, Incidents in the Life and Times of Rev. Alfred Brunson, A.M., D.D., Embracing a Period of Seventy Years. Written By Himself,* Volume II (Cincinnati: Hitchcock and Walton, New York: Philips and Hunt, 1879), 158, 175.

Chapter 3

1. Treaty with the Chippewa of Mississippi and Lake Superior, 9 U.S. Statutes 904.

2. Rhoda Gilman, "The Last Days of the Upper Mississippi Fur Trade," *Minnesota History* 42, no. 4 (1970): 122–40, 124.

3. Bethel Saler, "Negotiating the Treaty Economy: Race, Gender and the Transformation from an Indian to a White Territory in Northeastern Wisconsin, 1824–52" (Master's thesis, University of Wisconsin, 1992).

4. Thomas Jefferson, "President Jefferson to William Henry Harrison: February 27, 1803," in Francis Paul Prucha, *Documents of United States Indian Policy* (Lincoln: University of Nebraska Press, 1975), 22.

5. *Robert* H. *Keller.* 1978. "An *Economic History of Indian Treaties* in the Great Lakes Region," *American Indian Journal* 4 (February *1978*): 2–20, 3.

6. Gilman, "The Last Days . . . ," 124.

7. Treaty of Fond du Lac, 7 U.S. Statutes 290.

8. Treaty of Prairie du Chien, 7 U.S. Statutes 272.

9. William Whipple Warren, *History of the Ojibways*, 392–94.

10. Matt Hooley, "The Autoethnography of William Whipple Warren," *Wicazo Sa Review* 20, no. 2 (Fall 2012): 75–98, 86.

11. 1 Robert H. Keller, "The Chippewa Treaties of 1826 and 1836," *American Indian Journal* 9, no. 3 (Fall 1986): 27–32, 31.

12. See Ronald Satz "Chippewa Treaty Rights: The Reserved Rights of Wisconsin's Chippewa Indians in Historical Perspective," in *Transactions of the Wisconsin Academy of Sciences, Arts and Letters* 79, no. 1 (1991): 13–14.

13. Satz, *Chippewa Treaty Rights*, 33.

14. Robert H. Keller, "On Teaching Indian Treaties: Legal Jurisdiction in Chippewa Treaties," *Ethnohistory* 19, no. 3 (1972): 209–18, 215.

15. Explorer, *A Few Remarks On the Operations of the Companies: At Present Organized, for the Digging & Smelting of Copper and Other Ores, On Lake Superior and the Saint Croix River* [U.S.?]: [publisher not identified], [1845], 2.

16. Robert W. Swenson, "Legal Aspects of Mineral Resources Exploitation," in Paul W Gates, *History of Public Land Law Development* (New York: Arno Press, 1979): 699–764, 706.

17. David Dale Owen, *Report of a Geological Survey of Wisconsin, Iowa, and Minnesota* (Philadelphia: Lippencott, Grambo, 1852), 6.

18. Ibid., 53.

19. Ibid., 434.

20. Charles Whittlesey, "The Penokie Range, Wisconsin," *Proceedings of the Boston Society of Natural History* 9 (1863): 235–44, 236; Frederic Baraga, *A Dictionary of the Ojibway Language* (St. Paul: Minnesota Historical Society Press, 1992), 146.

21. James Clifton, "Wisconsin Death March: Explaining the Extremes in Old Northwest Indian Removal," *Transactions of the Wisconsin Academy of Sciences, Arts, and Letters* 5 (1987): 1–40.

22. Bruce M. White, "The Regional Context of the Removal Order of 1850," in James McLurken, ed., *Fish in the Lakes, Wild Rice, and Game in Abundance: Testimony on Behalf of the Mille Lacs Ojibwe Hunting and Fishing Rights* (East Lansing: Michigan State University Press, 2000): 141–328.

23. Charles Cleland, *Faith in Paper: The Ethnohistory and Litigation of Upper Great Lakes Indian Treaties* (Ann Arbor: University of Michigan Press, 2011), 58.

24. Bruce M. White, "The Power of Whiteness, or, The Life and Times of Joseph Rolette, Jr.," *Minnesota History* 56, no. 4 (1998–99): 178–97, 186.

25. United States, "List of persons to whom permits to locate mineral lands on the south shore of Lake Superior have been granted and leases issued upon them by the Secretary of War, up to June 16, 1846." United States, Department of War; Commissioner of Indian Affairs-Letters Received (hereafter COIA-LR) National Archives Microfilm (hereafter NAM), M 234 Roll 168, Watrous to Ramsey, Sept. 20. See also NAM 234 R 389–90, La Pointe Agency 1848–59.

26. Edmund Danziger, "They Would Not Be Moved: The Chippewa Treaty of 1854," *Minnesota History* 43, no. 5 (1973): 175–85, 178.

27. Robert A. Trennert, jr., *Alternative to Extinction: Federal Policy and the Beginning of the Reservation System, 1846–1851* (Philadelphia: Temple University Press, 1975).

28. Annual Report of the Commissioner of Indian Affairs (hereafter ARCIA) to the Secretary of the Interior for 1853, 21.

29. ARCIA 1855, 2.

30. Francis Paul Prucha, *American Indian Treaties: The History of an Anomaly* (Berkeley: University of California Press, 1994), 242.

31. See Charles J. Kappler, *Indian Affairs Laws and Treaties: Volume II: Treaties* (Washington D.C.: GPO, 1904), passim 612–56.

32. 1854 Treaty with the Chippewa, 10 U.S. Statutes 1109.

33. Charles Cleland, *Faith in Paper: The Ethnohistory and Litigation of Upper Great Lakes Indian Treaties* (Ann Arbor: University of Michigan Press, 2011), 218.

34. Ibid.

35. Ronald Satz, *Chippewa Treaty Rights*, 178.

36. *Prentice v. Stearns*, 113 U.S. 435 (1885); Benjamin G. Armstrong, *Early Life Among the Indians* (Armstrong and Wentworth: Ashland, Wisconsin, 1891), 40–41; italic emphasis added.

37. Armstrong, *Early Life Among the Indians*, 40.

38. Howard D. Paap, *Red Cliff, Wisconsin: A History of an Ojibwe Community, Volume I: The Earliest Years: The Origin to 1854* (St. Cloud, Minn.: North Star Press, 2013), 260.

39. J. P. Kinney, *A Continent Lost—A Civilization Won: Indian Land Tenure in America* (Baltimore: Johns Hopkins University Press, 1937), 97.

40. Rebecca Kugel, "Planning to Stay: Native Strategies to Remain in the Great Lakes, Post-War 1812," *Middle West Review* 2, no. 2 (2016), 1–26.

41. United States, *Half-breed scrip, Chippewas of Lake Superior: the correspondence and action under the 7th clause of the 2d article of the treaty with the Chippewa Indians of Lake Superior and the Mississippi, concluded at La Pointe in the state of Wisconsin, September 30, 1854 . . . Including the report of the commission appointed by the Secretary of the Interior, April 21, 1871, composed of Henry S. Neal, Selden N. Clark, Edward P. Smith, and R. F. Crowell: and the report of the commission appointed July 15, 1872, composed of Thomas C. Jones, Edward P. Smith, and Dana E. King.* U.S. House of Representatives, Executive Document 103. 42nd Congress, Second session. Washington: G.P.O., 1874, 55; emphasis added.

42. Peterson, *The People in Between: Indian-White marriage and the genesis of a Métis society and culture in the Great Lakes Region, 16780–1830* (PhD dissertation, University of Illinois at Chicago, 1981), 245–67.

43. One of the measures of their diversity as a community was the "Superior Chippewa Indian Choir," which included a number of familiar LaPointe mixed bloods. Mary Roy played the semiportable organ given to the choir by the Julius Ausrtrian and Leopold of the Lake Steamer Line. Vincent Cournoyer assisted and directed the singing of "Lizzie Renoir, Vincent Roy, Frank Duquet, Mary Houle, Angelique Soulier and the Morrison sisters." Chippewa Indian Historic Project Records, 1936–42, envelope 3, p. 11.

44. Meyer, *The White Earth Tragedy*, 89.

45. Cleland, *Faith in Paper*, 58.

46. Jacqueline Petersen, "Prelude to Red River: A Social Portrait of Great Lakes Métis," *Ethnohistory* 25, no. 1 (1978): 41–67. P. 45; italic emphasis added.

47. Theresa Schenck, *William W. Warren: The Life, Letters, and Times of an Ojibwe Leader* (Lincoln and London: University of Nebraska Press, 2007), 151.

48. Rebecca Kugel, *To Be the Main Leaders of Our People: A History of Minnesota Ojibwe Politics, 1825–1898* (East Lansing: Michigan State University Press, 1998), 87.

49. William Watts Folwell, *A History of Minnesota* (St. Paul: Minnesota Historical Society Press, 1956).

50. *Half-breed scrip, Chippewas of Lake Superior*, 15. The report found that the decision taken by the commissioner of Indian affairs in 1863 to suspend the requirement that mixed bloods reside "among or contiguous to the Chippewas of Lake Superior" created an opportunity for fraud that multiplied the intended beneficiaries by a factor of four.

51. Treaty with the Winnebago, 10 U.S. Statutes 1172; Treaty with the Chippewa, 10 U.S. Statutes 1165; Treaty with the Wyandottes, 10 U.S. Statutes 1159.

52. Treaty with the Chippewas, 10 U.S. Statutes 1165.

53. The first appearance of the phrase is in a 1793 Pennsylvania statute regarding the purchase of islands: "When the purchaser shall have made full payment for all the purchase-moneys of any such islands, it shall be lawful for the governor to grant him a patent, in the usual form of the land-office, vesting the same in him, his heirs and assigns for ever." John Purdon and Frederick C. Brightly, *A Digest of the Laws of Pennsylvania, from the Year One Thousand Seven Hundred to the Sixth Day of June, One Thousand Eight Hundred and Eighty-Three* (11th ed., rev., Philadelphia: Kay and Brothers, ps.), 1047. It would apparently come to be a real estate term of art over the course of the nineteenth century.

54. See, Robert W. McCluggage, "The Senate and Indian Titles, 1800–1825," *Western Historical Quarterly* 1, no. 4 (Oct., 1970): 415–25. Creeks, Choctaws, and Chickasaws were allotted in treaties signed in the 1830s without regard to bloodedness but largely for the purpose of making it possible for individual Indians to sell their allotment and move west across the Mississippi. See Mary Elizabeth Young, *Redskins, Ruffleshirts, and Rednecks: Indian Allotments in Alabama and Mississippi, 1930–1860* (Norman: University of Oklahoma Press, 1961).

55. Paul Gates, "Indian Allotments Preceding the Dawes Act," in John G. Clark, ed., *The Frontier Challenge: Responses to the Trans-Mississippi West* (Lawrence: University of Kansas Press, 1971): 141–70, 142.

56. Tanis Thorne, *People of the River: Mixed-Blood Families on the Lower Missouri* (PhD dissertation, University of California, Los Angeles, 1987), 21215.

57. Ibid., 176–77.

58. Patrick Wolfe, *Traces of History: Elementary Structures of Race* (London and New York: Verso, 2016), 187.

59. Theda Perdue, "Mixed Blood," in *Indians: Racial Construction in the Early South* (Athens: University of Georgia Press, 2005).

60. Rebecca Kugel, "Planning to Stay: Native Strategies to Remain in the Great Lakes, Post-War of 1812," *Middle West Review* 2, no. 2 (Spring 2016), 1–26, 14–15.

61. Thorne, *People of the River*, 177.

62. Ibid., 179.

63. Ibid., 181.

64. Ibid., 182.

65. Ibid., 179.

66. Amendments Proposed to an Indian Treaty. December 29, 1817. Committee on Public Lands. Indian Affairs No. 150. Fifteenth Congress, First Session, 149.

67. Treaty with the Wynadot, etc. 7 U.S. Statutes 178.

68. Kugel, "Planning to Stay."

69. Susan E. Gray, "Interlude: Of Two Worlds and Intimate Domains," in James Joseph Buss and C. Jospeh Genetin-Pilawa, *Beyond Two Worlds: Critical Conversations on Language and Power in Native North America* (Albany: SUNY Press, 2014), 161–80, 169.

70. Treaty with the Potawatomi, 7 U.S. Statutes 185.

71. Treaty with the Chippewa, 7 U.S. Statutes 203.

72. Treaty with the Wea, 7 U.S. Statutes 186.

73. Treaty with the Miami, 7 U.S. Statutes 300.

74. Treaty of Fond du Lac, 7 U.S. Statutes 290.

75. Ibid.

76. Treaty with the Potawatomi, 7 U. S. Statutes 317.

77. Treaty with the Chippewa, etc., 7 U. S. Statutes 320.

78. Treaty with the Sauk and Foxes, etc., 7 U.S. Statutes 328; italic emphasis added.

79. Treaty with the Winnebago, 7 U.S Statutes 323.

80. Bethel Saler, "Negotiating the Treaty Polity: Gender, Race and the Transformation of Wisconsin from Indian Country into an American State, 1776–1854" (PhD dissertation, University of Wisconsin-Madison, 1999), 193.

81. Treaty with the Chickasaw, 7 U. S. Statutes 450.

82. Treaty with the Wyandot, 11 U.S. Statutes 581.

83. Thorne, "People of the River," 207.

84. Ibid., 208–9.

85. Lewis Cass and Thomas McKenney to Thomas Barbour, September 11, 1826. *American State Papers (Indian Affairs) II*: no. 243, 682; italic emphasis added.

86. Thomas Ingersoll, *To Intermix with our White Brothers*, 157.

87. Ibid., 227.

88. Ibid., 234–35.

89. Treaty with the Sauk and Foxes, 15 U.S. Statutes 467.

90. Kinney, *A Continent Lost*, 124.

91. John Nichols, "The Translation of Key Phrases in the Treaties of 1837 and 1855," in James McClurken, *Fish in the Lakes, Wild Rice, and Game in Abundance* (East Lansing: Michigan State University Press, 2000): 514–24, 519.

92. Treaty of St. Peters, 7 U.S. Statutes 536; italic emphasis added.

93. Jennifer Brown and Theresa Schenck, "Métis, Mestizo and Mixed-blood," in Philip J. Deloria and Neal Salisbury, eds., *A Companion to American Indian History* (Malden, Mass: Blackwell, 2002), 321–38, 331.

94. Treaty with the Chippewa, 7 U.S Statutes 591.

95. Treaty with the Chippewa of Mississippi and Lake Superior, 9 U.S. Statutes 904; emphasis added.

96. Treaty with the Sauk and Foxes, etc., 7 U.S. Statutes 328.

97. Gustav O. Brohough, "Sioux and Chippewa Half-Breed Scrip and Its Application to the Minnesota Pine Lands" (Master's thesis, University of Wisconsin, 1906).

98. Arnold R. Alanen, "Homes on the Range: Settling the Penokee-Gogebic Iron Ore District of Northern Wisconsin and Michigan," in Robert C. Ostergren and Thomas R. Vale, eds., *Wisconsin Land and Life* (Madison: University of Wisconsin Press, 1997), 241–62, 245.

Chapter 4

1. Alfred Brunson Papers, Sub-agent Mss Letterbook. State Historical Society of Wisconsin.

2. Michael Witgen, *An Infinity of Nations*, 233. 345; Frederic Baraga, *A Dictionary of the Ojibwe Language* (St. Paul: Minnesota Historical Society, 1992), Part II, Ojibwe-English, 17.

3. Paul Spruhan, "A Legal History of Blood Quantum in Federal Indian Law to 1935," *South Dakota Law Review* 5 (2005): 1–50, 11; emphasis added.

4. Witgen, *Infinity of Nations*, 20, 14.

5. Gary Clayton Anderson, *Kinsmen of Another Kind: Dakota-White relations in the Upper Mississippi Valley, 1650–1862* (St. Paul: Minnesota Historical Society Press, 1997), 2: Pekka Hämäläinen, *The Commanche Empire* (New Haven and London: Yale University Press, 2008), 11.

6. See especially Pauline Strong, *Captive Selves, Captivating Others: The Poetics and Politics of Colonial American Captivity Narratives* (Routledge, 2018).

7. Henry Rowe Schoolcraft, *Schoolcraft's Expedition to Lake Itasca*, ed. Philip Mason (East Lansing: Michigan State University Press, 1993), appendix A: 126–27; italics in original.

8. Ibid., 120.

9. Schenck, *All My Relations*, 8.

10. Ella C. Brunson, "Alfred Brunson, Pioneer of Wisconsin Methodism," *Wisconsin Magazine of History* 2, no. 2 (December 1918): 129–48, 130.

11. Ibid., 131.

12. Alfred Brunson, *A Western Pioneer* (New York: Carlton and Lanahan, 1872–[79]), 207.

13. Alfred Brunson Papers, Sub-agent Mss Letterbook. State Historical Society of Wisconsin.

14. Jennifer Brown, "Linguistic Solitudes and Changing Social Categories," in Carol M. Judd and Arthur J. Ray, eds., *Old Trails and New Directions: Papers of the Third North American Fur Trade Conference* (Toronto: University of Toronto Press, 1978): 147–59, 158.

15. Treaty of La Pointe, 7 U.S. 591.

16. Theresa Schenck, *William W. Warren: The Life, Letters, and Times of an Ojibwe Leader* (Lincoln and London: University of Nebraska Press, 2007), 23–24.

17. Leonard Wheeler Papers, Diary, March 24, 1844, State Historical Society of Wisconsin.

18. Theresa Schenck, *All Our Relations*, 38–39.

19. Theresa Schenk, "The Cadottes: Five Generations of Fur Traders on Lake Superior," in Jennifer S. H. Brown, W. J. Eccles, Donald P. Heldman, eds., *The Fur Trade Revisited: Selected Papers of the Sixth North American Fur Trade Conference, Mackinac Island, MI, 1991* (East Lansing: Michigan State University Press, 1994), 189–98, 197.

20. Theresa Schenck, *All Our Relations*, 25.

21. Treaty with the Chippewa, 7 U.S. Statutes 591.

Chapter 5

1. "Relations of Indians to Citizenship," 7 Opinions of the Attorney General of the United States (1856), 746–66, 754.

2. Jacob Rader Marcus, *United States Jewry, 1776–1985* (Wayne State University Press, 1989); Lars Larson, *Chequamegon Bay and Its Communities I, Ashland, Bayfield, LaPointe: A Brief History 1659–1883* (Whitewater, Wisconsin, 2005), 69.

3. *New York Daily Tribune*, Monday June 26, 1854.

4. M606 Letters Sent by the Office of Indian Affairs. Volume 49: 0215. August 11, 1854.

5. M234 Letters Received Office of Indian Affairs, La Pointe Agency, 1824–81 (hence LROIA, LaPointe) Roll 391: 0004.

6. United States, Post Office, Selected Items Relating to Minnesota, Minnesota Historical Society Library.

7. 9 U. S. Statutes 904.

8. Rebecca Kugel, *To Be the Main Leaders of Our People: A History of Minnesota Ojibwe Politics, 1825–1898* (East Lansing: Michigan State University Press, 1998), passim.

9. See Robert Kuhiken's "Settin' the Woods on Fire: Rural Incendiarism as Protest," *Geographic Review* 89, no. 3 (July, 1999): 343–63.

10. LROIA, Lapointe. Roll 391: 0030,0101.

11. Ibid., Roll 391: 0045.

12. Ibid., Roll 391: 0044.

13. Ibid., Roll 391: 0025.

14. Nelson, Knute. "A Summary of Our Most Important Land Laws," *Annals of the American Academy of Political and Social Science* 33, no. 3 (1909): 127–35, 128.

15. Locally, the notice would first appear on page 3 of the July 10, 1855 issue of the *Superior Chronicle*, Superior, Wisconsin and ran for several weeks. It was accompanied by a notice to those who had "just and legal claims against the Chippewa Indians" to present them to Agent Gilbert before the next annuity payment in August.

16. LROIA, La Pointe, Roll 391: 0056.

17. Ibid., Roll 391: 0090.

18. Ibid., Roll 391: 0019.

19. Ibid., Roll 391: 0030; emphasis in original.

20. Ibid., Roll 391: 0115.

21. M606 Letters Sent by the Office of Indian Affairs. Volume 53, February 6, 1856.

22. Ibid., January 7, 1856.

23. LROIA, La Pointe, Roll 391: 0252.

24. Ibid.; emphasis added.

25. LROIA, La Pointe, Roll 391: 0284.

26. Ibid., Roll 391: 0288.

27. Ibid., Roll 391: 0282; italic emphasis added.

28. Henry Gilbert to Commissioner Manypenny, October 17, 1854. Reprinted as appendix 5 in Ronald N. Satz, "Chippewa Treaty Rights: The Reserved Rights of

Wisconsin's Chippewa Indians in Historical Perspective," *Transactions* 79 no. 1 (Madison: Wisconsin Academy of Sciences, Arts and Letters, 1991).

29. *The Daily Minnesotan*, Official Paper of the City, Saturday Morning, August 26, 1854.

30. See Katherine Neils Conzen, "The Winnebago Urban System: Indian Policy and Townsite Promotion on the Upper Mississippi," in Rondo Cameron, ed., *Cities and Markets: Studies in the Organization of Human Space* (Lanham, Md.: University Press of America, 1997), 269–310.

31. "Land Office Frauds," *The New York Times*, December 9, 1854.

32. "Relations of Indians to Citizenship," 7 Opinions of the Attorney General of the United States 746–66 (1856), 754.

33. Ibid., 749.

34. Ibid., 752.

35. Ibid., 752, 755. For Cushing's treatment of the Indian question, see *Congressional Globe*, 24th Congress, 2nd Session, 1 February 1837, 303–5, appendix.

36. Alice E. Smith. "Caleb Cushing's Investments in the St. Croix Valley," *The Wisconsin Magazine of History* 28, no. 1 (Sept., 1944): 7–19, 8.

37. "The Townsite of Superior City—Important Decision by the Secretary of the Interior," *Superior Chronicle*, June 26, 1858; "Western Land Frauds: More Blood in the Body than Shows in the Face-Land Frauds in the Northwest—The Superior City Controversy—Pre-emptions by Swedes and Indians," *New York Times*, July 19, 1858.

38. "Relations of Indians," 7 Opinions of the Attorney General, 756.

39. Ibid., 755; italic emphasis added.

40. Ibid., 746.

41. LROIA, La Pointe. Roll 391: 0368; italic emphasis added.

42. Treaty with the Chippewa, 7 U.S. Statutes 290.

43. LROIA, La Pointe, Roll 391: 0324.

44. Board of Commissioners of Public Lands: Surveyors' Field Notes, 1832–1865, electronic resource. University of Wisconsin Digital Collections.

45. Quoted in Horace V. Winchell, "The Lake Superior Iron-Ore Region, U.S.A.," *Transactions of the Federated Institution of Mining Engineers* XIII (London: Andrew Reid, 1898), 499.

46. *Ashland Weekly Press*, October 6, 1877.

47. Wisconsin and Lake Superior Mining and Smelting Company, *The Penokee Iron Range of Lake Superior: with reports and statistics showing its mineral wealth and prospects: charter and organization of the Wisconsin and Lake Superior Mining and Smelting Company. Wisconsin & Lake Superior Mining & Smelting Company* (Milwaukee: Starr & Son, Caloric Power Presses, 1860), 25–26; The 1860 federal census enumeration sheets for Bay Port Township in Ashland County, Wisconsin lists dwelling numbers 253–99 as "Unoccupied on mineral range."

48. Increase Lapham papers, Box 20, file 14, State Historical Society of Wisconsin.

49. A. N. Winchell, *Handbook of Mining in the Lake Superior Region* (Minneapolis: Brian and Learned, 1920), 9.

50. Milo M. Quaife "Increase Allen Lapham, First Scholar of Wisconsin," *Wisconsin Magazine of History* 1, no. 1 (1917): 3–15, 4; A. N. Winchell, *Handbook of Mining in the Lake Superior Region* (Minneapolis: Bryon and Learned 1920), 9; Erika Janik, "Citizen Scientist," *Wisconsin Natural Resources Magazine* (February 2007). http://dnr.wi.gov/wnrmag/html/stories/2007/feb07/lapham.htm. Visited September 27, 2017.

51. Wisconsin and Lake Superior Mining, 54; italic emphasis added.

52. Amorin Mello, "Wisconsin's Government Presumes Adverse Impacts Necessary for Mining Jobs," *Woods Person: Thoughts and Reports on What Is Happening in Wisconsin's North Woods*, May 7, 2013. Woodsperson.blogspot.com. Viewed February 10, 2016.

53. The author seems to be thinking of the Wisconsin and Lake Superior Mining and Smelting Company given the list of principle men he recalls.

54. *History of Milwaukee, Wisconsin: From Prehistoric Times to the Present Date* (Milwaukee Genealogical Society, 1881): 790–92; James Hansen, "A Roll of Mixed-blood Sioux, 1855–56," *Minnesota Genealogical Journal* 7 (November 1987): 601–20.

55. Lucy Eldersveld Murphy, *Great Lakes Creoles: A French-Indian Community on the Northern Borderlands, Prairie du Chien, 1750–1860* (Cambridge University Press, 2014).

56. Theresa Schenck, *All Our Relations*, 78–79.

57. Gail Morin, *Chippewa Half-Breeds of Lake Superior* (Pawtucket, R.I.: Quintin Publications, 1998), 169.

58. John S. Buck, "The Survey of the Penoka Iron Range and Incidents Connected with Its Early History," *Ashland Weekly Press*, December 8, 1877.

59. Frank A. Flower, *A History of Milwaukee from Pre-historic Times to the Present date, embracing a summary sketch of the Native Tribes and an Exhaustive Record of Men and events for the Past Century, etc. Volume 1* (Chicago: The Western Historical Company, 1881), pp. 790–91; italic emphasis added.

60. Buck, "The Survey of the Penoka Iron Range."

61. Bruce K. Cox, *Mines of the Pewabic Country of Michigan and Wisconsin, Volume 3, Wisconsin Iron* (Agogebic Press, LLC, 2005): 154–57.

62. Article IV, U.S. Constitution.

63. LROIA, La Pointe, Roll 391: 0333.

64. Board of Commissioners of Public Lands: Surveyors' Field Notes, 1832–1865. Interior Field Notes, General Description of Township 44N Range 2W; italic emphasis added.

65. The February 16, 1858, issue of the *Superior Chronicle* included a front-page article entitled "Iron Mines of Wisconsin," which noted the state geologist's recent report about the recently discovered, yet little known "iron wealth of Lake Superior" and the fact that "the best iron lands have been settled by pre-emptors under the 1841 law."

66. Gustav Brohough, "Sioux and Chippewa Half-Breed Scrip and its Application to the Minnesota Pine Lands" (Master's thesis, University of Wisconsin-Madison, 1906), 32.

67. Folwell, William Watts. *History of Minnesota*, Volume I, 485.

68. Schenck, *All Our Relations*, 107.

69. The south half of the northwest quarter of the Section 25 of Township 45 North, Range 1 West, U.S. Department of the Interior, Bureau of Land Management, General Land Office Records, http://www.glorecords.blm.gov/.

70. The south half of the southeast quarter of Section 27, Township 45 North Range 1 West.

71. Commissioner of Public Lands, Plat Map for T45N R1W (original). University of Wisconsin-Madison Library Digital Collection, http://images.library.wisc.edu/awareImageServer/SurveyNotesImageNav.jsp?collection=SurveyNotes&resource=PlatMaps/TN45/reference/004501WA.jp2. Surveys were done in 1847 and 1857. The map is dated 1858. Site visited October 31, 2014.

72. Warranty Deeds, Volume II, Iron County, Wisconsin Register of Deeds Office. Hurley, Wisconsin.

73. H. R. Executive Document No. 25–229, at 7 in Paul Spruhan, 2005. "A Legal History of Blood Quantum in Federal Indian Law to 1935," *South Dakota Law Review* 51, 13; italic emphasis added.

74. W. L. March, Secretary of War to Wm Medill, Commissioner of Indian Affairs. October 1, 1846. *Office copy of laws, regulations, etc. of Indian Bureau, 1950* (Washington: GPO, 1869), 74.

75. ARCIA, 1855, 19.

76. *Half-Breed Scrip, Chippewas of Lake Superior*, 61; italic emphasis added.

77. ARCIA, 1856, 4.

78. Ibid., 11.

79. Paul Wallace Gates, *Fifty Million Acres: Conflicts Over Kansas Land Policy, 1854–1890* (New York: Arno Press, 1954), 16.

80. United States, General Land Office. Wisconsin Local Office Tract Books, 1835–1909. Microfilm, State Historical Society of Wisconsin.

81. Affidavit of Julius Austrian. Interior Department Appointment Papers, 1849–1907. Roll 6, Superior Land Office 1854–1860.

82. Joel Allen Barber papers, 1832–1918. State Historical Society of Wisconsin.

83. Affidavit of John Howard, Interior Department Appointment Papers, 1849–1907. Roll 6, Superior Land Office 1854–1860.

84. Rebecca Kugel, "Planning to Stay: Native Strategies to Remain in the Great Lakes, Post-War 1812," *Middle West Review* 2, no. 2 (2016): 1–26.

85. In the late nineteenth century, the case of Jane Waldron, a mixed-blood Sioux, in a conflict with a full-blood over an allotment, led both state and federal officials to contend that mixed-bloods were citizens and not Indians, though they had recently been counted as Indians for purposes of ceding land. Waldron would eventually win and be regarded as Indian. See Paul Spruhan, "A Legal History of Blood Quantum in Federal Indian Law to 1935," *South Dakota Law Review* 51 (2006): 26–27.

86. LROIA, Roll 391: 0505, Thomas Hendricks, GLO to Charles Mix, Commissioner of Indian Affairs; italic emphasis added.

87. Ibid.

88. Ibid.

89. "Relations of Indians," 7 Opinions of the Attorney General, 746.

90. M606, Letters Sent by the Indian Division of the Office of the Secretary of the Interior, 1849–1903, Volume 59, 7.

91. *Half-Breed Scrip, Chippewas of Lake Superior*, 291.

92. Treaty with the Winnebago, 10 U.S. Statutes 1109. The phrase appears in an 1855 treaty with the Ottawa and Chippewa (11 U.S. Statutes 621) and in 1856, in a treaty with the Stockbridge and Munsee (11 U.S. Statutes 663); however, the first treaty only grants those fee patents after a ten-year period, and the second places a ten-year restriction on sale or transfer of the patent.

93. In the Treaty of 1836 with the Chippewa of Michigan (7 U.S. Statutes 503), the traders sought to distinguish three classes of mixed-bloods on the basis of the esteem with which they were held by their Indian relatives and "their capacity to use and take care of property." Letter of William Bell to President Jackson, November 13, 1836. LROIA, La Pointe, Roll 770: 0183.

94. Warrant Deeds, Volume II, Iron County, Wisconsin Register of Deeds Office. Hurley, Wisconsin.

95. LROIA, La Pointe, 1824–81 R 391 0510 Hendricks to Mix, August 13, 1858; italic emphasis added.

96. Records of the Office of Indian Affairs, Letters Sent, 59: 290, Mix to Hendricks, August 16, 1858.

97. 1860 United States Federal Census, LaPointe Township, Ashland County, Wisconsin, 11.

98. Private and Local Laws Passed by the Legislature of Wisconsin, 1859 (Madison, Wis.: Calkins & Proudfit, Printers, 1855–1872): 100–102. For a history of the company, see Bruce K. Cox, *Mines of the Pewabic Country of Michigan and Wisconsin*, Volume 3, Wisconsin Iron Agogebic Press, LLC, 2005, pp. 68–72.

99. The list was created working with the properties identified in the *La Pointe Iron Company of Ashland County, Lake Superior Wisconsin* (Chicago: Evening Post Print, 1871), the Wisconsin Local Office Tract Books, 1835–1909, and the U.S. Department of the Interior, Bureau of Land Management, General Land Office Records, at http://www.glorecords.blm.gov/default.aspx

100. Wisconsin and Lake Superior Mining and Smelting Company, *The Penokee Iron Range of Lake Superior: with reports and statistics showing its mineral wealth and prospects: charter and organization of the Wisconsin and Lake Superior Mining and Smelting Company* (Milwaukee: Starr and Son, 1860).

101. Both names appear in the Lake Pepin Half-Breed Affidavits, Record Group 75, Entry 529, Miscellaneous Reserve Papers, 1825–1907, Box 358, National Archives, Washington, D.C.

102. Treaty with the Sauk and Fox, et al., 7 U.S. Statutes 328.

103. Sioux Half-breed Scrip Act, 10 U.S. Statutes 304.

104. Brohough "Sioux and Chippewa Half-Breed Scrip," 35.

105. The outcome was similar for the mixed-blood members of the indigenous polities who signed the Treaty of Prairie du Chien in 1830 wherein a mixed-blood reservation was created, allotted and then disestablished, the mixed-bloods removing to their respective tribal reservations. See Snowden, Tyndall, and Smith, "American

Indian Sovereignty and Naturalization: It's a Race Thing," *Nebraska Law Review* 80, no. 2 (2001): 171–238, 193.

106. Pamela E. Klassen, *The Story of Radio Mind: A Missionary's Journey on Indigenous Land* (Chicago: University of Chicago Press, 2018), 97.

Chapter 6

1. Melissa Meyer, *The White Earth Tragedy: Ethnicity and Dispossession at a Minnesota Anishinaabe Reservation, 1889–1920* (Lincoln and London: University of Nebraska Press, 1994), 121. *Mahdosayquah*, a White Earth Minnesota Ojibwe woman spoke at a hearing in 1914 at the peak of conflicts over land ownership, allotment, and alienation of community resources characterizing mixed bloods.

2. Richard F. Morse, "The Chippewas of Lake Superior" in *Collections of the State Historical Society of Wisconsin, Volume III*, ed. Lyman Copeland Draper (Madison: State Historical Society of Wisconsin, 1905), 338–69, 362.

3. Meyer, *The White Earth Tragedy*, 121.

4. Theda Perdue, "Mixed Blood" Indians: Racial Construction in the Early South" 2003. Mercer University Lamar Memorial Lectures no. 45. Lamar Memorial Lectures.

5. Thomas N. Ingersoll, *To Intermix with Our White Brothers*, 92–95.

6. John D. Nichols, ed., "Statement Made by the Indians" A Bilingual Petition of the Chippewa of Lake Superior, 1864 (Center for Research and Teaching of Canadian Indian Languages: University of Western Ontario, 1988), 2; Neal et al., *Half Breed Scrip*, 57.

7. Nichols, "Statement," 23.

8. Ibid.

9. Frederic Baraga, *A Dictionary of the Ojibway Language* (St. Paul: Minnesota Historical Society Press, 1992), 124.

10. White, *The Middle Ground*, x.

11. John N. Dickinson, *To Build Canal: Sault Ste. Marie, 1853–1854 and After* (Columbus: Ohio State University Press, 1975), xvii.

12. Eric Olmanson, *The Future City on the Inland Sea: A History of Imaginative Geographies of Lake Superior* (Athens: Ohio University Press, 2007), 116.

13. Roy L. Martin, *History of the Wisconsin Central*, Bulletin No. 54 (The Railway and Locomotive Historical Society, 1941), 18.

14. Ibid., 26.

15. James W. Feldman, *Rewilding the Islands: Nature, History, and Wilderness at Apostle Islands National Lakeshore* (PhD dissertation, University of Wisconsin-Madison, 2004), 80.

16. Bruce K. Cox, *Mines of the Pewabic Country*, 68–72.

17. H. R. Aldrich, *The Geology of the Gogebic Iron Range of Wisconsin* (Wisconsin Geological and Natural History Survey, Bulletin 71. Economic Series no. 24, Madison, Wis.). Published by the State. 1929, 36.

18. Arnold Alanen, "Homes on the Range," 245.

19. Lake Pepin Half-Breed Affidavits, Record Group 75, Entry 529, Miscellaneous Reserve Papers, 1825–1907, Box 358, National Archives, Washington, D.C.

20. Bruce K. Cox, *Mines of the Pewabic Country*, 139–40.

21. Aldrich, *The Geology of the Gogebic Iron Range*, 36.

22. Ibid., 21, 24.

23. Aldich, *The Geology of the Gogebic Iron Range*, 18.

24. Lawrence Roe, *A History of Wisconsin Mining* (Madison: ROECO, 1991), 39.

25. Alanen, "Homes on the Range," 248.

26. Quoting from Mladenoff, "Vegetation Change on the Gogebic Iron Range (Iron County, Wisconsin) 1860 to the Present," in *Transactions of the Wisconsin Academy of Sciences, Arts and Letters* 68, 74–89, 81.

27. James A. Lake, *Law and Mineral Wealth: The Legal Profile of the Wisconsin Mining Industry* (Madison: University of Wisconsin Press, 1962), 78.

28. Mladenoff, "Vegetation Change," 88.

29. Personal Communication, September 2, 2015.

30. Vernon Carstensen, *Farms or Forests: Evolution of a State Policy for Northern Wisconsin, 1850–1932* (University of Wisconsin, College of Agriculture, 1958), 97.

31. Arnold Alanen "Homes on the Range," 253.

32. Robert J. Gough, "Richard T. Ely and the Development of the Wisconsin Cutover." *The Wisconsin Magazine of History* 75, no. 1 (Autumn 1991), 2–38.

33. By contrast, in the southern part of the ceded territory, relations between Potawatomis returning from Kansas in the last part of the nineteenth century who created the village of McCord, and the Finns were said to be cooperative.

34. David Mladenoff, "Vegetation Change," 128–29.

35. Michelle Steen-Adams, Nancy E. Langston, and David J. Mladenoff, "Logging the Great Lakes Indian Reservations: The Case of the Bad River Band of Ojibwe." *American Indian Culture and Research Journal* 34, no. 1 (2010) 41–66, 44.

36. Mladenoff, "Vegetation Change," 88, 111.

37. Ibid., 46.

38. *United States v. Cook*, 86 U.S. 591.

39. Anthony Godfrey, *A Forest History of Ten Wisconsin Indian reservations Under the Great Lakes Agency: Precontact to the Present* (Salt Lake: U.S. West Research, 1996), 39.

40. Steen-Adams et al., "Logging the Great Lakes," 56–57.

41. Ibid., 54–56.

42. Michelle Steen-Adams, "Change on a Northern Wisconsin Landscape: Legacies of Human History" (PhD dissertation, University of Wisconsin-Madison, 2005), 97.

43. David Wrone, "The Economic Impact of the 1837 and 1842 Chippewa Treaties," *American Indian Quarterly* 17, no. 3 (1993): 329–40, 332.

44. Robert Gough, *Farming the Cutover: A Social History of Northern Wisconsin, 1900–1940* (Lawrence: University Press of Kansas, 1997), 19.

45. Chantal Norrgard, *Seasons of Change: Labor, Treaty Rights, and Ojibwe Nationhood* (Chapel Hill: University of North Carolina Press, 2014), 63–107.

46. Ibid., 55.

47. Larry Nesper, *The Walleye War: The Struggle for Ojibwe Spearfishing and Treaty Rights* (Lincoln: University of Nebraska Press, 2002), 49–56.

48. Edmund Jefferson Danziger, *The Chippewas of Lake Superior* (Norman and London: University of Oklahoma Press, 1979), 100.

49. Edmund Jefferson Danziger, *Great Lakes Indian Accommodation and Resistance, 1850–1900* (Ann Arbor: University of Michigan Press, 2009), 213.

50. Danziger, *Great Lakes Indian*, 63.

51. Patricia Shifferd, "A Study in Economic Change: The Chippewa of Northern Wisconsin, 1854–1900," *The Western Canadian Journal of Anthropology* 6, no. 4 (1976): 16–41, 16.

52. Ibid., 217.

53. William Walker to Agent Durfee, August 30, 1881. Record Group 75, Records of the Bureau of Indian Affairs, LaPointe Agency, General Records, Letters Received from the Bad River Reservation, 1879–1924. National Archives, Chicago.

54. William Walker to Agent Durfee, April 10, 1882, RG 75, Letters Received.

55. Nawgawnab to Agent Durfee, July 18, 1883, RG 75, Letters Received.

56. Petition to Agent Durfee, June 18, 1883, RG 75, Letters Received.

57. Michelle M. Steen-Adams, Nancy Langston, and David J. Mladenoff, "White Pine in the Northern Forests: An Ecological and Management History of White Pine on the Bad River Reservation of Wisconsin," *Environmental History* 12 (July 2007): 595–629.

58. Gishhketawug and Edawegeshik to Agent Durfee, February 28, 1883, RG 75, Letters Received.

59. H. Price, Commissioner of Indian Affairs to the Secretary of the Interior, October 17, 1883, 48th Congress, 1st session, House of Representatives Executive Document No. 12.

60. William Walker to Agent Durfee, April 4, 1885, RG 75, Letters Received.

61. Ibid.

62. William Walker to Col. Robert Wagner, Special Agent, May 10, 1889, RG 75, Letters Received.

63. William Walker to Agent Leahy, January 15, 1890, RG 75, Letters Received.

64. Bad River Chiefs to the Commissioner of Indians Affairs, February 26, 1896, RG 75, Letters Received.

65. James Carrier, "Occidentalism: the world turned upside-down," *American Ethnologist* 19, no. 2 (May, 1992): 195–212, 198.

66. Roger Patterson to Agent Mercer, January 23, 1896, RG 75, Letters Received.

67. Roger Patterson to Agent Mercer, March 1, 1897, RG 75, Letters Received.

68. Roger Patterson to Agency, unclear addressee, September 4, 1897, RG 75, Letters Received.

69. Thirteenth Census of the United States 1910-Indian Population. Wisconsin, Ashland County, Bad River, Sheet no. 23b.

70. Annual Genealogical Roll of the Red Cliff Band, 1877; Schenck, *All Our Relations*, 96–97.

71. Thirteenth Census, 22a.

72. Danziger, *Great Lakes Indian Accommodation*, 231. Citing the agent's statistics, Danziger notes that of the 645 members of the community, all wore whiteman's clothing, 575 could read, 500 spoke English, and 95 percent held jobs.

73. Ibid., 243.

74. See Alexandra Harmon, Colleen O'Neill, and Paul Rosier, "Interwoven Economic Histories: American Indians in a Capitalist America," *The Journal of American History* 98, no. 3 (December 2011), 698–722, and Alexandra Harmon, *Rich Indians: Native People and the Problem of Wealth in American History* (Chapel Hill: University of North Carolina Press, 2010).

75. Danziger, *Great Lakes Indian Accommodation*, 89.

76. Shifferd, "A Study of Economic Change," 33–34; underlined in the original.

77. John S. Buck, "The Survey of the Penoka Iron Range and Incidents Connected with its Early History," *Ashland Weekly Press*, December 8, 1877.

78. "Western Land Frauds," *New York Times*, June 19, 1858.

79. Father Valentin, O.S.F., "A Friend of Roy," in *Miscellaneous Materials Related to Vincent Roy*, State Historical Society of Wisconsin.

80. Arthur Tenney Holbrook, *From the Log of a Trout Fisherman* (Norwood, Mass.: Plimpton Press, 1949), 98.

81. Chrysostomus Verwyst. O.F.M., *Life and Labors of Rt. Rev. Frederick Baraga, First Bishop of Marquette, Mich. To Which are Added Short Sketches of the Lives and Labors of Other Indian Missionaries of the Northwest* (Milwaukee, Wis.: M. H. Wiltzius & Co., 1900), 472; Fr. Oderic, O.S.F., "An Uncrowned King of the Chippewas," *The Franciscan Herald 9, no. 4 (March 1921).*

82. United States Census, 1860. Lapointe Township, Ashland County, Wisconsin, 18.

83. Thirteenth Census of the United States 1910-Indian Population, Wisconsin, Ashland County, Bad River, Sheet no. 8A.

84. Holbrook, *From the Log of a Trout Fisherman*, 44.

85. Eliza Morrison., *A Little History of My Forest Life: An Indian-White Autobiography by Eliza Morrison* (Tustin, Mich.: Ladyslipper Press, 2002), 51, 78, 145.

86. Ibid., 85.

87. Ibid., 104.

88. Ibid., 95.

89. Ibid., 79.

90. Ibid., 111.

91. Schenck, *All Our Relations*, 30.

92. United States Census 1860. La Pointe Township, Ashland County, Wisconsin, 11.

93. Holbrook, *From the Log of Trout a Fisherman*, 75.

94. Ibid., 54, 55.

95. Ibid., 124.

96. Ibid., 71.

97. Ibid., 72.

98. Ibid., 65.

99. Ibid., 145.

100. Thirteenth Census of the United States 1910-Indian Population, Wisconsin, Ashland County, Bad River, Sheet no. 8a.

101. Morrison, *A Little History*, 172.

102. Ibid., 180.

Chapter 7

1. Chief Doolittle at Proceedings of the Council held at Bad River from March 31–April 2, 1913, 25. BIA files Ashland, Wis.; Dr. Wooster at *Hearings before the Committee on Indian Affairs, House of* Representatives, 63rd Cong., 3rd Session, February 3, 1921, 18.

2. Melissa Meyer, *The White Earth Tragedy: Ethnicity and Dispossession at a Minnesota Anishinaabe Reservation, 1889–1920* (Lincoln and London: University of Nebraska Press, 1994).

3. Katherine Ellinghaus, "The Benefits of Being Indian: Blood Quanta, Intermarrige, and Allotment Policy on the White Earth Reservation, 1889–1920," *Frontiers: A Journal of Women Studies* 29, nos. 2/3: 81–105.

4. Thomas Biolsi, "The Birth of the Reservation: Making the Modern Individual among the Lakota" *American Ethnologist* 22, no. 1 (1995): 28–53, 35.

5. Loretta Fowler, *Tribal Sovereignty and the Historical Imagination: Cheyenne-Arapahoe Politics* (Lincoln and London: University of Nebraska Press, 2002), 29–43.

6. Paul Spruhan, "A Legal History of Blood Quantum in Federal Indian Law to 1935," *South Dakota Law Review* 51, 27–36.

7. David L. Beaulieu, "Curly Hair and Big Feet: Anthropology and the Implementation of Land Allotment on the White Earth Chippewa Reservation," *American Indian Quarterly* 8, no. 4 (Autumn 1984): 281–314, 287.

8. Carole Goldberg-Ambrose, "Of Native Americans and Tribal Members: The Impact of Law on Indian Group Life," *Law and Society Review* 28 (1994), 1123–48.

9. Beaulieu, "Curly Hair . . . ," 288.

10. Office of Indian Affairs, LaPointe Agency, Report of June 30, 1923, 2.

11. 1917 ARCOIA, Office of Indian Affairs, Annual Reports, La Pointe Agency, 18.

12. In a 2016 letter to Anthony Corbine at the Bad River Natural Resource Department, Linda Bristol of Bayfield Wisconsin concluded that the map was drawn before 1895 on the grounds that its author's obituary appears in the *Ashland Daily Press* in March of that year. She told Nesper that she found the map doing genealogical research and indicated that it may be from the Smithsonian. Phone conversation, January 17, 2019.

13. Edmund Danziger, *Chippewa Indians of Lake Superior* (Norman and London: University of Oklahoma Press, 1979), 108.

14. Danziger, *Chippewa Indians,* 102; Office of Indian Affairs, LaPointe Agency, Annual Reports between 1910 and 1924 report this number of local Indians working at Stearns Lumber Company.

15. Edmund Danziger, *Chippewa of Lake Superior,* 119.

16. Larry Nesper, "The 1914 Meeting of the Society of American Indians at UW-Madison," *Wisconsin Magazine of History* 102, no. 2 (Winter 2018): 28–37.

17. Ibid., 103.

18. And there is evidence of allotment beginning under the treat as early as 1867 with the patent of one Aie-ne-gan-bow entered into the Hearings before the Senate Committee on Indian Affairs on Matters Relating to Wisconsin Indians, 61st Congress, 2nd Session, p. 37. In 1911, the agent reported that allotment began in 1867, and to date, 1021 trust patents had been issued under the Treaty of Sept. 30, 1854. Office of Indian Affairs Annual Reports, 1910–39, La Pointe Agency, 28.

19. Anthony Godfrey, *A Forest History of Ten Wisconsin Indian Reservations under the Great Lakes Agency: Precontact to the Present* (Salt Lake: US West Research, 1996), 84.

20. Hearings before the Committee on Indian Affairs, United States Senate on Senate Resolution No. 263 (Washington: GPO, 1910), 532.

21. Ibid., 220.

22. Senate Hearings, 1910, 220.

23. Campbell to Clapp, February 14, 1922. *Samuel Campbell papers.* State Historical Society of Wisconsin.

24. *Proceedings of the La Pointe Band of Chippewa Indians, In General Council, Assembled at Odanah, Wisconsin, 1907* (State Historical Society of Wisconsin).

25. Samuel Campbell to Senator Clapp, April 15, 1912. *Samuel Campbell Papers,* General Correspondence, Box 1, Folder 1. State Historical Society of Wisconsin.

26. Senate Hearings, 1910, 208.

27. "Chief Ya Banse and the 'Lost Tribe,'" Chippewa Indian Historical Project, 1936–40. United States, Works Progress Administration, Reel 1, Envelope 1, no. 29.

28. Senate Hearings, 1910, 220–22.

29. Proceedings of the Council Held at Bad River from March 31–April 2, 1913 (Great Lakes Agency files, Ashland, Wisconsin).

30. "Wooster Leaves for Other Fields," *The Odanah Star*, October 23, 1914.

31. "Allotment List Recently Finished," *The Odanah Star*, November 13, 1914.

32. "Origins of the Lost Tribe," *The Odanah Star,* December 18, 1914.

33. Proceedings of the Council of the Chippewa Indians on the Bad River Reservation at Odanah, Wis. Sept. 8, 9, 10, 1919 (Great Lakes Agency files, Ashland, Wisconsin), 20.

34. Ibid., 23.

35. Ibid., 26.

36. Ibid., 30.

37. 13 United States Statutes at Large 182.

38. Proceedings Council, 1919, 41.

39. Ibid., 43.

40. Ibid., 56; italic emphasis added.

41. Office of Indian Affairs, LaPointe Agency, Narrative Reports, June 30, 1920, 25.

42. Hearings before the Committee on Indian Affairs, House of Representatives, 63rd Cong., 3rd Session, February 3, 1921, 21.

43. Thirteenth Census of the United States 1910-Indian Population. Wisconsin, Ashland County, Bad River, 3b; Senate Committee on Indian Affairs, Condition of Indian Affairs in Wisconsin, 61st Cong., 2nd Session on Senate Resolution 263 (Washington: GPO, 1910), 228.

44. House of Representatives Committee on Indian Affairs, Bad River Reservation Allotments, 66th Cong., 3rd Session (Washington: GPO), 14.

45. Register of Meeting of Association of American Indians at Madison, October 6–11. Papers of the Society of American Indians, State Historical Society of Wisconsin.

46. Thirteenth Census, 1a–25b.

47. House of Representatives Committee on Indian Affairs, 14.

48. Melissa Meyer, *The White Earth Tragedy.*

49. Ibid., 13.

50. The corpus is thirty-three nonsequential unenumerated pages of meeting minutes written by David English's father from a series of meetings in 1920, largely the memoirs of Blackbird for the chiefs and headmen pertaining to discrepancies in the treaty of 1854. On file at the Bad River Tribal Historic Preservation Office, Odanah, Wisconsin.

51. He testified that he was "15 or 16 years of age" at the time of the 1854 treaty. 1910 Senate Hearings, 201.

52. Ibid., 210.

53. Richard F. Morse, "The Chippewas of Lake Superior," in Lyman Copeland Draper, ed., *Collections of the State Historical Society of Wisconsin, Volume III* (Madison: Wisconsin Historical Society, 1905), 338–69, 345.

54. In 1892, the Treasury Department determined that the United States owed the Lake Superior Chippewa $92,302.69 for the difference in value of coin and Civil War–era devalued greenbacks, including $10,600.08 in arrearages, adding to the sense of being owed in the ninety-thousand-dollar range. (See Danziger, 1973, 182.)

55. "Treaty Commissioner Henry C. Gilbert's Explanation of the Treaty Concluded in 1854 with the Assistance of David B. Harriman," Appendix 5 in Ronald N. Satz, "Chippewa Treaty Rights: The Reserved Rights of Wisconsin's Chippewa Indians in Historical Perspective" Wisconsin Academy of Arts, Sciences and Letters 79, no. 1 (1991): 177–79.

56. Albert C. Stuntz, *Diaries 1858, 1863–1869, 1882* State Historical Society of Wisconsin. He surveyed the Wisconsin Chippewa reservations in 1863.

57. *Chippewa Half Breed Scrip*, 248; U.S. Department of Interior, Bureau of Land Management, General Land Office Records; U.S. Census, 1860, Bayfield Township, La Pointe, Wisconsin, 5; Thirteenth Census, 1910, Bad River, 20a.

58. Schenck, *All Our Relations*, 58.

59. U.S. Department of the Interior, Bureau of Land Management, General Land Office Records.

60. Chantal Norrgard, *Seasons of Change: Labor, Treaty Rights and Ojibwe Nationhood* (Chapel Hill: University of North Carolina Press, 2014), 20–42.

61. "My Parents: John B. Denomie and 0-musk-a-wa-si-nau-qua," *Chippewa Historical Project, 1936–40.* Reel 1, Envelope 12, no. 7. Denomie was also the subject of a short biographical essay in *Noble Lives of a Noble Race*, a 1909 publication of the Franciscan Sisters of Perpetual Adoration, written by their students at Bad River's St. Mary's School in celebration of the school's twenty-fifth anniversary.

62. Schenck, "The Cadottes: Five Generations of Fur Traders . . ."; Neal et al., Half Breed Scrip, 246, 250; U.S. Census, 1860, Bayfield Township, La Pointe, Wisconsin, 11; U.S. Department of Interior, Bureau of Land Management, General Land Office Records.

63. *Chippewa Half Breed Scrip*, 257; U.S. Department of Interior, Bureau of Land Management, General Land Office Records; Thirteenth Census, 1910, Bad River, 5b.

64. Richard Olney, "Sioux Mixed Bloods—Attorney General," 20 Opinions of the Attorneys-General, 742–46, 743, 745.

65. Circe Sturm, *Blood Politics: Race, Culture and Identity in the Cherokee Nation of Oklahoma* (Berkeley and Los Angeles: University of California Press, 2002), 39–43.

66. Patty Loew, *Newspapers and the Lake Superior Chippewa in the "Unprogressive" Era* (PhD dissertation, University of Wisconsin-Madison, 1998): 72–107.

67. Treaty with the Chippewa, 10 U.S. Statutes 1109, Article II, 2nd paragraph.

68. Loew, *Newspapers and the Lake Superior Chippewa.*

69. Ibid., 90–91.

70. Meyer, *The White Earth Tragedy*, 192.

71. Joseph Genetin-Pilawa, "In the Interests of Harmony and Good Government": Allotment Era Politics in the Great Lakes Region" (Master's thesis, Bowling Green University, 2002), 38.

72. Henry Gilbert to Commissioner Manypenny, October 17, 1854. Reprinted as appendix 5 in Ronald N. Satz, "Chippewa Treaty Rights: The Reserved Rights of Wisconsin's Chippewa Indians in Historical Perspective," *Transactions* 79, no. 1 (Madison: Wisconsin Academy of Sciences, Arts and Letters, 1991).

73. Jacqueline Peterson, *The People in Between: Indian-White Marriage and the Genesis of a Metis Society and Culture in the Great Lakes Region, 1680–1830* (PhD dissertation, University of Illinois, 1981), 158.

74. Michael D. Munnell, *American Indian Marriage Record Directory for Ashland County, Wisconsin, 1874–1907* (Chippewa Heritage Publications, 1993).

75. Ibid., v.

76. Thank you to Michael Shortreed, UW-Madison Department of Chemistry for the mathematical formula to derive these proportions.

77. "Scrip Act—Mixed Blood Chippewa Indians," *Chippewa Indian Historical Project*, Reel 1, Envelope 1, no. 31.

78. "Tom O'Connor," *Chippewa Indian Historical Project*, Reel 2, Envelope 16, unenumerated.

79. Indian Reorganization Act, 25 U.S. C. § 472.

80. Fifteenth Census of the United States, Wisconsin, Vilas County, Lac du Flambeau, Enumeration District 63–67; Ashland County, Odanah Village, Enumeration District 2–23.

81. Morin, *Chippewa Half-Breeds of Lake Superior*, 84.

82. Larry Nesper, "Historical Ambivalence in a Tribal Museum," *Museum Anthropology* 28, no. 2 (2005): 1–16.

83. Gail Guthrie Valaskakis, "The Chippewa and the Other: Living the Heritage of Lac du Flambeau," *Cultural Studies* 2, no. 3 (October 1988): 267–93, 268.

84. Ibid., 272.

85. Ibid., 274, 281, 282.

86. Schenck, *All Our Relations*, 73–75; Gail Morin, *Chippewa Half-Breeds of Lake Superior*, 94–95.

87. Morin, *Chippewa Half-Breeds*, 178–79; *State v Gurnoe*, 53 Wis. 2d 390 (1972).

88. U.S. Department of the Interior, Bureau of Land Management, General Land Office Records.

89. Chantal Norrgard, *Seasons of Change*, 59–60.

90. Patty Loew, *Seventh Generation Earth Ethics: Native Voices of Wisconsin* (Madison: Wisconsin Historical Society Press, 2014): 111–28.

91. Larry Nesper, "Simulating Culture: Being Indian for Tourists in Lac du Flambeau's Wa-Swa-Gon Indian Bowl," *Ethnohistory* 50, no. 3 (2003): 447–72.

92. Personal Communication, August 7, 2000.

93. Arthur Tenney Holbrook, "Antoine Dennis: Last of the Chippewa Mail Runners," *Wisconsin Magazine of History* 22, no. 4 (July 1939): 377–84.

94. Gail Morin, *Chippewa Half-Breeds*, 54.

95. General Land Office Records.

96. Gail Morin, *Chippewa Half-Breeds*, 33.

Conclusion

1. H. Craig Miner and William E. Unrau, *The End of Indian Kansas: A Study of Cultural Revolution, 1854–1871* (Lawrence: Regents Press of Kansas, 1978), 32.

2. Article III, Section 4. *Constitution of the State of Wisconsin, Adopted in Convention in Madison, on the first day of February, in the Year of Our Lord one thousand eight hundred and forty-eight.*

3. Though the Fourteenth Amendment on its face would appear to make Indians citizens, the Supreme Court found in *Elk v. Wilkins* in 1884 that it did not.

4. *General Allotment Act*, 24 U.S. Stat. 388, § 6.

5. Ronald N. Satz, "Chippewa Treaty Rights: The Reserved Rights of Wisconsin's Chippewa Indians in Historical Perspective," in *Transactions of the Wisconsin Academy of Arts, Sciences and Letters* 79, no. 1 (Madison, 1991); Larry Nesper, *The Walleye War: The Struggle for Ojibwe Spearfishing and Treaty Rights* (Lincoln: University of Nebraska Press, 2002).

6. Melissa Meyer, *The White Earth Tragedy*, 220.

7. *Survey of Conditions of the Indians of United States*, Hearings Before a Subcommittee on Indian Affairs, United States Senate, Seventy-first Congress, First Session (Washington: GPO, 1929).

8. David R. Wrone, "The Economic Impact of the 1837 and 1842 Treaties," *American Indian Quarterly* 17, no. 3 (1993): 329–40.

9. Arnold R. Alanen, "Homes on the Range: Settling the Penokee-Gogebic Iron Ore District of Norther Wisconsin and Michigan," in Robert C. Ostergren and Thomas R. Vale, eds., *Wisconsin Land Life* (Madison: University of Wisconsin Press, 1997), 242.

10. MNopedia, http://www.mnopedia.org/trading-posts-and-big-boxes-social-political-and-economic-importance-minnesota-business. Accessed November 7, 2017.

11. *Minnesota Chippewa Tribe et al on behalf of the Chippewas of Lake Superior v The United States of America, Docket #18-U.* Indian Claims Commission Decisions, vol. 25, 57.

12. *Minnesota Chippewa Tribe et al.*, vol. 35, 445.

13. Constitutions and By-Laws of the Bands of Lake Superior Chippewa Indians.

14. Bruce K. Cox, *Mines of the Pewabic Country of Michigan and Wisconsin, Volume 3: Wisconsin Iron* (Wakefield, Mich.: Agogeebik Press, 2005), 72.

15. Telephone conversation, Nesper-Thiede September 2, 2015.

16. *Woods Person: Thoughts and Reports on What Is Happening in Wisconsin's North Woods*, http://woodsperson.blogspot.com/2013/12/circles-of-friends-spheres-of-influence.html?q=circles+of+friends, visited December 19, 2017.

17. Circe Sturm's *Blood Politics: Race, Culture, and Identity in the Cherokee Nation of Oklahoma* (Berkeley: University of California Press, 2002) and Kristina M. Jacobsen's *The Sound of Navajo Country: Music, Language, and Diné Belonging* (Chapel Hill: University of North Carolina Press, 2017), who uses the term "social citizenship," bookend this growing literature.

18. Larry Nesper, *The Walleye War*.

19. Robert Ritzenthaler, "The Acquisition of Surnames by the Chippewa Indians," *American Anthropologist* 47 (1945): 175–77, 176.

20. Robert McGlory, "The Triumph of the Indians and Other Contrary Views of Richard Rodriguez, Gay Catholic Mexican Opponent of Multiculturalism," *The Chicago Reader*, April 1, 1993.

21. Richard White, *The Middle Ground: Indians, Empires, and Republics in the Great Lakes Region, 1650–1815* (Cambridge: Cambridge University Press, 1991).

22. Joel Austin, *Discovering the Penokees* (Iron River, Wis.: Sweetwater Visions, 2014).

Bibliography

Alanen, Arnold R. "Homes on the Range: Settling the Penokee-Gogebic Iron Ore District of Northern Wisconsin and Michigan." In Robert C. Ostergren and Thomas R. Vale, eds., *Wisconsin Land and Life*. Madison: University of Wisconsin Press, 1997: 241–262.

Aldrich, Henry. "The Geology of the Gogebic Iron Range of Wisconsin." PhD diss., University of Wisconsin-Madison, 1929.

American Institute of Mining Metallurgical and Petroleum Engineers, et al. *Handbook of Mining in the Lake Superior Region*. Minneapolis: Press of Byron & Learned Company, 1920.

Annual Geneological Roll of the Red Cliff Band of Chippewa Indians as Required by the Act of March 3, 1877, Section 2. Manuscript in possession of the author.

Armstrong, Benjamin G., and Thomas P. Wentworth. *Early life among the Indians: Reminiscences from the life of Benj. G. Armstrong: Treaties of 1835, 1837, 1842 and 1854: Habits and customs of the red men of the forest: Incidents, biographical sketches, battles, &c*. Ashland, Wis.: Press of A. W. Bowron, 1892.

The Ashland Press. Ashland, Wis.: Sam S. & Hank O. Fifield.

Austin, Joel. *Discovering the Penokees*. Iron River, Wis.: Sweetwater Visions, 2014.

Bad River Band of Lake Superior Chippewa Indians. *Minutes of Council Meeting, Bad River Reservation March 31, 1913*. Bureau of Indian Affairs, Great Lakes Agency. Ashland, Wisconsin.

———. *Proceedings Held at the Council of the Chippewa Indians on the Bad River Reservation September 8–10, 1919*. Bureau of Indian Affairs, Great Lakes Agency. Ashland, Wisconsin.

Baraga, Frederic. *Chippewa Indians, as Recorded by Rev. Frederick Baraga in* 1847. New York: Studia Slovenica, League of Slovenian Americans, 1976.

Baraga, Frederic, and John Nichols. *A Dictionary of the Ojibway Language*. St. Paul: Minnesota Historical Society Press, 1992.

Beaulieu, David L. "Curly Hair and Big Feet: Anthropology and the Implementation of Land Allotment on the White Earth Chippewa Reservation." *American Indian Quarterly* 8, no. 4 (1984): 281–314.

Benton-Banai, Edward. *The Mishomis Book: The Voice of the Ojibway*. Saint Paul, Minn.: Red School House, 1988.

Bieder, Robert E. "Scientific Attitudes toward Indian Mixed-Bloods in Early Nineteenth Century America." *Journal of Ethnic Studies* 8, no. 2 (1980): 17–30.

———. *Science Encounters the Indian, 1820–1880: The Early Years of American Ethnology.* Norman: University of Oklahoma Press, 1986.

Biolsi, Thomas. "The Birth of the Reservation: Making the Modern Individual among the Lakota." *American Ethnologist* 22, no. 1 (1995): 28–53.

Birk, Douglas A. "When Rivers Were Roads: Deciphering the Role of Canoe Portages in the Western Lake Superior Fur Trade." In Jennifer S. H. Brown, W. J. Eccles, and Donald P. Heldman, eds., *Fur Trade Revisited: Selected Papers of the Sixth North American Fur Trade Conference, Mackinac Island, Michigan, 1991.* East Lansing: Michigan State University Press, 1991: 359–375.

Block, Maurice. *In and Out of Each Other's Bodies: Theory of Mind, Evolution, Truth, and the Nature of the Social.* London: Routlege, 2016.

Bohaker, Heidi. "'Ninddodemag': The Significance of Algonquian Kinship Networks in the Eastern Great Lakes Region, 1600–1701." *The William and Mary Quarterly* 63, no. 1 (January 2006): 23–52.

Bourdieu, Pierre. "The Force of Law: Toward a Sociology of the Juridical Field." *Hastings Journal of Law* 38 (1977): 814–853.

Brohough, Gustav O. "Sioux and Chippewa Half-Breed Scrip and Its Application to the Minnesota Pine Lands." Master's thesis, University of Wisconsin-Madison, 1906.

Brown, Jennifer S. H. "Linguistic Solitudes and Changing Social Categories." In Carol M. Judd and Arthur J. Ray, eds., *Old Trails and New Directions: Papers of the Third North American Fur Trade Conference.* Toronto: University of Toronto Press, 1978: 147–159.

———. *Strangers in Blood: Fur Trade Company Families in Indian Country.* Vancouver: University of British Columbia Press, 1980.

———. "Fur Trade as Centrifuge: Family Dispersal and Offspring Identity in Two Company Contexts." In Raymond J. DeMallie and Alfonso Ortiz, eds., *North American Indian Anthropology: Essays on Society and Culture.* Norman: University of Oklahoma Press, 1994: 197–217.

———. Review of Keith Widder, "Battle for the Soul: Métis Children Encounter Evangelical Protestants at Mackinaw Mission, 1823–1837." *The American Historical Review*, 105, no. 2 (Apr., 2000): 543–544.

———. *An Ethnohistorian in Rupert's Land: Unfinished Conversations.* Edmonton: Athabasca University Press, 2017.

Brown, Jennifer S. H., W. J. Eccles, and Donald P. Heldman. *The Fur Trade Revisited: Selected Papers of the Sixth North American Fur Trade Conference, Mackinac Island, Michigan, 1991.* Mackinac Island: Michigan State University Press; Mackinac Island State Park Commission, 1994.

Brown, Jennifer S. H., and Laura Peers, "'There Is No End to Relationship among the Indians' Ojibwa Families and Kinship in Historical Perspective." *History of the Family* 4, no. 4 (1999): 529–555.

Brown, Jennifer S. H., and Jacqueline Peterson. *The New Peoples: Being and Becoming Métis in North America.* Lincoln: University of Nebraska Press, 1985.

Brown, Jennifer S. H., and Theresa Schenck, "Métis, Mestizo and Mixed-blood." In Philip J. Deloria and Neal Salisbury, eds., *A Companion to American Indian History*. Malden, Mass: Blackwell, 2002: 321–38.

Brunson, Alfred. *Alfred Brunson papers, 1815–1882*. State Historical Society of Wisconsin.

———. *A Western Pioneer: or, Incidents of the Life and Times of Rev. Alfred Brunson . . . Embracing a Period of Over Seventy Years*. Cincinnati, New York: Hitchchock and Walden; Carlton and Lanahan, 1872.

Brunson, Ella C. "Alfred Brunson, Pioneer of Wisconsin Methodism." *Wisconsin Magazine of History* 2, no. 2 (1918): 129–148.

Buck, John S. "The Survey of the Penoka Iron Range and Incidents Connected with Its Early History." *Ashland Weekly Press* December 8, 1877.

Butterfield, Consul Wilshire. *History of Crawford and Richland Counties, Wisconsin*. Springfield, Ill.: Union Publishing Company, 1884.

Callendar, Charles. "Great Lakes-Riverine Sociopolitical Organization." In Bruce G. Trigger, ed., *Handbook of North American Indians: The Northeast*. Washington D.C.: Smithsonian, 1978: 610–21.

Campbell, Samuel W. *Papers, 1881–1931*. State Historical Society of Wisconsin.

Carrier, James. "Occidentalism: The World Turned Upside-Down." *American Ethnologist* 19, no. 2 (1992): 195–212.

Carstensen, *Farms or Forests: Evolution of a State Policy for Northern Wisconsin, 1850–1932*. University of Wisconsin, College of Agriculture, 1958.

Clark, John Garretson, ed. *The Frontier Challenge: Responses to the Trans-Mississippi West*. Lawrence: University Press of Kansas, 1971.

Cleland, Charles E. *Faith in Paper: The Ethnohistory and Litigation of Upper Great Lakes Indian Treaties*. Ann Arbor: University of Michigan Press, 2011.

Clifton, James. "Wisconsin Death March: Explaining the Extremes in Old Northwest Indian Removal." In *Transactions of the Wisconsin Academy of Sciences, Arts, and Letters*, 1987: 1–40.

———. *Being and Becoming Indian: Biographical Studies of North American Frontiers*. Chicago, Ill.: Dorsey Press, 1989.

———. "Michigan's Indians: Tribe, Nation, Estate, Racial, Ethnic, or Special Interest Group?" *Michigan Historical Review* 20, no. 2 (1994): 93–152.

Comaroff, John. "Of Totemism and Ethnicity: Consciousness, Practice and the Signs of Inequality." *Journal of Anthropology* 52, nos. 3–4 (2010): 301–23.

Conzen, Katherine Neils. "The Winnebago Urban System: Indian Policy and Townsite Promotion on the Upper Mississippi." In Rondo Cameron, ed., *Cities and Markets: Studies in the Organization of Human Space*. Lanham, Md.: University Press of America, 1997: 269–310.

Culkin, William E. "Early Protestant Missions in the Lake Superior Country, Volume II: Journals of the Rev. Sherman Hall together with his letters to the Rev. David Greene, 1831–1844." Manuscript, State Historical Society of Wisconsin, 1936.

Cushing, Caleb. "Relations of Indians to Citizenship." *Opinions of the Attorney General* 70 (1856): 746–756.

Danziger, Edmund. "They Would Not Be Moved: The Chippewa Treaty of 1854." *Minnesota History* 43, no. 5 (1973): 175–185.

———. *The Chippewas of Lake Superior*. Norman: University of Oklahoma Press, 1978.

———. Great *Lakes Indian Accommodation and Resistance during the Early Reservation Years, 1850–1900*. Ann Arbor: University of Michigan Press, 2009.

Dewdney, Selwyn H. *The Sacred Scrolls of the Southern Ojibway*. Toronto, Buffalo: Glenbow-Alberta Institute, Calgary, Alta., by University of Toronto Press, 1975.

Dickinson, John N. *To Build a Canal: Sault Ste. Marie, 1853–1854 and After*. Columbus: Miami University, Ohio State University Press, 1981.

Doerfler, Jill. *Those Who Belong: Identity, Family, Blood, and Citizenship among the White Earth Anishinaabeg*. East Lansing: Michigan State University Press, 2015.

Edmunds, R. David. "'Unacquainted with the Laws of the Civilized World': American Attitudes toward Métis Communities in the Old Northwest." In Jacqueline Peterson and Jennifer S. H. Brown, eds., *The New Peoples: Being and Becoming Métis in North America*. Lincoln: University of Nebraska Press, 1985: 185–194.

Ellinghaus, Katherine. "The Benefits of Being Indian: Blood Quanta, Intermarrige, and Allotment Policy on the White Earth Reservation, 1889–1920." *Frontiers: A Journal of Women Studies* 29, nos. 2/3: 81–105.

Explorer. *A Few Remarks on the Operations of the Companies: At Present Organized, for the Digging & Smelting of Copper and Other Ores, on Lake Superior and the Saint Croix River*. United States?: publisher not identified, 1845.

Feldman, James W. "Rewilding the Islands: Nature, History, and Wilderness at Apostle Islands National Lakeshore." PhD diss., University of Wisconsin-Madison, 2004.

Flower, Frank A. *A History of Milwaukee from Pre-historic Times to the Present date, embracing a summary sketch of the Native Tribes and an Exhaustive Record of Men and events for the Past Century, etc., Volume 1*. Chicago: The Western Historical Company, 1881.

Folwell, William Watts. *A History of Minnesota*. St. Paul: Minnesota Historical Society, 1956.

Fowler, Loretta. *Tribal Sovereignty and the Historical Imagination: Cheyenne-Arapahoe Politics*. Lincoln and London: University of Nebraska Press, 2002.

Fried, Morton. "On the Evolution of Social Stratification and the State." In Stanley Diamond, ed., *Essays in Honor of Paul Radin*. New York: Columbia University Press, 1960: 713–731.

Gates, Paul W. *The Wisconsin Pine Lands of Cornell University: A Study in Land Policy and Absentee Ownership*. Ithaca: Cornell University Press, 1943.

———. *Fifty Million Acres: Conflicts over Kansas Land Policy, 1854–1890*. Ithaca: Cornell University Press, 1954.

———. "Frontier Land Business in Wisconsin." *The Wisconsin Magazine of History* 52, no. 4 (1969): 306–327.

———. "Indian Allotments Preceding the Dawes Act." In J. G. Clark, ed., *The Frontier Challenge: Responses to the Trans-Mississippi West*. Lawrence: University Press of Kansas, 1971: 141–170.

Genetin-Pilawa, Joseph. "'In the Interests of Harmony and Good Government': Allotment Era Politics in the Great Lakes Region." Master's thesis, Bowling Green University, 2002.

Gilman, Rhonda. "The Fur Trade in the Upper Mississippi Valley, 1630–1850." *Wisconsin Magazine of History* 58, no. 1 (1974): 2–28.

Godfrey, Anthony. *A Forest History of Ten Wisconsin Indian Reservations under the Great Lakes Agency: Precontact to the Present*. Salt Lake: U.S. West Research, 1996.

Goldberg-Ambrose, Carol. "Of Native Americans and Tribal Members: The Impact of Law on Indian Group Life." *Law and Society Review* 28 (1994): 1123–1148.

Gorham, Harriet. "Families of Mixed Descent in the Western Great Lakes Region." In Bruce Cox, ed., *Native People, Native Lands: Canadian Indians, Inuit, Métis*. Montreal: McGill-Queens University Press, 1987.

Gough, Robert. "Richard T. Ely and the Development of the Wisconsin Cutover." *The Wisconsin Magazine of History* 75, no. 1 (1991), 2–38.

———. *Farming the Cutover: A Social History of Northern Wisconsin, 1900–1940*. Lawrence: University Press of Kansas, 1997.

Gray, Susan E. "Interlude: Of Two Worlds and Intimate Domains." In James Joseph Buss and C. Jospeh Genetin-Pilawa, eds., *Beyond Two Worlds: Critical Conversations on Language and Power in Native North America*. Albany: SUNY Press, 2014.

Graybill, A. R. "Native-White Intermarriage and Family in 19th-century North America." *History Compass* 14, no. 3 (2016): 105–115.

Hagan, W. T. "Full-Blood, Mixed-Blood, Generic and Ersatz: The Problem of Indian Identity and American Indians." *Arizona and the West: A Quarterly Journal of History* 27, no. 4 (1985): 309–326.

Hall, Robert L. *An Archaeology of the Soul: North American Indian Belief and Ritual*. Urbana: University of Illinois Press, 1997.

Hallowell, A. Irving, "Ojibwe Ontology, Behavior and World View." In Raymond Fogelson et al., eds., *Contributions to Anthropology: Selected Papers of A. Irving Hallowell*. Chicago: University of Chicago Press, 1976.

Hämäläinen, Pekka. *The Commanche Empire*. New Haven and London: Yale University Press, 2008.

Hansen, James. "A Roll of Mixed-Blood Sioux, 1855–56." *Minnesota Genealogical Journal* 7 (1987): 601–620.

Harmon, Alexandra. *Rich Indians: Native People and the Problem of Wealth in American History*. Chapel Hill: University of North Carolina Press, 2010.

Harmon, Alexandra, Colleen O'Neill, and Paul Rosier, "Interwoven Economic Histories: American Indians in a Capitalist America." *The Journal of American History* 98, no. 3 (2011), 698–722.

Harper, Mattie. "French Africans in Ojibwe Country: Negotiating Marriage, Identity and Race, 1780–1890." PhD diss., University of California, Berkeley, 2012.

Hearings before the Committee on Indian Affairs. United States Senate on Senate Resolution 263. *Condition of Indian Affairs in Wisconsin*. Sixty-First Congress, Second Session. Washington: Government Printing Office, 1910.

———. House of Representatives. *Bad River Reservation Allotments.* Sixty-Sixth Congress, Third Session. Washington: Government Printing Office February 3, 1921.

Heath, Barbara J. "Commoditization, Consumption, and Interpretive Complexity: The Contingent Role of Cowries in the Early Modern World." In Barbara J. Heath, Eleanor E. Breen, and Lori A. Lee, eds., *Material Worlds: Archaeology, Consumption, and the Road to Modernity.* London: Routledge, 2019: 56–76.

Hickerson, Harold. "The Sociohistorical Significance of Two Chippewa Ceremonials." *American Anthropologist* 68, no. 1 (1963): 67–85.

———. "The Genesis of Bilaterality among Two Divisions of Chippewa," *American Anthropologist* 68, no. 1 (1966): 1–26.

———. *The Chippewa and Their Neighbors: A Study in Ethnohistory.* New York: Holt, Rinehart and Winston, 1970.

History of Crawford and Richland Counties, Wisconsin: together with sketches of their towns and villages, educational, civil, military, and political history, portraits of prominent persons, and biographies of representative citizens; History of Wisconsin: embracing accounts of the pre-historic races, and a brief account of its territorial and state governments. Springfield, Ill.: Union Publishing Company, 1884.

History of Milwaukee, Wisconsin: from prehistoric times to the present date, embracing a summary sketch of the native tribes and an exhaustive record of men and events for the past century, describing in elaborate detail the city as it now is, its commercial, religious, educational and benevolent institutions, its government, courts, press and public affairs, its musical, dramatic, literary, scientific and social societies, its patriotism during the late war, its development and future possibilities and including nearly four thousand biographical sketches of pioneers and citizens. Chicago: Western Historical Co., 1881.

Hoffman, Walter James. "The Midewiwin or 'Grand Medicine Society' of the Ojibwe." *Smithsonian Institution, U. S. Bureau of Ethnology Report No. 7.* Washington D.C.: Government Printing Office, 1891: 149–299.

Hogendorn, Jan S., and Marion Johnson. *The Shell Money of the Slave Trade.* New York: Cambridge University Press, 1986.

Holbrook, Arthur Tenney. *From the Log of Trout Fisherman.* Norwood, MA: Plimpton Press, 1949.

Hooley, Matt. "The Autoethnography of William Whipple Warren." *Wicazo Sa Review* 20, no. 2 (2012): 75–98.

Horsman, Reginald. *Race and Manifest Destiny: The Origins of American Racial Anglo-Saxonism.* Cambridge, Mass.: Harvard University Press, 1981.

Hosmer, Brian. "Reflections on Indian Cultural "Brokers": Reginald Oshkosh, Mitchell Oshkenaniew, and the Politics of Menominee Lumbering." *Ethnohistory* 44, no. 3 (1997): 493–509.

Ingersoll, Thomas N. *To Intermix with our White Brothers: Indian Mixed Bloods in the United States from the Earliest Times to the Indian Removals.* Albuquerque: University of New Mexico Press, 2005.

Innis, Harold. *The Fur Trade in Canada: An Introduction to Canadian Economic History.* New Haven: Yale University Press, 1930.

Jacobsen, Kristina M. *The Sound of Navajo Country: Music, Language, and Diné Belonging.* Chapel Hill: University of North Carolina Press, 2017.

Janik, Erika. "Citizen Scientist." *Wisconsin Natural Resources Magazine.* February 2007. https://dnr.wi.gov/wnrmag/html/stories/2007/feb07/lapham.htm. Accessed March 15, 2016.

Jenkins, Richard. "Different Societies? Different Cultures? What Are Human Collectivities?" In Sinisa Malesevic and Mark Haugaard, eds., *Making Sense of Collectivity: Ethnicity, Nationality and Globalization.* London: Pluto Press, 2002: 12–32.

Jenks, Albert Ernest. "The Wild Rice Gatherers of the Upper Lakes: A Study in American Primitive Economics." *Annual Report of the Board of Regents of the Smithsonian Institution,* 1901; Lincoln, Neb.: J & L Reprint Co., 1977.

Kappler, Charles J. *Indian Affairs Laws and Treaties: Volume II: Treaties.* Washington D.C.: Government Printing Office, 1904.

Keller, Robert H. 1978. "An *Economic History of Indian Treaties* in the Great Lakes Region." *American Indian Journal* 4 (1978): 2–20.

———. "The Chippewa Treaties of 1826 and 1836." *American Indian Journal* 9, no. 3 (1986): 27–32.

Kemble, Rebecca. "Bad River Chippewa Take a Stand against Walker and Mining," *The Progressive,* May 28, 2013.

King, Thomas F. *Places That Count: Traditional Cultural Properties in Cultural Resource Management.* Walnut Creek, CA: Altamira Press, 2003.

Kinney, Jay P. *A Continent Lost, a Civilization Won: Indian Land Tenure in America.* New York: Arno Press, 1975.

Klassen, Patricia E. *The Story of Radio Mind: A Missionary's Journey on Indigenous Land.* Chicago: University of Chicago Press, 2018.

Knute, Nelson. "A Summary of Our Most Important Land Laws." *Annals of the American Academy of Political and Social Science* 33, no. 3 (1909): 127–13.

Kohl, Georg. *Kitchi-gami: Travels Round Lake Superior.* London: Chapman and Hall, 1860.

Krug, Merton E. *DuBay: Son-in-Law of Oshkosh.* Appleton, Wis.: C. C. Nelson Publishing Company, 1946.

Kugel, Rebecca. *To Be the Main Leaders of Our People: A History of Minnesota Ojibwe Politics, 1825–1898.* East Lansing: Michigan State University Press, 1998.

———. "Reworking Ethnicity: Gender, Work Roles, and Contending Redefinitions of the Great Lakes Métis, 1820–42." In R. David Edmunds, ed., *Enduring Nations: Native Americans in the Midwest.* Urbana and Chicago: University of Illinois Press, 2008: 160–181.

———. "Planning to Stay: Native Strategies to Remain in the Great Lakes, Post-War 1812." *Middle West Review* 2, no. 2 (2016): 1–26.

Kuhiken, Robert. "Settin' the Woods on Fire: Rural Incendiarism as Protest." *Geographic Review* 89, no. 3 (1999): 343–363.

Lake, James A. Law *and Mineral Wealth: The Legal Profile of the Wisconsin Mining Industry*. Madison: University of Wisconsin Press, 1962.

Langston, Nancy. "Iron Mines, Toxicity, and Indigenous Communities in the Lake Superior Basin." In J. R. McNeill and G. Vrtis, eds., *Mining North America: An Environmental History Since 1522*. Berkeley: University of California Press, 2017: 313–38.

Lapham, Increase Allen. *Increase A. Lapham papers, 1825–1930*. State Historical Society of Wisconsin.

Lapham, Increase Allen, and P. R. Hoy. *Fauna and Flora of Wisconsin*. Madison: Wisconsin State Agricultural Society, 1852.

Lapointe Iron Company. *La Pointe Iron Company of Ashland County, Lake Superior, Wisconsin*. Chicago: Evening Post Print, 1871.

Larson, Lars. *Chequamegon Bay and Its Communities: A Brief History, 1659–1883*. Whitewater, Wis.: L. Larson, 2001.

Loew, Patty. "Newspapers and the Lake Superior Chippewa in the 'unProgressive' Era." PhD diss., University of Wisconsin-Madison, 1998.

———. *Seventh Generation Earth Ethics: Native Voices of Wisconsin*. Madison: Wisconsin Historical Society Press, 2014.

Marcus, Jacob Rader. *United States Jewry, 1776–1985*. Detroit: Wayne State University Press, 1989.

Martin, Lawrence. *The Physical Geography of Wisconsin*. Madison: Published by the State, 1932.

Martin, Roy L. *History of the Wisconsin Central*. Boston: Railway and Locomotive Historical Society, 1941.

Mason, Carol I. "A Sweet Small Something: Maple Sugaring in the New World." In James Clifton, ed., *The Invented Indian: Cultural Fictions and Governmental Policies*. New Brunswick and London: Transaction Publishers, 1994: 91–106.

McCluggage, Robert W. "The Senate and Indian Titles, 1800–1825." *Western Historical Quarterly* 1, no. 4 (1970): 415–42.

McClurken, James M. et al. *Fish in the Lakes, Wild Rice, and Game in Abundance: Testimony on Behalf of Mille Lacs Ojibwe Hunting and Fishing Rights*. East Lansing: Michigan State University Press, 2000.

McDonnell, Michael A. "Rethinking the Middle Ground: French Colonialism and Indigenous Identities in the Pays d'en Haut." In Gregory D. Smithers and Brooke N. Newman, eds., *Native Diasporas: Indigenous Identities and Settler Colonialism in the Americas*. Lincoln: University of Nebraska Press, 2014: 49–62.

———. *Masters of Empire: Great Lakes Indians and the Making of America*. New York: Hill and Wang, A Division of Farrar, Straus and Giroux, 2015.

McGlory, Robert. "The Triumph of the Indians and Other Contrary Views of Richard Rodriguez, Gay Catholic Mexican Opponent of Multiculturalism." *The Chicago Reader*, April 1, 1993.

Mello, Amorin. "Wisconsin's Government Presumes Adverse Impacts Necessary for Mining Jobs." *Woods Person: Thoughts and Reports on What Is Happening in Wisconsin's North Woods*, May 7, 2013. Woodsperson.blogspot.com. Viewed February 10, 2016.

Meyer, Melissa L. *The White Earth Tragedy: Ethnicity and Dispossession at a Minnesota Anishinaabe Reservation, 1889–1920*. Lincoln: University of Nebraska Press, 1994.

Miller, Christopher L., and George R. Hamell. "A New Perspective on Indian-White Contact: Cultural Symbols and Colonial Trade." *The Journal of American History* 73, no. 2 (1986): 311–328.

Miner, Craig H. and William E. Unrau. *The End of Indian Kansas: A Study of Cultural Revolution, 1854–1871*. Lawrence: Regents Press of Kansas, 1978.

Minnesota Chippewa Tribe et al on behalf of the Chippewas of Lake Superior v The United States of America, Docket #18-U. Indian Claims Commission Decisions, Vols. 25, 35.

Mladenoff, David J., and Evelyn A. Howell. "Vegetation Change on the Gogebic Iron Range (Iron County, Wisconsin) 1860 to the Present." *Transactions of the Wisconsin Academy of Sciences, Arts and Letters*, 1980: 74–89.

Mladenoff, David J., Lisa A. Schulte, and Janine Bolliger. "Broad-Scale Change in the Northern Forests: From Past to Present." In D. M. Waller and T. P. Rooney, eds., *The Vanishing Present: Wisconsin's Changing Lands, Waters, and Wildlife*. Chicago: University of Chicago Press, 2008: 61–73.

Morin, Gail. *Chippewa Half-Breeds of Lake Superior*. Pawtucket, R.I.: Quintin, 1998.

Morrison, Eliza. *A Little History of My Forest Life: An Indian-White Autobiography*. Tustin, Mich.: Ladyslipper Press, 2002.

Morse, Richard F. "The Chippewas of Lake Superior." In *Collections of the State Historical Society of Wisconsin, Volume III*, ed. Lyman Copeland Draper. Madison: State Historical Society of Wisconsin, 1905: 338–369.

Munnell, Michael D. *American Indian Marriage Record Directory for Ashland County, Wisconsin, 1874–1907*. Duluth, Minn.: Chippewa Heritage Publications, 2003.

Murphy, Lucy Eldersveld. *Great Lakes Creoles: A French-Indian Community on the Northern Borderlands, Prairie du Chien, 1750–1860*. New York: Cambridge University Press, 2014.

Murphy, Lucy Eldersveld, and Wendy Hamand Venet. *Midwestern Women: Work, Community, and Leadership at the Crossroads*. Bloomington: Indiana University Press, 1997.

National Archives, Washington, D.C. Records of the Bureau of Indian Affairs. Record Group 75, Entry 529, Miscellaneous Reserve Papers: Lake Pepin Half-Breed Affidavits, 1825–1907, Box 358.

Nesper, Larry. *The Walleye War: The Struggle for Ojibwe Spearfishing and Treaty Rights*. Lincoln: University of Nebraska Press, 2002.

———. "Simulating Culture: Being Indian for Tourists in Lac du Flambeau's Wa-Swa-Gon Indian Bowl." *Ethnohistory* 50, no. 3 (2003): 447–472.

———. "Historical Ambivalence in a Tribal Museum." *Museum Anthropology* 28, no. 2 (2009): 1–16.

———. "Law and Ojibwe Indian 'Traditional Cultural Property' in the Organized Resistance to the Crandon Mine in Wisconsin." *Law and Social Inquiry* 36, no. 1 (2011): 151–169.

———. "The 1914 Meeting of the Society of American Indians at UW-Madison." *Wisconsin Magazine of History* 102, no. 2 (Winter 2018): 28–37.

Nesper, Larry, and Chantal Norrgard. *Mashkii Ziibii: Human Water and Landscape Report.* Report prepared for the Bad River Band of Lake Superior Chippewa Indians, 2014.

Nichols, John. *"Statement Made by the Indians": A Bilingual Petition of the Chippewas of Lake Superior, 1864.* London, Ont.: Centre for Research and Teaching of Canadian Native Languages, University of Western Ontario, 1988.

———. "The Translation of Key Phrases in the Treaties of 1837 and 1855." In James McClurken, *Fish in the Lakes, Wild Rice, and Game in Abundance.* East Lansing: Michigan State University Press, 2000: 514–524.

Norrgard, Chantal. *Seasons of Change: Labor, Treaty Rights, and Ojibwe Nationhood.* Chapel Hill: University of North Carolina Press, 2014.

The Odanah Star. Odanah, Wisconsin. 1912–1916. State Historical Society of Wisconsin.

Oderic, Fr., O.S.F., "An Uncrowned King of the Chippewas." *The Franciscan Herald* 9, no. 4 (March 1921).

Olmanson, Eric D. *The Future City on the Inland Sea: A History of Imaginative Geographies of Lake Superior.* Athens: Ohio University Press, 2007.

Olney, Richard. "Sioux Mixed Bloods—Attorney General." *Offiical Opinions of the Attorneys-General of the United States,* Volume 20: 742–46. Washington: Government Printing Office.

Overholt, Thomas W., and J. Baird Callicott. *Clothed-in-Fur and Other Tales.* New York: University Press of America, 1982.

Owen, David Dale, et al. *Report of a geological survey of Wisconsin, Iowa, and Minnesota: and incidentally of a portion of Nebraska Territory.* Philadelphia: Lippincott, Grambo & Co., 1852.

Paap, Howard D. *Red Cliff, Wisconsin: A History of an Ojibwe Community, Volume I: The Earliest Years: The Origin to 1854.* St. Cloud, Minn.: North Star Press, 2013.

Pastor, John. *What Should a Clever Moose Eat?: Natural History, Ecology, and the North Woods.* Washington, D.C.: Island Press, 2016.

Perdue, Theda. *"Mixed Blood" Indians: Racial Construction in the Early South.* Athens: University of Georgia Press, 2003.

Peterson, Jacqueline. "Prelude to Red River: A Social Portrait of Great Lakes Métis." *Ethnohistory* 25, no. 1 (1978): 41–67.

———. "The People in Between: Indian-White Marriage and the Genesis of Metis Society and Culture in the Great Lakes Region, 1680–1830." PhD diss., University of Illinois at Chicago, 1981.

———. "Many Roads to Red River," In Jennifer Brown and Jacqueline Peterson, *The New Peoples: Being and Becoming Métis in North America.* Lincoln: University of Nebraska Press, 1985.

———. "Rocking the Cradle of the Plains: The Emergence of a New Aboriginal People in Northern North American." (Paper given at the Society for Ethnohistory Meeting in Winnipeg, Canada, October 2017).

Podruchny, Carol. *Making the Voyageur World: Travelers and Traders in the North American Fur Trade.* Lincoln and London: University of Nebraska Press, 2006.

Price, Hiram. *Commissioner of Indian Affairs to the Secretary of the Interior, October 17, 1883*. Forty-Eighth Congress, First session, House of Representatives Executive Document No. 12.

Proceedings of the La Pointe Band of Chippewa Indians, In General Council, Assembled at Odanah, Wisconsin, 1907. State Historical Society of Wisconsin.

Proceedings of the Council held at Bad River from March 31–April 2, 1913. Great Lakes Agency files. Ashland, Wisconsin.

Proceedings Council of the Chippewa Indians on the Bad River Reservation at Odanah, Wis. Sept 8, 9, 10, 1919. Great Lakes Agency files. Ashland, Wisconsin.

Prucha, Francis Paul. *Documents of United States Indian Policy*. Lincoln: University of Nebraska Press, 1975.

———. *Indian Policy in the United States: Historical Essays*. Lincoln: University of Nebraska Press, 1981.

Purdon, John, and Frederick C. Brightly, compilers. *A Digest of the Laws of Pennsylvania, from the Year One Thousand Seven Hundred to the Sixth Day of June, One Thousand Eight Hundred and Eighty-Three* Philadelphia: Kay and Brothers, 1885.

Quaife, Milo M. "Increase Allen Lapham, First Scholar of Wisconsin." *Wisconsin Magazine of History* 1, no. 1 (1917): 3–15.

Ray, Arthur J. "Indians as Consumers in the Eighteenth Century." In Carol M. Judd and Arthur J. Ray, eds., *Old Trails and New Directions: Papers of the Third North American Fur Trade Conference*. Toronto: University of Toronto Press, 1980: 255–271.

———. *Indians in the Fur Trade: Their Role as Trappers, Hunters, and Middlemen in the Lands Southwest of Hudson Bay, 1660–1870*. Toronto: University of Toronto Press, 1998.

Ray, Arthur J., and Donald B. Freeman, *Give Us Good Measure: An Economic Analysis of Relations between the Indians and the Hudson's Bay Company Before 1763*. Toronto: University of Toronto Press, 1978.

Reynolds, Glenn C. "A Native American Water Ethic." *Transactions of the Wisconsin Academy of Sciences, Arts and Letters* 90 (2003): 143–161.

Rich, E. E. *The Fur Trade and the Northwest to 1957*. Toronto: McClelland and Steward Limited, 1967.

Rictor, Daniel K. "War and Culture: The Iroquois Experience." *The William and Mary Quarterly* 40, no. 4 (1983): 528–559.

Ritzenthaler, Robert E. "The Acquisition of Surnames by the Chippewa Indians." *American Anthropologist* 47 (1945): 175–177.

———. "Southwestern Chippewa." In Bruce G. Trigger, ed., *Handbook of North American Indians, the Northeast*. Washington D. C.: Smithsonian, 1978: 743–759.

Robinson, H. M. *The Great Fur Land; or, Sketches of Life in the Hudson's Bay Territory*. New York: G. P. Putnam's Sons, 1879.

Roe, Lawrence A. *A History of Wisconsin Mining*. Madison, Wis.: ROECO, 1991.

Ross, Frank E. "The Fur Trade of the Western Great Lakes Region." *Minnesota History* 19, no. 3 (1938): 271–307.

Roy, Vincent. *Miscellaneous Materials Related to Vincent Roy, 1861–1862, 1892, 1921*. State Historical Society of Wisconsin.

Sahlins, Marshall. *Stone Age Economics*. New York: Aldine, 1972.

———. *Islands of History*. Chicago: University of Chicago Press, 1985.

———. "The Economics of Develop-Man in the Pacific." *Anthropology and Aesthetics* 21 (1992): 12–25.

———. *What Kinship Is—And Is Not*. Chicago: University of Chicago Press, 2013.

Sahlins, Marshall, and David Graeber. *On Kings*. Chicago: Hau Books, 2017.

Saler, Bethel. "Negotiating the Treaty Economy: Race, Gender and the Transformation from an Indian to a White Territory in Northeastern Wisconsin, 1824–1852." Master's thesis, University of Wisconsin-Madison, 1992.

———. "Negotiating the Treaty Polity: Gender, Race and the Transformation of Wisconsin from Indian Country into an American State, 1776–1854." PhD diss., University of Wisconsin-Madison, 1999.

———. *The Settlers' Empire: Colonialism and State Formation in America's Old Northwest*. Philadelphia: University of Pennsylvania Press, 2015.

Satz, Ronald N. *Chippewa Treaty Rights: The Reserved Rights of Wisconsin's Chippewa Indians in Historical Perspective*. Madison: Wisconsin Academy of Sciences, Arts, and Letters, 1991.

Schenck, Theresa M. "The Cadottes: Five Generations of Fur Traders on Lake Superior." In Jennifer S. H. Brown, W. J. Eccles, Donald P. Heldman, eds., *The Fur Trade Revisited: Selected Papers of the Sixth North American Fur Trade Conference, Mackinac Island, MI, 1991*. East Lansing: Michigan State University Press, 1994: 189–198.

———. *The Voice of the Crane Echoes Afar: The Sociopolitical Organization of the Lake Superior Ojibwa, 1640–1855*. New York: Garland Publications, 1997.

———. *William W. Warren: The Life, Letters, and Times of an Ojibwe Leader*. Lincoln: University of Nebraska Press, 2007.

———. *All Our Relations: Chippewa Mixed Bloods and the Treaty of 1837*. Centre for Rupert's Land Studies at the University of Winnipeg and Madison, Wisc.: Amik Press, 2010.

Schoolcraft, Henry Rowe, and Philip P. Mason. *Schoolcraft's Expedition to Lake Itasca and the Discovery of the Source of the Mississippi*. East Lansing: Michigan State University Press, 1993.

Scheider, David. *American Kinship: A Cultural Account*. Chicago: University of Chicago Press, 1980.

Schorger, A. W. "The Beaver in Early Wisconsin." *Transactions of the Wisconsin Academy of Science, Arts and Letters* 54: 149–179.

Schultz, Jerry. Review of Melissa Meyer, *The White Earth Tragedy*. In *Great Plains Research* 4, no. 2 (1994): 332–334.

Shifferd, Patricia. "A Study in Economic Change: The Chippewa of Northern Wisconsin, 1854–1900." *The Western Canadian Journal of Anthropology* 6, no. 4 (1976): 16–41.

Sleeper-Smith, Susan. *Indian Women and French Men: Rethinking Cultural Encounter in the Western Great Lakes*. Amherst: University of Massachusetts Press, 2001.

———. *Rethinking the Fur Trade: Cultures of Exchange in an Atlantic World*. Lincoln: University of Nebraska Press, 2009.

———. Indigenous Prosperity and American Conquest: Indian Women of the Ohio River Valley, 1690–1792. Chapel Hill: University of North Carolina Press, 2018.

Smith, Alice E. "Caleb Cushing's Investments in the St. Croix Valley." *The Wisconsin Magazine of History* 28, no. 1 (1944): 7–19.

Snowden, John Rockwell, Wayne Tyndall, and David Smith. "American Indian Sovereignty and Naturalization: It's a Race Thing." *Nebraska Law Review* 80, no. 2 (2001): 171–238.

Spruhan, Paul. "A Legal History of Blood Quantum in Federal Indian Law to 1935." *South Dakota Law Review* 5 (2005): 1–50.

Society of American Indians. *The Papers of the Society of American Indians.* Register of Meeting of Association of American Indians at Madison, October 6–11.

St. Mary's Industrial School. *Noble Lives of a Noble Race.* Minneapolis: Brooks Press, 1909.

Steen-Adams, Michelle Marie. "Change on a Northern Wisconsin Landscape: Legacies of Human History." PhD diss., University of Wisconsin-Madison, 2005.

Steen-Adams, Michelle, Nancy E. Langston, and David J. Mladenoff. "White Pine in the Northern Forests: An Ecological and Management History of White Pine on the Bad River Reservation of Wisconsin." *Environmental History* 12 (2007): 595–629.

———. "Logging the Great Lakes Indian Reservations: The Case of the Bad River Band of Ojibwe." *American Indian Culture and Research Journal* 34, no. 1 (2010): 41–66.

Strong, Pauline. *Captive Selves, Captivating Others: The Poetics and Politics of Colonial American Captivity Narratives.* London: Routledge, 2018.

Stuntz, Albert C. *Diaries 1858, 1863–1869, 1882.* State Historical Society of Wisconsin.

Sturm, Circe. *Blood Politics: Race, Culture, and Identity in the Cherokee Nation of Oklahoma.* Berkeley: University of California Press, 2002.

The Superior Chronicle. Superior, Douglas County, Wis.: Ashton and Wise.

Survey of Conditions of the Indians of United States. Hearings Before a Subcommittee on Indian Affairs, United States Senate, Seventy-first Congress, First Session. Washington: Government Printing Office, 1929.

Swenson, Robert W. "Legal Aspects of Mineral Resources Exploitation." In Paul W. Gates, ed., *History of Public Land Law Development.* New York: Arno Press, 1979: 699–764.

Tanner, Helen Hornbeck. *Atlas of Great Lakes Indian History.* Norman: University of Oklahoma Press, 1987.

———. "The Career of Joseph La France, Coureur De Bois in the Upper Great Lakes." In *The Fur Trade Revisited: Selected Papers of the Sixth North American Fur Trade Conference, Mackinac Island, Michigan, 1991.* East Lansing: Michigan State University Press, 1994: 171–188.

Thorne, Tanis. "People of the River: Mixed-Blood Families on the Lower Missouri." PhD diss., University of California, Los Angeles, 1987.

Tipton, John. *The John Tipton Papers.* Indianapolis: Indiana Historical Bureau, 1942.

Turner, Frederick Jackson. *The Character and Influence of the Indian Trade in Wisconsin: A Study of the Trading Post as an Institution.* New York: B. Franklin, 1970.

United States. Treaty with the Potawatomi. U.S. Statutes at Large 7 (1818): 185.

———. Treaty with the Wyandot, etc. U.S. Statutes at Large 7 (1818): 178.

———. Treaty with the Chippewa. U.S. Statutes at Large 7 (1819): 203.

——— Treaty with the Wea. U.S. Statutes at Large 7 (1819): 186.

———. Treaty of Prairie du Chien. U.S. Statutes at Large 7 (1825): 272.

———. Treaty with the Miami. U.S. Statutes at Large 7 (1826): 300.
———. Treaty of Fond du Lac. U.S. Statutes at Large 7 (1826): 290.
———. Treaty with the Chippewa, etc. U.S. Statutes at Large 7 (1829): 320.
———. Treaty with the Sauk and Foxes, etc. U.S. Statutes at Large 7 (1830): 328.
———. Treaty with the Winnebago. U.S Statutes at Large 7 (1830) 323.
———. Treaty with the Potawatomi. U. S. Statutes at Large 7 (1832): 317.
———. Treaty with the Chickasaw. U.S. Statutes at Large 7 (1834): 450.
———. Treaty of Washington. U.S. Statutes at Large 7 (1836): 503.
———. Treaty of St. Peters. U.S. Statutes at Large 7 (1837): 536.
———. Treaty of La Pointe. U.S, Statutes at Large 7 (1842): 591.
———. Treaty with the Wyandot. U.S. Statutes at Large 11 (1842): 581.
———. Treaty with the Chippewa of Mississippi and Lake Superior. U.S. Statutes 9 (1847): 904.
———. Treaty of La Pointe. U.S. Statutes at Large 10 (1854): 1109.
———. Treaty of Washington. 10 U.S. Statutes at Large 10 (1855): 1165.
———. Treaty with the Winnebago. U.S. Statues at Large 10 (1855): 1172.
———. Treaty with the Sauk and Foxes. U.S. Statutes at Large 15 (1859): 467.
———. *Half-breed scrip, Chippewas of Lake Superior: the correspondence and action under the 7th clause of the 2d article of the treaty with the Chippewa Indians of Lake Superior and the Mississippi, concluded at La Pointe in the state of Wisconsin, September 30, 1854 . . . Including the report of the commission appointed by the Secretary of the Interior, April 21, 1871, composed of Henry S. Neal, Selden N. Clark, Edward P. Smith, and R. F. Crowell: and the report of the commission appointed July 15, 1872, composed of Thomas C. Jones, Edward P. Smith, and Dana E. King*. U. S. House of Representatives, Executive Document 103. 42nd Congress, Second session. Washington: Government Printing Office, 1874.
———. *The Territorial Papers of the United States: The Territory of Wisconsin, 1836–1848*. Washington: National Archives and Records Service, General Services Administration, 1971.
———. *The New American State Papers, Indian Affairs*. 13 vols. Wilmington, Del.: Scholarly Resources, 1972.
———. Records of the Wisconsin Superintendency of Indian Affairs, 1836–1848 and the Green Bay Subagency, 1850.
United States Bureau of Indian Affairs. *Annual Report of the Commissioner of Indian Affairs*. Washington: Government Printing Office, 1853.
———. *Letters Sent by the Office of Indian Affairs, 1824–1881*. National Archives microfilm publications microcopy no 21. Washington, D.C.: National Archives and Records Administration, 1963.
United States Department of the Interior. Interior Department Appointment Papers: Wisconsin, 1849–1907. Washington, D.C.: National Archives and Records Administration.
United States General Land Office. *Wisconsin Local Office Tract Books, 1835–1909*. State Historical Society of Wisconsin.
United States Indian Claims Commission. *Indian Claims Commission Decisions* 25 Boulder, Colo.: Native American Rights Fund, 1878.

United States Office of Indian Affairs. *Office copy of laws, regulations, etc. of Indian Bureau, 1850*. Washington: Government Printing Office, 1869.

———. *Letters Received by the Office of Indian Affair, La Pointe Agency, 1824–81*. In National Archives microfilm publications. Microcopy, no. 234.

———. Records, 1910–1939. *Narrative Reports, La Pointe Agency*.

United States Supreme Court. *United States v. Cook*, 86 U.S. 591 (1873).

United States War Department. "List of persons to whom permits to locate mineral lands on the south shore of Lake Superior have been granted and leases issued upon them by the Secretary of War, up to June 16, 1846." Np.

United States Works Progress Administration. *Chippewa Indian Historical Project, 1936–42*. State Historical Society of Wisconsin.

Valaskakis, Gail Guthrie. "The Chippewa and the Other: Living the Heritage of Lac du Flambeau." *Cultural Studies* 2, no. 3 (1988): 267–293.

Van Kirk, Sylvia. *Many Tender Ties: Women in Fur-Trade Society, 1670–1870*. Norman: University of Oklahoma Press, 1983.

Vecsey, Christopher T. *Traditional Ojibwa Religion and Its Historical Changes*. Philadelphia: American Philosophical Society, 1983.

Vennum, Thomas. *Wild Rice and the Ojibway People*. St. Paul: Minnesota Historical Society Press, 1988.

Verwyst, Chrysostomus. *Life and Labors of Rt. Rev. Frederick Baraga, First Bishop of Marquette, Mich. To Which are Added Short Sketches of the Lives and Labors of Other Indian Missionaries of the Northwest*. Milwauke: M. H. Wiltzius & Co., 1900.

Vogel, Virgil J. *Indian Names on Wisconsin's Map* Madison: University of Wisconsin Press, 1991.

Waller, Donald M., and Thomas P. Rooney. *The Vanishing Present: Wisconsin's Changing Lands, Waters, and Wildlife*. Chicago: University of Chicago Press, 2008.

Whittlesey, Charles. "The Penokie Range, Wisconsin." *Proceedings of the Boston Society of Natural History* 9 (1863): 235–244.

William W. Warren. *History of the Ojibway People: Its History and Construction*. 2nd ed. Edited and annotated with an introduction by Theresa Schenck. St. Paul: Minnesota Historical Society Press, 2009.

Wheeler, Harriet, and Leonard Wheeler. *Wheeler Family Papers, 1833–1965*. State Historical Society of Wisconsin.

White, Bruce. "Give Us a Little Milk": The Social and Cultural Significance of Gift Giving in the Lake Superior Fur Trade." In Thomas C. Buckley, ed., *Rendezvous: Selected papers of the Fourth North American Fur Trade Conference, 1981*. Norman: University of Oklahoma Press, 1984: 185–197.

———. "The Meanings of Merchandise in the Ojibwa Fur Trade." In Sylvia Depatie et al., eds. *Vingt ans après, Habitants et marchands: Lectures de l'histoire des XVII et XVIII siècles canadiens*. Montreal, Que.: McGill-Queen's University Press, 1998: 115–37.

———. "The Power of Whiteness, or, The Life and Times of Joseph Rolette, Jr." *Minnesota History* 56, no. 4 (1998–99): 178–197.

———. "The Regional Context of the Removal Order of 1850," in James McLurken, ed., *Fish in the Lakes, Wild Rice, and Game in Abundance: Testimony on Behalf of the Mille Lacs Ojibwe Hunting and Fishing Rights*. East Lansing: Michigan State University Press, 2000: 141–328.

White, Richard. *The Middle Ground: Indians, Empires, and Republics in the Great Lakes Region, 1650–1815*. New York: Cambridge University Press, 1991.

Widder, Keith R. *Battle for the Soul: Métis Children Encounter Evangelical Protestants at Mackinaw Mission, 1823–1837*. East Lansing: Michigan State University Press, 1999.

Winchell, A. N. *Handbook of Mining in the Lake Superior Region*. Minneapolis: Bryon and Learned, 1920.

Winchell, Horace V. "The Lake Superior Iron-Ore Region, U.S.A." *Transactions of the Federated Institution of Mining Engineers* XIII. London: Andrew Reid, 1898.

Wisconsin. Board of Commissioners of Public Lands. *Surveyors' Field Notes, 1832–1865*. State Historical Society of Wisconsin.

Wisconsin and Lake Superior Mining and Smelting Company. *The Penokee Iron Range, of Lake Superior: With Reports and Statistics Showing its Mineral Wealth and Prospects: Charter and Organization of the Wisconsin and Lake Superior Mining and Smelting Company*. Milwaukee: Starr & Son, 1860.

Wisconsin, State of. *Constitution of the State of Wisconsin, Adopted in Convention in Madison, on the first day of February, in the Year of Our Lord one thousand eight hundred and forty-eight*.

———. *Private and Local Laws Passed by the Legislature of Wisconsin*. 20 volumes. Madison: State Printer, 1853–1972.

Witgen, Michael J. "The Rituals of Possession: Native Identity and the Invention of Empire in Seventeenth-Century Western North America." *Ethnohistory* 54, no. 4 (2007): 639–668.

———. *An Infinity of Nations: How the Native New World Shaped Early North America*. Philadelphia: University of Pennsylvania Press, 2012.

Wolfe, Patrick. "Land, Labor, and Difference: Elementary Structures of Race." *American Historical Review* 106, no. 3 (2001): 866–905.

———. *Traces of History: Elementary Structures of Race*. London and New York: Verso, 2016.

Wrone, "The Economic Impact of the 1837 and 1842 Chippewa Treaties." *American Indian Quarterly* 17, no. 3 (1993): 329–340.

Young, Mary Elizabeth. *Redskins, Ruffleshirts and Rednecks: Indian Allotments in Alabama and Mississippi, 1830–1860*. Norman: University of Oklahoma Press, 1961.

Index

Italicized numbers refer to illustrations

www.ingramcontent.com/pod-product-compliance
Lightning Source LLC
LaVergne TN
LVHW040158080826
844660LV00001B/28

* 9 7 8 1 4 3 8 4 8 2 8 5 9 *